Nonprofit
Strategic
Positioning

Nonprofit Strategic Positioning

Decide Where to Be, Plan What to Do

Thomas A. McLaughlin

WILEY

John Wiley & Sons, Inc.

For general information on our other products and services, or technical support, please contact our Customer Care Department within the United States at 800–762–2974, outside the United States at 317–572–3993 or fax 317–572–4002.

Wiley also publishes its books in a variety of electronic formats. Some content that appears in print may not be available in electronic books.

For more information about Wiley products, visit our Web site at *www.wiley.com*

McLaughlin, Thomas A.
   The art of strategic planning for nonprofits / Thomas A. McLaughlin.
      p. cm.
   Includes index.
   ISBN-13: 978–0–471–71749–2 (cloth : alk. paper)
   ISBN-10: 0–471–71749–5 (cloth : alk. paper)
  1. Nonprofit organizations -- Management. I. Title.
HD62.6.M392 2006
658.4'012--dc22   2005031931

10 9 8 7 6 5 4 3 2 1

Contents

Acknowledgments

Since this book attempts to break new ground in strategy formulation for nonprofit organizations, many individuals have influenced its development.

Twelve years after the fact, I must thank Allan Bergman and Michael Morris. If this were a drug instead of a book it could be said that they participated in the first round of live human trials, although none of us thought of it that way at the time. Roxanne Spillett, Glenn Permuy, Ronnie Jenkins, and so many of the national and regional staff members at Boys & Girls Clubs of America have always been ready to explore these and others of my ideas for the past several years.

Paul Clolery unflinchingly runs my columns in the Nonprofit Times, where I was able to test-drive some of the concepts articulated here. Small amounts of the narrative first appeared in a different form in that publication.

My former colleague Jim Heller showed me that one can go further with a smile, a joke, and a relentlessly focused facilitative technique than with just the first two alone. David Donaldson showed me group techniques that proved invaluable long after I lost track of him and realized what he had done for me.

Winston Fairchild and the Blue Ridge Institute—which is a far less stuffy experience than the name implies—gave me one of my first extended opportunities to air these ideas, and the group's enthusiasm for them came at a critical time. Irv Katz, George Kessinger, John Huber, and Michael Weekes did the same thing, with comparable results. Don Kozera challenged me to think more deeply about some of these approaches, and

Janet Larson and her volunteers provided a brief but encouraging new type of proving grounds for this approach.

Kathy Cloninger, Marla Bobowick, Paula Van Ness, Katie Burnham, and several others agreed to be readers of various parts of the manuscript. Jan Masaoka was an early booster of strategic agendas, one of the key elements of the implementation phase of strategic positioning. Jim Mecone has become a new and instinctive champion of this approach.

Barry Friedman allowed me to unleash some of these ideas on a few small herds of innocent graduate students. The students always seemed to connect with the material, and in the process I relearned from them the power of ideals and a commitment to a vision of society far greater than what can be expressed in a single book.

Most of all, I want to thank my colleague Stacey Zelbow. Never has anyone read one of my manuscripts with such care, insight, and focus. The depth of her tough critiques is exceeded only by the extent of her support. The book is much better than it would have been without her contributions.

About the Author

Thomas A. McLaughlin has more than 25 years of experience as a nonprofit manager, trade association executive, and management consultant. He is nationally recognized as an expert in nonprofit mergers and alliances, strategic positioning, and financial management. He is a nonprofit management consultant with Grant Thornton in Boston, and is on the faculty of the Heller School of Social Policy and Management at Brandeis University. A frequent speaker at nonprofit-oriented events nationwide, he has been quoted in numerous industry and national publications. Tom is a monthly columnist and contributing editor for *The NonProfit Times*. He is also the author of *Streetsmart Financial Basics for Nonprofit Managers, 2e* and of *Nonprofit Mergers and Alliances*, both published by Wiley.

Introduction

In times of change, learners inherit the Earth, while the learned find themselves equipped to deal with a world that no longer exists.

—E. HOFFER

This idea for this book first occurred to me when I published a column in the *Nonprofit Times* suggesting that the classic S.W.O.T. analysis (Strengths, Weaknesses, Opportunities, and Threats) in traditional strategic planning was misleading and wrongheaded. I argued that one never gets anywhere by concentrating overly much on weaknesses, that "threats" is just another term for competitors, and that opportunities lie in the unique interaction between what the environment demands and what the organization can supply.

On publication day I awaited the response, preparing to be shunned forever as a strategy consultant—and was shocked by the outpouring of support. Most of the feedback had the same theme—this is the way it really works, we modified S.W.O.T. a long time ago, we always focus on strengths, and so on.

On the market today there are many books containing many good forms and checklists one can use for strategy formulation. Many of these actually focus on operations, but some do operate on a strategic level. Both can be useful. In fact, some could even be useful as an independent companion to this book.

Why be so inviting of others' work when it could easily be interpreted as a competing approach? Because, in truth, it really is not a competing approach. This is a book about strategic thinking, not about forms and checklists. We will provide some of the latter, but only as few as are absolutely necessary to introduce a new way of thinking about strategy. And they will largely be confined to the back of the book, as easily accessed as ignored.

Strategic planning is a famously unsatisfying undertaking. We will go into some of the specific reasons for that later in the book, but here's a simple hunch as to the fundamental reason why that's true: *it is too hard*. Practically everyone agrees that strategic planning should be a regular practice, but when the exercise itself is widely regarded as painful or too time-consuming, it is not difficult to see why organizations would avoid it.

By streamlining the thinking behind it as well as some of the process of creating the strategy, we will try to make it easier to incorporate the elements of strategic positioning into everyday management. By making some of that thinking more intuitive and easier to connect to daily experience we will make its relevance clearer. And by offering greater clarity about roles and responsibilities, we will suggest ways of making the entire process more manageable.

BRIGHT LINES BETWEEN ROLES

We derive some of that clarity by drawing bright lines between strategy planning and work planning, between board and staff, and between leaders and managers. Most of all, we draw sharp distinctions between thinking and doing. Each belongs in strategic positioning, though in different ways.

In the end, this is a book about ideas, an extended exploration of a certain kind of thinking. Most managers are long on activity and short on concepts, because they have to be if they want to be effective. It is not surprising then that their books about strategy usually have the same emphases. We flip that formulation on its head in the belief that ideas come before action. Only when one is clear about the conceptual context can the kind of planned actions and decisions undertaken by managers be truly effective. What's more, management without a good strategic framework is unsatisfying for managers themselves in the long term. Frenetic activity without a guide is absorbing and even exhilarating in the short run, but in the long run it leads to feelings of drift and burnout.

It is not an exaggeration to say this book is an attempt to show the primacy of ideas in management. It offers an integrating overlay for use in making decisions and choices and allocating resources and supervising people. We speak in the book of institutional ego—of what it is that the entire organization "wants"—because that's not a bad way to conceive of strategy. It is the way that an organization collectively sees what it wants to become in the future, and that gives logic and shape and purpose to the actions and decisions it takes in order to get there.

Strategy is often regarded as either the private province of brilliant leaders or the earnest thoughts offered during a "strategic planning retreat," but in reality it is larger than both of these limited sources. If strategy is the primary guideline for management action, and if it is to mean anything to the vast majority of people in an organization, it has to be clear and engaging. Even brilliant leaders need brilliant managers to be engaged in the strategy, and the simplest way to ensure that is to make it a product that they help create, not one that is received as part of the job, like a stack of office supplies.

If there is a hidden message in the book, it is this: strategy is for everyone. For very practical reasons, it has to be produced by a manageably small group of people, but the preparation for it is an appropriate time to include a diversity of voices, and implementation will be far smoother and more seamless if everyone in the organization feels a responsibility for carrying it out.

The mythology surrounding strategy is often just thinly disguised hero literature. Even in the nonprofit sector, strategy implementation is frequently couched in terms best suited for unique individuals. Strategies are described approvingly as "breakthrough," or "daring," or "high performance." These are terms rarely ascribed in other contexts to entire organizations—truthfully, have you ever encountered *any* organization of any appreciable size that you would consider "daring" or that consistently delivers "high performance?"

Strategy works best when it is understood and embraced by the largest number of people possible. For something to be understood and embraced by a wide array of people it has to be clear and comprehensible. Consequently, the central discipline in strategic positioning is to craft a clear and comprehensible response to an extraordinarily complex set of factors. The strategy must operate at the highest conceptual level and be useful in making the most minute operating decisions.

A STREAMLINED APPROACH

Strategic positioning is a streamlined approach to strategy formulation. This is true for several reasons. First, the clear distinction between the roles of the board and the executive helps prevent the confusions and misunderstandings that often accompany traditional approaches. It is a waste of time—and possibly worse—for board members to be involved in anything having to do with operations, including planning them. This is one reason why conventional approaches to strategy formulation are often confusing and unsatisfying. Strategic positioning allows each group to do what it does best.

Second, strategic positioning maximizes in-person time by facilitating discussion via a simple and easy-to-understand agenda. One of the pitfalls of some planning processes is spending far too much time on blue-sky or feel-good discussion with no point and less practical usefulness. To get some idea of the value that is available to a planning group, multiply the number of hours each individual staff member or volunteer puts into it by some conservative approximation of their economic value such as $20 or $30. Strategic positioning keeps that number as low as possible both out of respect for people's time and because it aims for quality of hours, not quantity.

Finally, strategic positioning done well relies on offline work by participants. In the future scan that is the first major step in the process, offline research and documentation of future fact-based trends and patterns is suggested to be carried out by individuals who then share their newfound knowledge with the whole group. This micro-planning builds a broad institutional knowledge base in the entire organization in the most efficient way possible.

It will not go unrecognized that a streamlined approach means less cost in staff time and consultant fees. To the extent that this frees up resources that could be devoted to the mission, it is to the good. But it is a secondary benefit. The primary benefit is that the process itself does not become a distraction. Strategy formulation and reformulation should be organizationally instinctive, and that will not happen if the process of achieving it causes rolled eyes and whispered complaints.

Nonprofit leaders of the future need a bulging toolkit that includes contributions from fields ranging from finance and human resources to technology and public relations. Strategic positioning is just one of those tools. Like those other pieces, strategic positioning is simply one way of thinking about a complex task that goes well beyond checklists and spreadsheets. Yet it is every bit as powerful a tool as are those management devices. Use it wisely and well.

Nonprofit
Strategic
Positioning

Preplanning

At Brandeis University, the Heller School for Social Welfare was founded in 1952 as a kind of policy utopia for those interested in social welfare matters. In 2001, after great discussion but relatively little disagreement, it changed its name to the Heller School for Social Policy *and Management* (italics added).

When the Kennedy School of Government was created at Harvard University, about the same time, one of its major revenue streams came from mid-career federal government officials, who received scholarships and other support to earn a graduate degree. Today, that emphasis has faded and one of the school's major components is dedicated exclusively to nonprofit management. Across the river at the Harvard Business School, social enterprise is one of the most popular concentrations. At Boston University, the management school changed the title of its Public Management Program to the Nonprofit Management Program.

Colleges and universities as institutions do not usually lead trends. As economic entities, they respond to them. Their students and faculty members often help lead trends, but the institutions themselves lag behind for a complex set of reasons. When a few large educational institutions make even apparently superficial changes such as these, it is a sign that something fundamental has occurred in the economy as a whole.

And it has. The number of nonprofit public charities—501(c)(3)'s, as they are known—has grown steadily for many years and now exceeds one million. Other types of nonprofits such as associations and advocacy groups have also grown significantly. The sector employs about 1 in every 25 people, producing a similar share of the gross domestic product (GDP).

The nonprofit corporation has changed considerably. In the middle of the twentieth century nonprofits were economic afterthoughts. Government was the only widely understood type of economic institution not organized expressly to make a profit. In effect, there were two sectors of the economy—the private business sector and the governmental sector. Today, there are indisputably three sectors—the private business sector, the governmental sector, and the nonprofit sector.

In contrast to for-profits, which are usually organized to pursue an opportunity for private gain, nonprofit organizations are usually organized in response to a dysfunction in society. The orphanages of the nineteenth century came into being largely because the pressures of the newly developing industrial age—including economic dislocation, and death and injury suffered by parents caused in the brutal factory working conditions—created a whole new class of parentless children. Visiting nurse associations arose in response to the demonstrably unsafe conditions of early industrial age hospitals. AIDS service providers scrambled into existence to deal with a new scourge, and so on.

Americans love voluntary association. In colonial America, Benjamin Franklin, the writer Daniel Defoe, and the preacher Cotton Mather urged the formation of voluntary associations for purposes such as fire services, widows' support, and seafarers' pensions. Many of their efforts bore fruit, and we have not stopped connecting with each other in this way since then. Whether it is a church, a professional group, an under-ten soccer league, or an Irish step dancing club, we freely associate with each other to accomplish goals that are not directly related to profit or government. Most of the time these groups are essentially forums. Often highly informal, they may not have any special legal standing. In all cases, they are based on trust.

THE INTERMEDIARY SECTOR

The result is that the nonprofit sector is a giant intermediary layer between private individuals and the government. It is where conflicts get worked out, or, better still, prevented from occurring. The nonprofit vehicle allows for people to form ties outside of close family circles, and to create personal pathways that may not have existed before.

There is now even some emerging research into the role that voluntary associations play in civil order. Political scientist Ashutosh Varshney studied cities in India and discovered a simple but intriguing pattern. Cities that had achieved a good level of social, political, and economic integration through voluntary groups were far more likely to avoid the ethnic conflicts that decimated cities with less integration. Networks of peace committees, for example, were able to quash inflammatory rumors before they spread.

On the negative side, this intermediary position is one of the reasons why nonprofits are widely held to be slow to change, difficult to manage, and beset with ambiguities. The instinct to preserve, the need to be trusted, and the imperative to react to social dysfunction all combine to discourage the relatively abrupt changes such as bankruptcies, buyouts, and mergers that often characterize the for-profit sector.

Also a factor, especially in the past, is the fact that many nonprofits are small corporations. If the majority of nonprofits were for-profit organizations, they would be considered small to medium-sized businesses, at best. Even today, with the growth of many nonprofits, only about 4 percent have revenues over $25M. As single entities, they are engines of integration, not economic change.

It is not hard to envision the way the old mental model of operating a nonprofit got started. These small corporations probably sprang from the passion of a local person or two and his or her circle of friends and acquaintances. They had perhaps two or three staff persons at most, and when it came to stuffing envelopes and decorating for the special fundraising dance each year, it was impossible to distinguish between board members and staff.

Governance emerged in a similar way. The board was expected to be hands-on in the management of the agency, including keeping the records and sometimes supervising the staff. The executive director, called such probably to distinguish the position from that of the president or chairman of the board, had first-among-equals power but was never expected to act like a true CEO—a good thing, because until last year he was quite likely to have been, say, a staff person in a large local manufacturing company.

This little group acted like a true association—a voluntary joining of diverse people who shared a common interest and who knew how to get along with each other. Just about everything was done pretty informally, and there was a great deal of improvising, sharing, and good faith effort. It worked out.

Then things started to get serious. In the health care sector there arose a need for more and bigger hospitals, their demand for capital funding fulfilled partly by the federal government starting in the 1950s. Human and social services became a recognized need by many levels of government, and reform movements started to help retarded children, the mentally ill, runaways, and young students. Nursing homes were created for the care of the elderly, and the old orphanages—no longer needed thanks to safer factories, government aid to families, and birth control—turned into special education schools. Established groups such as the YMCA found themselves with sudden company. United Ways, once the primary fundraisers for a market-controlling segment of social service nonprofits, were reduced to funding a smaller percentage share of a much larger sector.

At the same time government as a provider of service was reaching a kind of maximum cap beyond which taxpayers were not interested in going. The acceptability of large-scale government-provided services was beginning to fade. Just as important, needs got more complex and subtle and fast-changing, while the population itself grew inexorably. The for-profit sector, which knows how to produce mass quantities of goods and services and how to sniff out profitable opportunities, was either uninterested or uninvited. Into this vacuum was drawn the nonprofit sector. Already providing many services, nonprofits were asked to expand them and to come up with new ones. Separately, the IRS clarified their definition of a private foundation, formalizing a funding vehicle that would become increasingly popular in lieu of or as a supplement to government funding.

This giant outsourcing experiment has now become permanent. Although it has amounted to privatization in many quarters, the more potent change is that government has begun to give the nonprofit sector a legitimacy that it never had before. Even where government has no direct funding role, it has accepted nonprofits as equal partners to a degree unheard of a few years ago. Today governments deliberately create nonprofits to carry out activities that they would have attempted to do themselves in prior generations. Partly this is a reaction to the generalized mistrust of government, and partly it is a frank recognition that nonprofit public charities often have lower-cost structures and can raise private dollars more readily than can governments.

Governments are not the only source of demand for nonprofits' services, but they are a bellwether of what is happening in the larger economy. Whether it is YMCAs or PTAs or art museums, most people have made more use of some type of nonprofit organization's services than even a few years ago.

As a result of this spiraling demand and newfound acceptance, nonprofits must improve their management. It is not an accident that the numbers of degree-granting graduate-level programs in nonprofit management has skyrocketed in recent years. Nor is it an accident that CEOs with business credentials are often sought as leaders of these organizations.

The biggest obstacle to accomplishing this necessary task is not money, it is that mental model mentioned above. The common problems associated with nonprofits—poor cash flow, inadequate recordkeeping, and lax management, to mention a few—are just symptoms of the larger and more profound inability or unwillingness to do powerful strategic thinking. This is why entrepreneurs often chafe when they find themselves on a nonprofit's board of directors. They are accustomed to a pace and a way of thinking that is often missing in nonprofits.

Fairly or not, for-profit CEOs are often associated with grand thinking. It would be a sad commentary if it were to be true that only the opportunity to earn huge riches prompts people to set lofty and compelling goals for their organizations. More likely is that, until recently, nonprofits were not typically seen as having the capacity to achieve great things. Even more likely is that the world used to be divided neatly into two groups, for-profit and nonprofit, and never were the two expected to coincide or get close. Now that the bright lines between the two groups have blurred, there is greater interchange between them, and greater recognition that management skill does not grow from the tax code.

FOR-PROFIT VERSUS NONPROFIT

Underlying this blurring between the two camps has been the growing recognition of the impact that nonprofits can have. For-profit companies often target instrumental areas of our lives, those products and services that help us get things done. That is why for-profits process and distribute food, build houses, and run airlines. Nonprofits, on the other hand, often show up at transitional periods of our lives, doing things like running hospitals, schools, shelters, museums, and nursing homes. They also serve functions that for-profits are ill-equipped to do, such as advocate policies, promote community economic development, and conduct research.

Nothing established nonprofits' legitimacy in the national economy more profoundly than the fall of the Berlin Wall and the end of the Soviet Union. Without a monolithic external threat, our national attention turned inward. It is not a coincidence that this coincided with a period of sustained prosperity, and it is not a coincidence that that prosperous period essentially ended on September 11, 2001 as the nation realized that it had a new and more decentralized international enemy. Conflict absorbs resources, and international conflicts absorb resources that would otherwise have gone to internal purposes.

International conflicts tend to tip the scales in favor of innovations in national security, not innovations in civil society. Nonprofits' role in smoothing civil matters gets pushed to the background in the face of external crisis. This suggests that nonprofits will need to consolidate the gains made during the 1990s until the pendulum swings back in favor of internal issues again. The best way to do this is to craft a sound strategy and then follow it with solid implementation.

That is why we will concentrate on the thinking that goes into crafting a sound strategy as well as some ways to implement one. Each will help nonprofits solidify their role in their respective futures. More important, a well implemented strategy will ensure that a nonprofit will have its proper impact. Many for-profit firms do not need to do much more than get a few hundred tasty meals out every evening, or manufacture an interesting perfume. Nonprofits are expected to do a lot more, usually with a lot less. The pressure is on to get the basics right. Strategic positioning can help.

The Logic of Strategic Positioning

Strategic planning has been hijacked by middle managers, bureaucrats, and consultants masquerading as strategic thinkers. It is no accident that the beautifully printed and bound strategic plan that sits unread on a shelf has become a staple of comedians and cartoonists. Through a series of subtle changes over the years, the typical strategic plan has turned into a hopelessly complex and unachievable collection of small ideas leading nowhere in particular.

Partly this is because true strategy is highly cerebral, and most of us spend our time dealing with tangible, recognizable, noncerebral things. Most people are just not comfortable in a world of symbols and concepts, and so it is not surprising that such a fuzzy concept as strategy would get reduced to tools encouraging busywork and frenzied activity in the name of strategy. This dilutes the power of a good strategy and confuses everyone, especially the people who should be responsible for carrying it out.

There is also an economic incentive to misdirect the planning process. Whenever an organization undertakes something as potent as a strategy, there will be no shortage of those who would spend as many hours churning out minutiae as there is money available to pay them. Some of these will be employees, others outsiders. Everywhere, even in small organizations, one will find the bureaucratic impulse: to turn something new and foreign and challenging into something recognizable, predictable, and safe.

This is as it should be. Every organization needs to be able to take new ideas and directions and turn them into routine, familiar activities. This is the process of operationalizing strategy, and in many ways it is at the heart of productivity. The engine of production that any organization should represent—whether that production is of services or manufactured goods— needs the framework and guiding principles of a strategy in order to work its mundane magic of forms, measurements, policies, and procedures. This is the essence of good operational planning.

But turning strategy into a predictable production line is the exact opposite of what we call strategic positioning. Strategic positioning is about choices and decisions in uncharted waters. It is relentlessly forward-looking, and it is capable of imposing a uniquely tailored discipline on external realities that are as likely to be predictable and methodical as they are chaotic and random. Strategy is, in short, an act of institutional will.

So, it is an understandable impulse to retreat from the ambiguities of strategy to the comforting familiarity of operations. And the truth is that organizations need to plan both strategy and operations. An old-time for-profit CEO is said to have remarked that he'd rather have a half-good idea executed properly than an excellent idea executed moderately well. Experience supports his preference. In the early 1980s IBM's personal computer was, technologically, no better than average. But with the weight of the company's superior marketing and distribution systems behind it, it was an instant hit.

Another uncomfortable reality for all managers is that implementation is just plain hard to do. It can be tedious, demanding, and not the slightest bit glamorous, and if one is not careful things can fall apart in a nanosecond. Nonprofits are at a special disadvantage in implementing strategy for a whole variety of reasons, not the least of which is that implementation efforts do not usually get a lot of resources or respect.

The key is to be clear about the difference between strategy and implementation, or operations planning. This is a theme to which we will return repeatedly.

WHAT STRATEGIC POSITIONING IS NOT

This is not a book of recipe cards and checklists. There will be some of those, but as few as necessary, and we have tucked most of them into back corners that you can visit or not as you please. There are many books on strategic planning out there filled with good, usable forms and checklists. Truthfully, all but the section on implementation is probably compatible with the best of those tools, because this is a book about strategic thinking, not a book on how to fill out forms.

Strategic positioning is also not about creating high-performing organizations, achieving breakthroughs, or establishing Big, Hairy, Audacious Goals (or BHAGs, as the strategy wonks would say). There is a theme of promethean effort running through much of the literature on strategy, as well as management literature in general, that we explicitly reject. This underlying assumption by business thinkers of superhuman effort is an unfortunate albeit understandable result of our tendency to talk about how organizations work by focusing on the individuals in them rather than on the delicate balance between individuals and the systems in which they work.

We do not wish to discourage leaders from trying to create high-performing organizations, or from using hard-to-achieve outcomes as motivating tools. But they have nothing to do with strategy. Strategic objectives can be accomplished by flashy, high-octane leadership or by plodding, one-step-at-a-time management. Casting strategic effectiveness as something that can only be achieved by demigods does a disservice to the vast majority of leaders and managers who will rightfully never view themselves as mythical figures.

Mostly, strategic positioning as we describe it here is a process of systematic thinking on a plane where leaders and managers do not often get to spend time together. As you will understand early in this book, planning strategy is about deciding where an organization wants to *be*, while operations and work planning are about what it will *do* to get to where it wants to be. Many nonprofit managers, of necessity, spend the vast majority of their time *doing*. They operate in environments that are underfunded, undercapitalized, and underresourced, which is a functional definition of crisis mode. To compensate, they simply work harder. The curse of the nonprofit sector is this very busyness, because it causes managers to miss messages from consumers and funders alike, and to fail to lead their communities on public policy issues or shape public dialogs that affect their constituencies and their missions.

It is also very unsatisfying and can lead to burnout, leaving the sector, or cynicism. A consulting colleague once described this as the Whack-a-Mole syndrome, named after the carnival game in which mechanical moles pop up through holes to challenge the foam hammer-wielding player to whack them down and earn a point. The game starts slowly enough, the better to build false confidence, but after a time virtually every player is flailing wildly, trying to hit everything in sight and finally collapsing out of sheer exhaustion and a terminal lack of strategy. The price at the carnival is embarrassment and a few lost dollars, but in real life the price is lost opportunities to fulfill a public good.

Strategic positioning is also not just about a carefully selected Saturday in April when the entire board, a group of managers, and various others gather off-site to think grand thoughts, returning in five years to do it all again. One of the enduring problems with conventional strategic planning is that it is the intellectual equivalent of mobilizing a small army. Successful or not, once done, few want to do it again any time soon.

By streamlining the strategy formulation process, we will make it more readily accessible, self-reinforcing, and easier to incorporate into daily affairs. Strategy formulation should be ongoing and instinctual, which is one of the reasons that we reject the recipe card approach. The irony is that a strategic position should be more durable than a conventional strategic plan and thus not require constant tinkering. A conventional strategic plan is likely to be obsolete the day it is finished, if only because of the voluminous detail that typically goes into it. A strategic position ideally should be elegantly simple, easy to understand, and useful in any reasonably foreseeable circumstances. It is the work plan that supports it that can be expected to change frequently. Those expecting a monumental work product to emerge from a strategic positioning process will be disappointed. If it takes more than a single sheet of paper or two to describe the strategic position, something is probably wrong.

INTRODUCING WILLOWS' END ASSISTED LIVING

To make the concepts in this book clearer and more concrete, we will use an organization called Willows' End Assisted Living Center, or WEAL. This composite nonprofit organization is an elder service organization whose strategic positioning process will be described at various points in the book as a way of illustrating key concepts and practices. Their desired strategic position can be summed up in this single sentence:

> To be a flagship elder service organization at the crossroads of community learning about care for the elderly.

How Willows' End got to this strategic position will be clearer with each section. It will be clear that this single sentence was the product of much analyzing, synthesizing, and dreaming. We start with it to show the conceptual simplicity for which strategic positioning strives. This expression of a desired strategic position will be easy for everyone connected with the organization to understand and ascribe to, and it should last for the next 5–10 years, and possibly much longer. Its simplicity belies the complexity of thinking that produced it. Why a flagship, rather than a leader? What does it mean to be at the crossroads of community learning instead of being the major source? What does community learning in an elder service context require? Those participating in the process, which included many in the organization, will have history-based answers for these questions, but one does not need to know all that to use the strategy fully.

The simplicity and potential elegance of strategic positioning are embedded in this simple end point. Which formulation would be most concrete and helpful to the people who work and volunteer for Willows' End—this simple declaration of intent or the contents of a three-ring, two-inch-thick "strategic planning" binder?

THE PROCESS OF STRATEGIC POSITIONING

The QuickStart material in the toolkit will give the reader a good overview of the process of strategic positioning, but for our purposes we will summarize it briefly. Strategic positioning consists of the following steps:

Reaffirm the mission statement.
Scan the organization's future for projected trends and patterns based on current realities.
Scan for the organization's internal strengths.
Decide where you want to be in 5–10 years.
Craft a succinct statement of the desired strategic position.
Devise a work plan for getting there.

Because successful managers have found ways to be successful at developing work plans, and because work plans vary tremendously with each organization's unique elements, we will focus mostly on the first five steps where the strategy is truly developed. Organizations need both good strategy and good work plans, but the harder part for most groups is developing the strategy.

Reaffirming the mission statement may take five minutes, or it may take a lot longer. This is the time to deal with things like a persistent lack of clarity, or like mission drift in which the stated mission gets stretched over time to accommodate new revenue sources.

Next comes a clear-eyed scan of the future. This is a conceptual exercise intended to open eyes and broaden visions throughout the organization. It is also a fact-based undertaking. No anecdotes are desired unless they enrich understanding. Good strategies are based on fact, not good stories. To make this step easier, we will suggest seven categories into which most trends and patterns will fit. Some or all of these will apply to every nonprofit: choose the ones that apply to yours.

Once future trends are documented, it is time to look inward for strengths. A good strategy is built on strengths, either those that already exist or those that can be acquired. Strengths for these purposes are not the intangibles or the personal ones (which do have their place) but those that are systemic, replicable, and recognizable by outsiders. These are the things that the organization can use to respond to those trends and patterns expected to be true in the future. These strengths can be categorized in many of the same categories as the previous step.

After this comes an expression of organizational ego. Knowing what you know about future trends and patterns, and with a reasonable although not constrictive grounding in your strengths, decide where you want your organization to be in the next 5–10 years. How you will get there is not relevant at this point, nor is the presence or absence of audaciousness in the goal. All that matters is that the desired strategic position be a comfortable choice for the organization as a whole.

Traditional strategic planning often confuses strategy with work planning, so the group of board and staff that have formulated the strategic position should now step aside and hand over to the chief executive the responsibility for crafting a plan that will achieve the desired strategic position. This is a critical component of strategic positioning that is based on the very different roles of leaders and managers, and of board members and senior executives. One of the chief executive's and his or her staff's first jobs is to craft a polished and easy-to-understand statement of the desired strategic position. The next step is to create a work plan that will accomplish it. This is the type of work that is often confused with strategy development. In a full strategic positioning project, it is the final step, not the only step.

CHARACTERISTICS OF STRATEGIC POSITIONING

Strategic positioning is unrelated to organization size. It can be used with startup entities, and it will help ongoing organizations' strategy development to be much simpler and clearer. It can also be scaled up to accommodate larger, complex institutions, or miniaturized to support small ones.

In strategic positioning one can also be as bold as one wishes or as incrementally cautious as the prevailing culture dictates. It supports thinking big—or small—because the desired degree of organizational stretch has nothing to do with the usefulness of a strategic position.

One of the enduring and richly deserved criticisms of traditional strategic planning is that it suffers from the Shiny New Thing Syndrome. Planners retire to a pleasant weekend getaway and immerse themselves in new possibilities, exciting innovations, and ambitious fundraising plans. These are all deeply moving new things and everyone forgets that, come Monday morning, the doors will still have to open, the staff must keep programs open and services flowing, and the books and records will still need to be maintained. Where will the resources and personal energy for the Shiny New Thing come from?

The wishful alchemy that results when good intentions cozy up with a steadfast denial of management realities is what discredits most strategic planning processes. Those who come up with Big Hairy Audacious Goals are rarely the ones who have to implement them, and so there is every chance for a gap between intention and execution. Strategic positioning overcomes that by insisting on, first, a sound and factually based projection of where the organization wants to be and, second, a management-based work planning process for how to get there.

It is entirely conceivable that an organization going through a strategic positioning process might decide that it is exactly where it wants to be and that, therefore, the entire work plan will consist of ways to keep itself there. This notion alone may seem odd to those conditioned to equate strategy

SCALING UP FOR LARGE ORGANIZATIONS

While the actual planning group for a strategic positioning process (step four: decide where to be in 5–10 years) works best if it is small and manageable (7–12 members), large organizations can still use the process in an inclusive way by arranging for widespread participation in mission reaffirmation and in the first two steps of future and internal scans. Think of the process as being a way to build a common voice from the ground up. Large organizations can invite participation through written means such as surveys as well as in-person meetings akin to focus groups or ad hoc committees. To systematize data collection using any kind of group meeting, create heterogeneous groups by rank. For instance, create groups for entry-level support staff, or for tenured faculty, or for specialized clinicians. The heterogeneous aspect is important because it tends to establish a broadly acceptable range for discussion. The concentration on people from the same approximate level of the organizational chart is important because mixing differing levels of power in the same group will often silence some groups, while giving undue influence to others.

A caution to large organizations intending to be inclusive in the planning process: be sure to document suggestions and insights, issue at least a summary of them, and (hopefully) reflect some of them in the eventual strategic position, or the resident cynics will be able to gloat that they were right after all.

development with the Shiny New Thing, but only if one assumes that organizations move forward mainly in heroic leaps and bounds. In truth, most organizations change incrementally, and some start the strategic positioning process in an enviable place.

True market leaders or dominant organizations, of which there are few in the nonprofit sector, will be the ones most likely to be in this kind of position. In those cases, the strategy will be essentially a hold-the-line approach, with the greatest pressure being on management to decide how to execute a work plan that preserves their position. Even there, however, the perception that dominant organizations in their field need only keep doing what they have been doing is misleading. Chances are that the dominant or leading organization got that way not by holding to a static position but by continually reading its future environment correctly and by build-ing an enduring management capacity to make the necessary adjustments.

WHY DO IT AT ALL?

We end this section with some thoughts on the topography of strategic positioning. More precisely, we end with an attempt to explain why an organization should want to go through a strategic positioning process at all. The effort is time-consuming, potentially confusing, and downright foreign to the way many people think. Worse, it is often unsatisfying and unhelpful.

Start with the reasonable premise that most human beings want to do the right thing, but that it is not always clear what that is and that in any case there are a variety of external factors such as time pressures, short-sighted incentives, and mission-based demands that make it hard to do so. Add to that the naturally fractious nature of most groups. It is not easy to get every-one rowing in the same direction, and even when the oars are working right, conflicting personalities can be a wildcard.

On the other hand, groups have some advantages, primary among which is the quality of their decisions. James Surowiecki in his book *The Wisdom of Crowds* tells the story of Francis Galton, a scientist and researcher who studied an ox weight–judging contest in his Plymouth, England home-town 100 years ago. The object of the contest was to guess how much a particular ox would weigh once it was slaughtered and dressed. The cor-rect answer was 1,866 pounds. When Galton calculated the average of the 800 entrants' guesses he was astonished to find that the average guess was . . . 1,867 pounds.

There is an almost inverse trade-off between the timeframe of a decision and its consequences, and the number of people who should make it. In battlefield conditions, the officer in charge is the one by definition and position who should make the decisions. But in strategic positioning, which is intended to endure for years and provide eloquent guidance to all, it should be the crowd.

That is not to say that anarchy reigns in strategic positioning. Rather, just as individual board members and staff members have wisdom, so does the group doing the planning. It is the responsibility of those in charge to figure out how to tap into that wisdom, and how to bring it forward in a way superior to that which any one participant might have been capable of producing on his or her own.

Tapping into the group's wisdom is crucial for another reason. It is well known that any group needs to feel a sense of ownership for an idea to be accepted and acted upon. This is especially true for nonprofits, which typically do not use top-down corporate strategies combined with major financial incentives to ensure desired behavior. The alternative is to create a widespread sense of investment in the chosen strategy. This is not just altruism or everybody's-a-winner sappiness. Ego in its many forms, not money, is the currency of the nonprofit world, and there is no stronger force than the group whose values and sense of worth are routinely upheld by playing a part in decision making.

Nonprofit managers need tools, and a strategic position is one of the most effective. So is the process that leads to its development because, done properly, it creates the same alignment of interests that implementing a strategic position creates. A good strategic position puts a house in order at the highest level and gives planners, decision makers, and even casual observers a durable guide to action. Still, it is at most a good starting point. How it fits with the rest of the tools available to a manager is the subject of the next section.

The Formal Points of Control

As stated previously, for the most part nonprofits respond to some sort of dysfunction or gap in society. Virtually all health and human service nonprofits attempt to deal with illness, disability, or a social issue of some kind. Environmental nonprofits seek to avoid or mitigate pollution, preserve some aspect of the future, or both. Research institutes try to create knowledge where there is none or where it is incomplete, while others provide information or education. Many other nonprofits, including most arts groups, try to provide physical access to the arts or to lower barriers to people's enjoyment of the arts.

The implications of this single fact cannot be underestimated. For-profits are usually created to fill gaps too, but not of the same kind. For-profits are asked to produce goods and services that are needed in the economy, but they are not typically remedial goods or services. Food distribution companies fill a need, as do garment makers and air freshener manufacturers. Mutual fund managers fill a different kind of need, cab drivers yet another, and so on. But the public needs that nonprofits attempt to fill usually involve explicit social improvement (at least, as the nonprofits see it).

This need is the nonprofit starting point, the central reason for being of the organization. How the founder and succeeding generations marshal resources and people to fill that gap or respond to that dysfunction turns out to be a unique blend of action and accident, but as long as the original need remains valid the nonprofit's claim on society's support is valid.

So, if the equation starts with need, and if the nonprofit exists to execute responses to that demand, what's the link between need and execution? That is the role of vision. A commodity in short supply during any generation, vision is what allows a uniquely driven individual—or a very small group of individuals—to envision a panorama of the way things might be. Their vision might be one of social justice, an end to a terrible disease, a world free of a particular kind of prejudice, or any one of a number of things.

We all have visions. The beauty pageant winner who wishes for World Peace has a vision. The frustrated commuter who sits in rush hour traffic and has a flash of inspiration for how to make traffic flow better has a vision. The anthropologist who wants to preserve a rare culture for future generations has a vision. Of course, there is a huge distance between those relatively common visions and the creation of an institution designed to execute a response to them. There are three reasons for this distance.

First, vision is an intensely personal thing. It does not matter how sappy or preposterous a vision might sound to others, because it is unique to the individual. Lying at the connection between emotion and intellect, vision is practically impossible to replicate for others. Even those who share the same general vision of preserving an endangered culture may have such radically different notions of what that means that for all purposes they are two completely different ideas.

What they can do is talk in emotional terms. They can share hopes, and they can inspire each other. They can talk about what gave rise to their visions, and they can describe the conditions they would like to see arise in the future. The visions may well be complementary and parallel, but in the end they are not likely to be identical.

The second reason why most visions do not go anywhere is that they are not sustainable. To be converted into a functioning organization, a vision needs to consume the holder. In this respect, a vision is different from a simple idea. Many creative people have many good ideas. Fewer have something as sweeping and all-encompassing as a vision.

Think of it this way. With the number of nonprofit public charities in this country over a million, one can guess that perhaps tens of thousands came into existence as a mechanical outgrowth of one kind or another— an existing public charity needs to form another one for legal or liability-related reasons, for example. Take away another several hundred thousand because they are local affiliates or chapters of larger national systems such as the scouting organizations, United Ways, YMCAs, and the like, and thus they all share the same root vision. These entities may have been formed as the result of a passionate belief in the local application of a national model, and they were almost certainly formed out of one or more person's passion and energy, but they cannot truly be said to be products of a unique vision. The real vision was what created the first version of the model many years ago.

The remaining number—a few hundred thousand?—are the products of a unique vision that was compelling enough for someone to conceive of, launch, and nurture a nonprofit organization.

The difficulty of translating the vision into an organization that can realize the vision is the third reason why so few visions actually get brought to fruition, especially in the nonprofit world. Starting a nonprofit from zero is one of the most difficult undertakings in the American economy, harder even than starting a for-profit company, because capital is so difficult to obtain in the nonprofit sector. Whereas investors will invest in a for-profit in hopes of reaping financial gains later on, no such gains are possible in a nonprofit. Moreover, few lenders will make a loan, and no institutional funders will contribute to an endowment campaign until the nonprofit is established.

FOR ESTABLISHED NONPROFITS

The vision calculus is different for an established organization. For these groups, the initial founding vision has long since been spent, and one or more generations of successors have passed through the leadership positions. If the founding vision is such an individualized, visceral thing, what becomes of it as it moves through the years? Who preserves the vision, adapts it to current realities if necessary, and uses it to drive the organization?

There is only one role in the organization situated so as to be able to steward the vision through succeeding generations: the CEO. While many in a nonprofit may have a vision, only the chief executive is in a position to act on it in a comprehensive fashion. This is what the chief executive's psychic investment is all about. Others may very well have the same—or greater—level of emotional and intellectual engagement with the organization, but it is the CEO who is naturally positioned to take maximum advantage of it.

This is why the most compelling requirement for any CEO of a nonprofit organization is to be able to invest his or her psychic energy in the group and its mission. It is why in a positive, growing culture, the excitement is palpable. Conversely, the CEO without a vision for what the organization can be will, over time, run into difficulty. It is one of the reasons why CEO's hired straight from the for-profit sector often fail—they do not even realize that this level of psychic energy is demanded, and that they are the only ones who can provide it.

WHEN THE VISION IS GIVEN ITS VEHICLE

Nonprofit organizations have a handful of formal points of control with which to carry out the vision: mission, strategy, organizational structure, and resources. Exhibit 3.1 shows the relationship between them.

In a nonprofit organization, the mission moves the heart, while the strategy guides the mind. The mission is the first formal statement of intention that the outside world can understand, the necessarily rough translation of the founding vision into a form that all can understand. Its purpose is primarily emotional. It is the thing that engages outsiders and connects insiders more readily than almost anything else. Because the vision is so inaccessible—especially because eventually the original vision holder moves

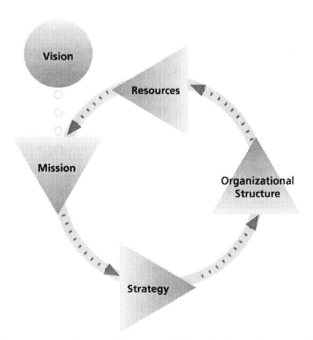

EXHIBIT 3.1   **Formal Control Points in a Nonprofit
Organization**

on—the mission becomes the most important emotional control point. More on how that works later.

STRATEGY

Strategy is for the head, not the heart. People look for guidance when making professional decisions, and the organization's strategy should be the first place they look (values and ethics should be so ingrained that they are not a matter of "choice"). A good strategy will be broad enough to be valid in just about any reasonable set of circumstances, yet powerful enough to help make finely calibrated choices. It will facilitate coordinated action throughout an organization as very different people with very different roles theoretically make compatible choices and decisions.

Many nonprofit organizations in the twentieth century set about to replicate themselves in every corner of the country in order to serve as many people as possible. Groups as different as the Make-A-Wish Foundation, Boys and Girls Clubs, Habitat for Humanity, Associations for Retarded Citizens (ARCs), and the American Cancer Society all set out to create dozens if not hundreds of chapters or affiliated organizations as part of their strategy. In some cases, those affiliates sprang up so quickly, with the "central office" being formed only later, that the growth strategy simply happened rather than being guided.

In any event, they were consciously following a growth strategy, and they did everything to make rapid growth for their affiliates easy. They readily gave permission to use the organization's name and logo, they established governance structures that encouraged rapid multiplication, and they constantly publicized or aided publicity of their mission. These were all formal, deliberate choices based on a desire for growth.

Other groups embrace a different kind of strategy. Associations do not typically exist in a highly competitive future, so their strategies often tend to be member service-oriented. Associations will emphasize education and brokering relationships between and among members as a primary strategy for achieving their missions. On the other hand, health care providers frequently do operate in competitive situations and their strategies reflect this. They must segment their markets and the services they provide in order to make the best use of their resources, so an overarching strategy is critical to their success.

IT'S ABOUT THE MONEY

One Washington-based headquarters of a nationally known system had for years organized itself to lobby the federal government on behalf of its members. But when, in preparation for a strategic planning project, they surveyed their affiliates about the things they most needed, the message came back very clearly: *money*. In past years, the federal government *had* been a reliable source of funding, so lobbying was a logical choice. That had changed steadily, and now their lobbying focus was more policy-oriented. What members needed now was a more sophisticated approach to money such as collaborative bond issues, planned giving campaign consulting, and brand-oriented fundraising. In response, the headquarters changed its entire strategy for serving members.

Organizational Structure

Clear strategies lead to deliberate choices of organizational structure, which is the next step along the continuum of control points. How one chooses to put the organization together, in both the corporate and the management control senses, determines a great deal about its success or failure.

The groups mentioned earlier created national organizational structures to make proliferation easy, defining success itself as more affiliates. They often created regional offices staffed with people good at program development, assembled a board of directors in tune with the growth imperative, offered financial support for starting new affiliates, and advocated on behalf of the larger cause with government officials. These were all logical organizational responses to a growth strategy. In a similar fashion, for the past several years, many of these same groups have adopted a strategy of deepening impact, corporate efficiency, and management development in order to further their mission. As a result, their organizational structures have begun to change too.

RESOURCES

The final formal control point in any organization is the resources that it allocates to its various efforts. The effect of alignment between mission, strategy, and organizational structure is to narrow the acceptable

ALIGNMENT DETERMINES RESOURCES

Aligning mission, strategy, and organizational structure narrows the acceptable ranges of resource allocation. Good alignment increases the organization's effectiveness. Unfortunately, it also makes it that much harder to change the organization when the future demands it. The satisfaction derived from the operation of a well aligned organization tends to outweigh all but the strongest signals from the outside world.

ranges of resource allocation. This is why the budget process often seems so anticlimactic—it is. By the time numbers go onto paper, all those previous choices effectively narrow the playing field considerably. Still, the nature of the resources committed to a strategy predetermines a lot about its eventual fate.

FEEDBACK LOOP

The loop comes full circle when the amount of resources available signals something about the feasibility of the mission. If the mission has been well chosen, the strategy for accomplishing it is sound, and the organizational structure is well thought out, the quantity of resources available makes a compelling statement about the marketability of the mission. It is like biofeedback for the organization. Ideally, the resources that can be marshaled are just as strong and powerful as the mission. Money not only talks, it enunciates with excruciating clarity.

DECIDING WHERE TO BE

There is an old saying that culture eats strategy for breakfast. It is true—informal controls are far more potent than formal ones. But the formal control points are easier to see, easier to understand, and easier to write about. Moreover, informal control mechanisms are unpredictable, highly unique to every organization, and perishable. Worse, deliberately trying to use them to change the organization can backfire.

In a sense, the phrase "strategic plan" is a contradiction in terms. A strategy is very different from a plan. Strategy is only meaningful as the guiding force behind a series of parallel, hopefully integrated actions. Following a strategy involves constant adjustments based on feedback from multiple sources.

In strategic positioning, a strategy is about what an organization wants to *be*, while planning is about what an organization is going to *do*. A good strategy should be expected to last for a few years, while a good plan will be changed virtually every time someone touches it. Strategy is the thing that guides an organization to a desired state of affairs that is presumed to accomplish the organization's mission and goals. The implementation of the strategy consists of a set of activities.

Another important but easy-to-miss distinction—strategy should be easy to understand. Operational plans often take on the same inscrutable qualities as a tax return, with the same result. Accumulate more than a handful of variables for a group of managers, and two things will happen: the plan is ignored, or it is updated once—and then it is ignored.

Yet another difference between strategy and plans is that plans and evaluation methodologies can always be gamed. Careers and paychecks are ultimately at stake in any system of measurement, which is a prescription for game playing. Just about any detailed method of planning, regulating or evaluating human activity can be challenged from a number of angles, and the only effective counterbalance is the human element—which effectively undercuts pure rationality.

The misconception underlying the presumed importance of work plans is a holdover from the industrial age of production, which began in the early nineteenth century in the United States and ended for all purposes in the late twentieth. This misconception is that purposeful human activity—such as work—can be reduced to the smallest of tasks and precisely standardized indefinitely. This is the legacy of Frederick Winslow Taylor and his "scientific method" of organizing factory production. Taylor's logic, carried to an extreme, removes virtually all free judgment and discretion from the individual worker and either replicates it exactly in the process itself or leaves it up to management.

Taylor's work was discredited to some degree in his lifetime, but it persists as an extremely powerful, subconscious model even today. Labor-management conflict is the partial legacy of scientific management. In the public arena, the persistent sincere belief that the government has plenty of money if it can just be made more efficient is another example of the powerful hold of scientific management. The idea of industrialization itself is very valid, as we will discuss later, but we now know how to make it take shape in a different way today.

The irony is that, to properly industrialize, an organization must first be creative enough to see an opportunity and bold enough to take a risk, neither of which can occur through a precise methodology. Which returns us to our initial point that strategic positioning is about thinking and guiding, not fine-scale measurement and recipe following. It is just as disciplined and demanding, but operates on a different level from traditional strategic planning. More important, it is about strength and opportunity and growth, not weaknesses and threats. Grand structures are built on solid foundations, not quicksand.

STRATEGIC POSITIONING CAN BE USED BY ALL NONPROFITS

Different organizations require different emphases in the strategic positioning approach. No matter what type or size of nonprofit, the strategic positioning method will work, but different aspects may be emphasized depending on the type of organization involved. We will cover a few common examples, starting with nonprofit federations, those systems of local nonprofit affiliates that have a single national headquarters and often share a brand name.

Nonprofit Federations

Someday, local affiliates of the large national federated systems will skip over most of this book and go right to the implementation section. Why? Because, rightfully speaking, local affiliates ought not to have to reinvent the wheel by creating a strategic position for themselves. This is an enormous waste of time and talent for something that should be done once, on the national level, for all affiliates. That is right, we said the national federated systems—essentially, most of the household name nonprofit systems—should determine the strategic position of every single one of their affiliates.

This will take some explaining. If the proposition is frightening to you, it is probably because you thought you heard that the national office should create the same strategic plan for all affiliates, and that *is* a frightening proposition—if one equates a strategic plan with an implementation plan.

The main reason why the national headquarters of such groups do not create a unified strategic position for all affiliates is because . . . they never have. A secondary reason is because few leaders have thought in those terms. The idea that the national office in Washington or New York or wherever should create a single implementation plan for all affiliates is massively wrong. But a strategic position as we have defined it makes sense for many reasons. A strategic position is about where an organization wants to be, and, given roughly comparable socioeconomic circumstances, the nature of this position is not going to change much from location to location. What will change is the details of implementation. So, one role of a national organization could easily be to decide the universal long-term desired strategic position for its movement, while leaving the details of how it gets there up to each affiliate.

Why should not Boys & Girls Clubs of America adopt as its desired strategic position being the foremost out-of-school-hours youth development organization in America? Why would not Girl Scouts of the USA declare its desire to be the premier character-development option for girls in each of the 312 areas where it operates? Without using our terminology, United Way of America began moving in this direction during the early part of the twenty-first century when it began to position itself as the primary community impact organization in the country. Goodwill Industries International has acted comparably by declaring its intention to serve 20 million people by the year 2020. In so many words, this is a declaration of intent to be the largest rehabilitation services organization in the country.

The concept of a strategic position is ideally suited to national federations. While based on facts and grounded in reality, it is highly conceptual and, therefore, durable. It would not take much for most federations to create a national strategic position that fits Brooklyn as well as Boise, and it would make everyone's roles in the movement clearer.

By aligning strategy with mission in these organizations, a single national strategic position would dramatically boost effectiveness because local efforts would not be fragmented and possibly in conflict with the national intent. Also, to be candid, most affiliates of these federations are small organizations whose leadership, both staff and board, are usually better at operations and execution than they are at strategy. So, why not play to their strengths and ask them to implement a strategic position that works for the entire country? Such a strategy would also make it easier to protect and promote the brand name because it would stand for something much more consistent and appealing.

Very Large Nonprofits

Strategic positioning can also be used by entities smaller than an entire organization such as a department or a division of a large nonprofit. As long as the entire organization has created a desired strategic position, smaller segments of the entity can base their work planning on that position. In larger and more complex organizations, there is little alternative anyway. While strategy is set from the top down, it gets implemented from the bottom up. The executive/board level of leadership decides where the organization wants to be, and the mission services figure out what they can do to get there. Strategy often fails in larger systems because leaders try to do too much implementation planning themselves. Top-down detail management rarely works in a large organization. This is perhaps the origin of the oft-quoted phrase that "90 percent of all strategic plans fail"—of course they do, if leaders do not resist the temptation to handle details from the top.

Larger organizations will find strategic positioning scalable, as long as they start with an overall strategic position. This is difficult because large organizations have so many different involvements and so many services that they offer planners an irresistible opportunity to drown in details. Yet by concentrating on a single overall strategic position, even the most complicated groups can devise a workable starting point.

Take universities, for instance. Seemingly one of the most complicated of nonprofits, there are only a few thousand in the country, and when you closely examine each one you will usually see unique characteristics in everything from geography to target market to courses of study. Higher education is substantially driven by consumers, and so the schools sort themselves on this basis. It is hard for a large organization to truly serve many different segments of a market, which is why there is a consistency in what they do, even if the details are different. The Ivy League universities all look considerably different from each other yet they consistently serve the same elite student population. State university systems, with some exceptions, often target the lower-middle-class student market (although that is changing steadily as tuitions rise across the board).

Or take hospitals, an even more segmented future. To the untrained eye, one sprawling hospital campus may look the same as any other. But, to survive today, virtually every hospital has to have a clear strategic position and the infrastructure to support it. Large medical centers look very different from community hospitals, which in turn look very different from rural providers.

It is when these large nonprofits begin changing their strategic positions that they can confuse people—and themselves. When strategy changes and execution follows shortly afterward, the confusion is temporary, but when they change their strategies and not their execution, they create a jumble of conflicting plans that endanger themselves. This is yet another example of how closely linked an organization's strategic position and its implementation plans have to be. Larger nonprofits must set their desired strategic position and then monitor their entire operation to be sure the individual departments and divisions are implementing the desired strategy.

Associations and Professional Societies

Associations and professional societies can also use strategic positioning. However, for these organizations above all others, boundaries are a problem no matter how they go about formulating strategy. Whether the membership is individuals or business entities, membership in an association is voluntary, unlike in a federation where members are tied together in a variety of ways such as a common brand name or an effort to offer comparable programming. Members of an association tend to have a keen appreciation of the larger future picture, especially if they have joined a trade association or a professional society partly to help lobby a governmental agency.

Leaders of associations and professional societies tend to see their membership group as synonymous with the industry, so developing a strategy for the field is the same thing as developing a strategy for the association. It is not. Associations and professional membership societies have to be careful not to strategize about things that they have no hope of controlling. Members tend to think that by changing the association they can change the industry, whereas the only thing they can hope to change is the association to which they all belong.

By focusing first on a strategic position *for the association*, leaders can make the boundaries clearer between the things they can influence and the larger future for all members. The inescapable fact is that the association, whether a society or a trade association, exists in order to accomplish things for its members. Strategy for the association, therefore, is a matter of determining what it should try to accomplish. Thinking in terms of a strategic position makes this easier, and then the implementation planning phase will emphasize the point.

WHO DOES STRATEGY? SELECTING THE TEAM

In strategic positioning the answer to this question is not as simple as it may sound. Take the for-profit world as a starting point. In the for-profit world, strategy is usually the exclusive domain of executives, who are, or are employed by, the firm's owners. The executives craft the strategy and have unquestioned responsibility for implementing it. This also gives them unquestioned authority, or at least as much authority as a bureaucracy permits.

The big differentiating point is who owns the company's capital, because owning capital is what confers authority in the for-profit world. So, the default source of strategic thinking is ownership, whether the capital is in the hands of the executives/owners, the stockholders, or an outside investor. This is one of the ways that for-profits are accurately perceived as being run in a top-down fashion. They have to be. Concentrating capital also concentrates accountability. Never mind that the owner of capital only needs to be accountable to him or herself. In a capitalist society the capital itself confers rights and authority. Or, to put it a slightly different way, putting one's capital at risk as majority owner gives power.

The situation is very different in nonprofits, where no one can own the organization's capital. Without that direct line of authority and responsibility, the picture is blurry. Who has authority in a nonprofit? Who has responsibility for its strategy? The answer is—it depends on who takes it. It is not conferred automatically but rather comes from an always-unique blend of personality, character, ideas, and knowledge.

This is one of the things that distinguishes the nature of business in a nonprofit from a that in a for-profit. Because the route to leadership positions in a nonprofit is through ideas and personality and character rather than through simple ownership of capital, there is a more diverse population of leaders in the nonprofit sector. It is easier to gain an executive position in a nonprofit without personal wealth. Moreover, nonprofit leaders can focus more clearly on the mission without having to factor in demands to increase personal wealth.

In a nonprofit, then, entrepreneurial strategic insight can come from anyone in the organization, which means that the planning process has to find a way to enable those insights instead of shutting them out. Owners of a for-profit perhaps can be forgiven for nervously listening only to those closest to the ownership structure, but that still limits the possible voices and range of ideas. Traditional nonprofit strategic planning often leans toward inclusiveness in the planning process, but it does so more out of a vague egalitarian impulse than a deliberate effort to identify good ideas and the talent to carry them.

HOW TO IDENTIFY THEM

A strategic positioning process needs leaders as participants. The problem is that organizational leaders do not come to work with "L" on their backs. On the other hand, with a little practice it is not hard to recognize leaders wherever one finds them.

Two things that leaders are not: first, leaders are not leaders within a nonprofit simply because they are leaders outside of it. The Fortune 500 CEO lionized on the cover of the national business magazine last month is not automatically a leader on the board of directors of a nonprofit. Second, leaders do not necessarily have official positions. Titles do not provide leadership, people do. There is a big body of literature on leadership going back at least as far as Machiavelli's *The Prince* and even Sun Tsu's *The Art of War*, and we are not going to even try to outclass those sources here. But a handful of signs of leadership might be helpful.

Good leaders have a single job—to help their organizations cope with change. By contrast, managers' job is to help their organizations cope with

CEOs who spend too little time on conceptual work spend too much time on supervising, which is why this type of leader is seen as a micromanager.

complexity—often the complexity created by change. To do their job, strategic leaders absolutely must display two distinguishing characteristics (see Exhibit 3.2). First, they must deal primarily with concepts and ideas. Ideas precede action, which is why college professors get their greatest degree of satisfaction twenty years after a course ends and their former students get a chance to act on all those ideas that they absorbed. Most people in most organizations spend most of their time operating in either the direct service zone or in a supervisory capacity. The circle diagram shows the nature of these three types of work, in rough proportion to their actual existence. Direct service, or production in a manufacturing setting, occupies the greatest amount of time and energy and dollars in a company, while supervisory work takes up considerably less. Conceptual work takes up the least time of all, because so few people do it and because there's usually less time for it than for the other two types of work.

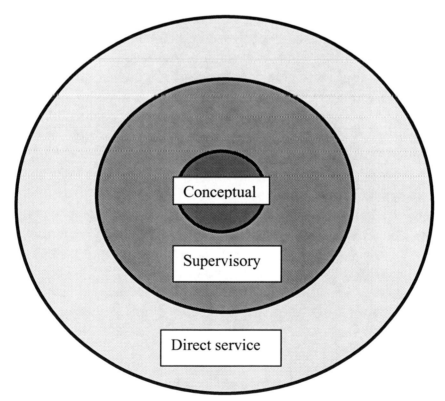

EXHIBIT   3.2   Strategic Leadership Skills

The entrepreneurial leader's second distinguishing characteristic is a relentless orientation to the future. This is the harder of the two tasks, especially in smaller organizations when the day-to-day demands of management seem simply overwhelming. It is hard to think about the long-term future when a program director has just resigned to take a better-paying job, an agency vehicle was involved in a fender bender at rush hour, and a funding source is threatening cutbacks for next year. Still, it has to be done.

The good part is that a half hour of future thinking is far more powerful than a half hour of problem solving. In a strange way, though, it is harder than solving the next problem that might come along. Problems do not often present themselves as neat packages with a clear-cut beginning, middle, and end, but at least the important ones are unmistakable. They tend to pound on the door and demand attention, and there's something to be said for the comfort one can draw from recognizing and acting upon a big problem.

Thinking toward the future is a lot messier. Not only does the entrepreneurial leader have to identify an important current trend, but he or she also has to bet correctly that it is going to continue to be worth paying attention to. This doubles one's chances of being wrong—if it is not an important trend now or if it turns out not to be important in the future, one wastes a lot of peoples' time and probably a lot of resources.

Fortunately, there is a way to orient one's thinking. Our attitudes toward the future are derived from our general orientation to time, which drives many major personal decisions in the workplace. The timeline in Exhibit 3.3 shows common orientations toward time.

Each segment of this timeline represents typical time orientations in an organization. The smallest segment is the solid part of the bar under "today." This represents the direct service zone. Many mission people in a nonprofit have this present-day orientation toward time. How many times have you heard someone say that one of the reasons that they chose their type of work is because "I can leave the job at work when I go home at night?"

Attitudes about the future are derived from our general orientation to time.

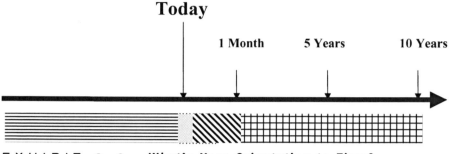

EXHIBIT 3.3   What's Your Orientation to Time?

This is a very present-oriented attitude about time. What this person is say-ing is that time for him or her is measured in hours and days. That person does not look back, and does not usually spend a lot of time looking ahead.

Managers, on the other hand, have to have a slightly broader orientation toward time. They show up as the diagonal lined segment to the right of direct service. Managers need to be worried about the present day—did Maxie show up for his shift? Do we have enough supplies on hand?—but they also need to be concerned about the future. Exactly how far into the future they routinely operate is usually determined by their natural business cycle. For instance, managers in a development department will be intensely oriented to the current campaign. Grant writers will be oriented to foun-dations' grant application cycles. Theater managers will be heavily focused on the current play, and so on. If there is no natural business cycle, man-agers will tend to be oriented to the number of weeks ahead of time for which they make up the staff schedule.

MISSION PEOPLE AND SUPPORT PEOPLE

For shorthand purposes, we will occasionally refer to mission people or support people. Mission peoples' primary responsibility puts them directly in line with others charged with actually carrying out the tasks that accomplish the mission. Support people are positions such as bookkeeper and information technology manager, which do not focus on the mission but instead help others accomplish it.

The most striking and powerful orientation to time is that of professionals, represented here by the horizontal lines. *Most professionals are oriented backward in time.* Think about it. Accountants deal mostly with transactions that have already occurred. Lawyers advise clients about cases that have already been decided and precedents that have been set. Physicians take in-depth medical histories and perform tests that can only show that a heart attack occurred, not predict the next one.

There is nothing wrong with these orientations to time. In fact, they are quite appropriate for the nature of the work that these professionals do. But for many individuals their professional orientation to time cements their approach to management. They tend to define the future as the next case, or the next symptom, or the new set of completed transactions to be recorded. Professionals unable to get out of this time orientation tend to make poor managers and leaders because they cannot get out of the habit of operating in the past or the very short-term future. Often they are not even aware of how much they instinctively look backward. These are the people on a board of directors who instinctively try to tug the organization back to some previous preferred state of affairs, who are lukewarm to innovation, or who resolutely refuse to consider new ventures "until we can manage what we are doing already."

The huge time segment unaccounted for so far is the future, the box-weave segment stretching out five and ten years. This is leadership territory, because it is the only place where things can be materially different from the way they are now. It is territory that is there for the asking, but few people in any organization ask for it. True leaders are comfortable in this zone, in part because it is very compatible with conceptual work.

These characteristics explain why leaders can be found anywhere in an organization, and they help get at one of the advantages nonprofits have in that leadership can more easily come from ideas and concepts rather than ownership of capital. The recipe card for selecting people to help plan strategy, then, is to find people in the organization who are focused on the future and who are comfortable operating with concepts and ideas. These are like DNA markers for successful participants.

When assembling a group of people to create a strategic position, look for participants with these traits. The process will be much more effective, take less energy, and be more likely to produce a successful entrepreneurial strategy.

CONSIDER INCLUDING WILDCARDS

While on the subject of picking strategy participants, let us put in a plug for what we call wildcards. These are people who would not ordinarily get a seat at the planning table because they are not part of the management-board pool of potential planners. Direct service employees and consumers are obvious choices as wildcards. Including people who have a street-level point of view about the same organizational realities that management and board members see from a distance gives new meaning to the term diversity. It also challenges possible convenient but mistaken assumptions that formal leadership might hold. Most important, it confers a subtle legitimacy on the planning process and helps communicate its outcome throughout the organization. The same leadership criteria apply here too — pick the people who can operate comfortably with concepts and ideas and who have a relentless focus on the future.

MCLAUGHLIN'S LAW OF TASK FORCE LEADERSHIP

Any task group, such as a board of directors or a senior management team, can only have a limited number of leaders as defined earlier. The actual number will vary by task group, but the formula for calculating the total number of leaders remains constant. This is McLaughlin's law:

> The total number of leaders in any task-oriented group is never greater than the square root of its membership.

The math is simple, as long as you paid attention in middle school. Take the total number of members of the task group and calculate that number's square root. So, if you have a task group of 25 people, you will have a maximum of 5 leaders. If you have a group of 100, there will be no more than 10 leaders.

Note that we said "maximum" number of leaders. You may have a maximum of five leaders but in practice only three people truly are leaders. Or two. Or, gulp, zero. These are all possibilities, but you will never have, say, 17 leaders out of 25 possibles. There just is not room enough.

Here's the implication of this law. The leaders are the ones you want to participate in a planning process, so do everything you can to get them there. Volunteer them to a committee, make a personal pitch, get someone on the board to nominate them—just get them. Never let a planning process involve just the officers of the board solely by virtue of their offices. The risk of not including enough of the leadership core is too great.

It can get crowded in that planning meeting, so try to limit the total numbers. There is a natural instinct to include dozens and dozens of people in these planning processes and that is honorable at the same time that it is doomed to fail. Once a meeting like this includes more than about 9–15 people it gets out of hand. Not that anything bad will happen; it is just that nothing much at all is likely to happen.

The two organizational population centers to draw from are the board of directors and the staff. In most instances, agencies with a manageably sized board and a comparable senior management team will produce no more than a dozen or so people. That still leaves room for a wildcard or two and possibly even the political must-have who is not really a leader at all but will make everyone's life miserable if he or she is not included.

CONSULTANT OR FACILITATOR? OR NOTHING AT ALL?

The classic question is whether to use an outside expert in a strategic planning process. The real question is who is going to own the process? Strategic positioning, like any kind of process, needs to be managed. Most people do not understand the concept of process, equating it with a meeting or a discussion. As a result, they tend to conceive of a planning process as being a group of people working together to follow an established series of steps. Their image of a planning process is akin to a group of aproned people gathered in the space between a thick butcher-block table and an industrial stove, studying a complex recipe to decide who is going to prepare the ingredients, who is going to sauté, and who is going to assemble.

Unhappily, it is not that simple. A successful strategic positioning process is a journey in thinking. It is an exercise in analysis, creativity, and implementation that asks participants to imagine the future based on the past. There can be no predetermined road map, and the end point—itself a misleadingly definitive-sounding concept—cannot even be described until one is close to it. The magic comes not from reaching certain points but from the group's reaction to the concepts it grasps and to the aspirations to which that understanding gives rise. The success comes not from finishing the process but from following up on those aspirations.

If this sounds like a maddeningly imprecise process, it is. That is why it helps to have someone own the process, whose primary responsibility is not to a specific party but to the effectiveness of the dialog. That is what a facilitator does. Most people today understand and accept the need for a facilitator in a planning process like this, but there is less agreement in practice on exactly what that person or persons should look like and what they should do. Here are some guidelines.

A good facilitator is, first and foremost, independent. When participants are intensely engaged in a planning process, their objectivity is one of the first things to go. Whether it is because of intellectual excitement or political posturing or any of a hundred other factors, they tend to get carried away by the emotional wind gusts, and it is the role of the facilitator to keep them on course.

We resist the term "objective" here. What human being is truly objective in any situation? Objectivity is a mirage, especially in a value-laden process such as strategic positioning. All human beings, particularly in a professional setting, have axes to grind and will always fall short in some way of complete objectivity. Independence, on the other hand, is attainable.

The essence of independence is not that an individual does not have any vested interests or personal agendas but that his or her interests and agendas are clearly different from those of insiders. Since the axes this person grinds are recognizably not the same as those of all the other participants, he or she can be presumed free of the emotional baggage and tactical skirmishing that consume insiders.

Who fulfills the criteria for independence is fairly simple. Only someone from outside the organization can be truly independent, meaning a member of that despised minority known as management consultants. But not just any consultant. Exclude regular consultants that are well known by the organization, unless they are in the rare category of consulting outsiders who have not accumulated much political baggage in their previous projects. And exclude those who are generalists. Facilitation is a rare skill.

Distinguish between a consultant who acts as a facilitator and one who acts as a facilitator and a resource, and seek the latter. Straight facilitators know how to make the process work but will probably lack knowledge of the industry. Facilitators who know the field bring a crucial dimension.

Sometimes a parsimonious CEO is tempted to use an internal person as the facilitator. Bad idea. Perhaps under extremely limited circumstances—such as a board member who has barely attended his or her first board meeting and has demonstrable facilitative skills—you could get away with using an internal person. But in strategic positioning, as in life, you tend to get what you pay for.

One thing is certain, however: no guiding force at all leads to planning drift. This process is about change and choice, and the embarrassing fact is that most groups of human beings do not easily chose to change without at least some nudge. One of the functions of a facilitator, no matter where they came from or what they are paid, is to, skillfully and subtly, *nudge*.

Prepare

One of the first things to do to prepare for strategic positioning is to check that mission statement. Without stock options, cushy salaries, or nosey shareholders, nonprofits do not have many control tools available to them. Your mission statement is one of the few, so use it.

THEME IDENTIFICATION PERCENTAGE ("TIP SCORE")

Try this test. Analyze your mission statement and break it into as many different key ideas as it contains. A key idea is usually expressed by a noun ("poverty," "music") or a significant adjective ("rural," "symphonic"). Generally, you will find no more than about three or four key ideas per sentence; there just is not much room for more than that, and often there will be less. In a reasonably short mission statement, one might find five to ten key ideas.

Ask the board (or staff members, or a mixed group) to write the mission from memory on a piece of paper. Check each written summary for the number of key ideas from the actual mission statement that appear, and calculate the total number of matches against the total number of possible matches. If ten people did the exercise and there were ten key ideas in their mission statement, there would be a possible 100 matches. If there were in fact a total of 30 matches from the 10 people, the score would be 30 percent.

We call this the Theme Identification Percentage Score (or TIP), and we have found that most nonprofits score in the 5–25 percent range. Anything over 25 percent, in our experience, suggests a strong mission

INTRODUCING WILLOWS' END
ASSISTED LIVING CENTER

To illustrate these points, we reintroduce the Willows' End Assisted Living Center, a 120-bed assisted living center located in a converted factory building in the Willows' End neighborhood in a large town. We will use Willows' End, a composite of many related organizations, to illustrate some of the key points and concepts in the strategic positioning process.

For Willows' End's first in-process appearance, we concentrate on its mission statement, which currently reads as follows:

To care for older adults with dementia, and support their caregivers, friends, and family.

In reviewing the statement, planners noted that "care for" sounded bland, and that 'support' could mean many things. Some also felt that the reference to caregivers in the same sentence as friends and family was redundant and possibly confusing. Others argued that "caregivers" as used should refer to anyone who gave care to older adults with dementia, and that in effect it also suggested that Willows' End would support its own staff of caregivers.

Willows' End's strategic positioning committee decided as part of its preplanning work that the existing mission statement is adequate— for now. The points raised were perhaps valid, but not worth pursuing at this time. They decided to revisit the mission statement within three years.

Note: we will include examples of the application of many tools and techniques using Willows' End periodically throughout the rest of the book.

statement. Scores over 50 percent are very unusual and suggest a highly mission-oriented organization.

WHAT TO DO ABOUT IT

If your mission statement is less than memorable, the solution might be as simple as a few mechanical fixes. Here are some of them.

Make It Pass the Business Card Test

If your mission cannot be written comfortably on the back of a business card, it is too long. Mission statements tend to get wordy for one reason: Group Write. Nothing will ruin a good mission statement faster than a Mission Statement Writing Committee. Whether through political correctness or the inability to make stylistic choices, committees are not good at writing short statements (on the other hand, committees are great at writing long statements, cf. the United States' Constitution). Avoid this tendency by setting a simple ground rule at the beginning of any planning session: *no wordsmithing*. Appoint a committee of one to write the mission statement, with everyone else acting as reviewers of the draft.

Make It Conform to the Deli Principle

The second problem with your mission statement may be that it violates the Deli Principle. Go to any deli and order a peanut butter and jelly sandwich. Chances are excellent that you will get exactly what you want. But try to order a ham and cheese with a trace of spicy mustard, lettuce, tomatoes, and hot peppers on a sesame bulky roll sliced in half with a pickle wrapped separately on the side. Guaranteed, the counter person will ask you to repeat at least part of that order. Why? Because you exceeded his or her capacity to manage variables.

Most of us can only hold up to about seven variables in our mind at any one time (it is why phone numbers originally had seven digits). Mission statements violate the Deli Principle when they have an excessive number of variables. We call these variables moving parts, and the more moving parts an object has the more likely it will be to break down. Moreover, the more complicated something seems, the more likely people will not understand it. Either way, the mission statement will not work.

How do you simplify a mission statement? One place to start is by getting rid of extra adverbs. Adverbs tell *how* one does something, which is usually superfluous in a mission statement because it should concentrate on describing *what* one plans to do. In fact, process-related information is not typically helpful in a mission statement at all. The fact that your organization intends to carry out its mission "enthusiastically" is of no interest to most people.

Another candidate for elimination is adjectives. Our perennial favorite adjective for deletion is the adjective *quality*, as in "we deliver high-quality

WHAT'S WRONG WITH THIS MISSION STATEMENT?

"With inclusiveness and diversity, we provide the highest-quality services to disadvantaged service recipients and those with special challenges. We are committed to maintaining a supportive, open, empowering working future dedicated to individual choice and the preservation of human dignity."
    (What isn't wrong with it?)

services. . . ." Is it really necessary to say this? Can we not just take it for granted that that is what you intend to do? Whoever would say they intend to deliver mediocre services, anyway?

Make It Active

Another way to improve the mission statement is to write it in the active voice. The passive voice is always a bit stilted and distancing. Saying "our clients will be given . . ." instead of "we will give our clients . . ." subtly suggests passivity and reactive thinking. The cooling effect of the passive voice dilutes a mission statement's power.

Make It Say Something

Strategy is about making choices, and so are mission statements. Trying to make the mission statement do too much is a sure way of making it do too little. So is making the mission statement speak only about process, which is the surest way to create an insipid mission statement. In the end, no one cares very much about the precise way you are going to go about serving your mission, and over time it will probably change anyway. One respected nonprofit began as a small institution in the 1920s with a single mission—"to provide health care to the poor." Eight decades later it is still doing the same thing, except that it has grown into a respected community hospital, a teaching institution, and a major community force. Yet there was never a word about creating a hospital in the original mission statement. What's more, if it turned itself into a completely different kind of institution tomorrow it could still be just as faithful to its original mission.

Clean It Up

Make your mission statement broom-clean in other ways. Lose the jargon and the highly technical references. Forget the clichés. Geographic references may not be as important as you think. Funding sources should be honored during fancy public dinners, not by putting them in the mission statement. The reason for all of these prohibitions is the same—avoiding clutter and unnecessary restrictions. The geographic reference that seems so obvious today may feel like a set of handcuffs tomorrow, and funding sources can change with alarming speed.

Sell It

A mission statement is the first formal touchstone of a nonprofit organization. It is what helps others define your organization, and it is the one management statement with which insiders most readily identify. It is therefore a management tool. Sell it with the same enthusiasm that you'd give to a promising donor or a willing foundation.

It is said that repetition is the essence of advertising. That makes a case for finding ways to get the mission statement out in front of people repeatedly. One of the most obvious yet most effective ways to get the message out is to post it. Print the mission statement in a nice format and frame it tastefully for hanging in waiting areas, hallways, meeting rooms, offices, and just about any other location you can think of except for restrooms.

There's an ulterior motive in this seemingly obsessive self-promotion. People need to know quickly whether this is an organization that they want to be involved with, and the mission statement is a powerful shorthand if it is the first thing that they see. Prospective funders immediately have a way of gauging their "fit" with the organization, and jobseekers decide whether they want to work for the place or not. Even outsiders who work regularly with the nonprofit can use a periodic reminder of what the organization is supposed to be all about.

WAYS TO "SELL" YOUR MISSION STATEMENT

Award/recognition Pieces
Business cards
Fax cover sheets
In the lobby/waiting rooms
Newsletter masthead
On board agendas
On business cards
On fax cover sheets
On formal stationery
On invoices
On thank you notes
On the back of envelopes
On the newsletter's masthead
On the website
On voicemail greetings
On website
On your vehicles
Reading it at board meetings
Screen savers

The box above contains some concrete suggestions for promoting your mission that cost little or nothing (some suggestions are only practical for very short, powerful mission statements). Many organizations will find unique opportunities in their own operations.

WHEN THE MISSION IS PREESTABLISHED

In many cases the mission is a given. Many of the name-brand nonprofit systems such as Boys & Girls Clubs or Make-A-Wish Foundations require that their affiliates use the same mission statement. In these cases, there is little mystery about the mission, so the groups need not labor over the actual statement and can focus instead on the mechanical aspects of using it to its fullest extent.

TAP INTO THE EMOTION

Note something about this section: so far it has all been about cognitive, intellectual kinds of things. Yet a good mission statement will tug at the heart strings of even the most aloof, unemotional board member. It is a compelling mission that will most readily distinguish nonprofits from their for-profit counterparts, so why not use it?

Most board and staff members will make their own emotional connection with the mission if you let them. Much of the preceding material is about how to make that connection easier. But it has also been about making private, individual connections—what happens when a person reads a mission statement, or how a mission can be made easier to remember. To really use the power of a mission, use the power of a group.

Most people connected with a nonprofit will have their own story to tell about the mission statement, or will develop one early in their relationship with the group. It will not work to force people to tell those stories, and it will seem hokey anyway. An alternative is to create a culture where people can reference those stories easily and naturally. Strangely, it will take some work to make it seem natural, but it can be done.

Boards of directors can have the easiest time of it. They can begin meetings with a story about a consumer, for example, or the nominating committee can ask about a potential candidate's personal connection with the mission. Board members often have a vast pool of emotional attachment to the organization, or at least they could have if they were properly invited to do so.

DO NOT FORGET THE VISUALS

One often overlooked way of tapping into the emotional power of a mission is through visual means. Hanging photographs around the office, or including meaningful pictures in official communications is a great way to give permission to stakeholders to tap into the collective emotional identification with the mission.

Scan Your Future

Traditional nonprofit organizations wait for their future to define market needs, which usually happens through the actions of government funders or foundations. Strategically minded nonprofits try to recognize those needs and then look for ways to fund responses to them. It is a subtle but hugely important difference. Both types of organizations must study their future as part of strategic positioning, but they will look in different places for different things.

No doubt about it, the massive amount of government funding that has gone into the nonprofit sector in recent decades has been a good thing. But one of the ways it is been counterproductive is that it has quietly turned nonprofits into domesticated black bears, no longer afraid of contact and willing to hang around the back porch for the next feeding. That's not to say that reduced government funding is a good thing, just that government-funded nonprofits as a class risk losing the vitality that made them such an attractive partner in the first place.

The seductive thing about government funding is that it excuses the nonprofit from having to do market research, which is just a more formal and slightly narrower way to scan one's future. If the government says it is a problem and offers money to solve it, well then it is definitely a problem. The downside to this dynamic has two parts. First, it discourages nonprofits from being more aware of their future by encouraging them to think of that future through the government's eyes. Philosophically that's not a bad thing, but in practical terms it means that nonprofits may uncritically absorb the arm's-length character of government thinking.

Governments are not good individual problem solvers; nonprofits are. Governments are good at recognizing problems, processing a consensus about what to do, possibly securing some resources, and then finding a way to get things done. Government gets into trouble when it tries to deal at the individual level. Government units are not good at running waiting rooms, helping desperate single moms, identifying promising artists, doing surgery, or supplying extra blankets to homeless shelters during a sudden cold snap. One of the reasons why in the nineteenth century massive, dehumanizing governmentally operated institutions came into being to deal with social problems, such as mental illness and law-breaking juveniles, is that the nonprofit sector was simply not developed enough to take on the challenge itself. Had it been able to do so, many of those solutions would undoubtedly have looked very different.

The second downside to government funding, then, is that it can have the effect of separating the nonprofit from its community. When community needs get filtered through the governmental lens and are backed by funding, the nonprofit's attention is inevitably split. Given enough time and enough government funding, that split can grow wide, deep, and nearly permanent. After the split comes a kind of complacency.

It is not that the individuals involved in either the governmental unit or the nonprofit are complacent about the social need. What they become complacent about is the more or less steady stream of money and attention dedicated to the need. Government is slow to start up and slow to close down. Where it clicks into a rhythm is in the middle, when it has figured out how to make a process run consistently and keep it in a steady direction. In this aspect, it is not much different from any large bureaucracy, which needs to operate predictably and uncritically.

One of the intentions of a future scan is to disturb this steady state in order to rethink fundamental assumptions about need. Some developmental disability service providers needed to do this several years after the crack epidemic in the late 1980s and 1990s, when the demands of their normal client population were skewed tremendously by the unique physical and mental damage that babies of mothers addicted to crack suffer. As a result, their population service profile changed significantly. Those who anticipated the change well enough in advance had a better chance of adjusting their services and funding sources to adapt.

Organizations using substantial volunteer time that paid attention to their future began rethinking their assumptions during the 1980s as well. The average volunteer shifted dramatically away from the long-term model of a volunteer assignment over time to a decidedly short-term focus, preferring one-day or one-project assignments over long-term relationships. Organizations in touch with their future were not surprised by this switch because they correctly read the signals of squeezed family time and higher productivity demands from employers and were able to respond with what has by now become a widely accepted one-day model for many volunteers. This is the essence of a strategic response.

This forced rethinking of the organization's basic assumptions about the future is one of the reasons for studying the future in the first place. In truth, this future scanning process is all about institutional learning, with hopes that a few opportunities will present themselves somewhere along the line. The desired result of the process itself is mutual education.

The bedrock need here is survival. Most institutions and the people who work in them spend most of their time managing the details and grinding out the work with little chance to think about the larger context in which they operate. There is rarely time for reflection, let alone careful observation of macro trends. Yet it is precisely those trends that will shape the nonprofit's future. If the future scan does nothing else, it should provide a

POOR, MISSHAPEN COMMUNITY

What word in the English language is more used and abused than "community"? It has to be in the top 10, right? For these purposes, we will define community as the geographic area of service defined entirely by the nonprofit itself. This takes it down somewhat from its often lofty perch, but we need the word to refer to something very tangible and understandable. At the same time, geographic area does not necessarily mean "administrative borders." We do not care if your community crosses state lines, city lines, or even socioeconomic lines—the boundaries you draw on a map, however crude or imprecise they may be, define your community.

chance to catch up on the big, sweeping developments that will govern many of tomorrow's details.

A FEW BIG TRENDS

For the most part, what it takes to succeed at running a for-profit business is similar to what it takes to succeed at running a nonprofit. There are differences, of course, but the similarities dominate because social norms, laws, and the realities of economics do not change to accommodate a particular tax classification. More important, what it takes to succeed in running either type of organization is changing.

It has become widely accepted that our economy has moved decisively in a new direction in recent decades. Since the early part of the nineteenth century the primary economic task had been to industrialize society, to find ever newer and better ways of organizing companies and individuals to produce more and better goods. This was in contrast to the prior generations when the primary economic task was finding newer and better ways to farm. There was always a service-oriented part of the economy, but in the industrializing society that began almost 200 years ago production of services was secondary to the production of goods.

Somewhere in the late 70s to 80s we started shifting to an economy where the primary economic task was the production and use of information. Again, farming still existed, and industrial-age production still existed, but a kind of tipping point was reached and we moved into an information-based economy. With that change has come many associated changes. And, again, what it takes to succeed in the for-profit world still turns out to look a lot like what it takes to succeed in the nonprofit world (we are talking about fundamental economic tasks, not personality judgments).

With the shift in the nature of the major economic tasks came shifts in the way that nonprofits responded to the demands of their newly information-based future. The coping tools and styles needed in the industrial non-profit economy began to give way to the tools and styles needed in the information-based nonprofit economy. Here are a few of the big changes we are seeing. Note that some are well under way, while others may only be at the beginning. No matter: the "from' category represents what used to work well, the "to" column category what works well now.

From Command and Control to Shape and Influence

An industrialized economy must operate in a fairly strict command-and-control style. When the major task is producing large numbers of consumer goods, the people in charge have to have close control or else the assembly line will implode and profitability will vaporize. Nonprofits that were the assembly line equivalents in the industrial era include large residential care providers for the developmentally delayed, mentally ill, and adjudicated delinquents. Museums and large opera houses are industrial-style nonprofits too. Universities are perhaps the ultimate assembly line, producing millions of college graduates.

Of course, many, if not most, of these models will carry over well into the furthest reaches of the information economy also. But there will be two significant changes. First, we will not be producing as many of these models in the future, and some of the old ones will shut down. New energies in the sector will produce different-looking institutions. Second, even the older models that survive will over time begin to look partly like the newer institutions. Museums are now online, as are universities. Opera houses will see rock concerts more than *La Boheme*. And large residential service providers will move toward home-based programming and outreach.

What does the concept of shaping and influencing mean as an alternative to command-and-control? The latter requires strict hierarchical organizations with defined roles for all participants and relatively little room to maneuver outside of those bounds. In an economy where shaping and influencing are the primary means of getting things done, organizations will be flatter. It is not an accident that the recession of the early 1990s, which coincided with a stepped-up movement toward the new information-based economy, saw some of the largest layoffs in the formerly untouchable middle manager ranks in corporate America, and the elimination of a layer of overhead in nonprofits (does anyone remember the days before voicemail?).

On a person-to-person level, shaping and influencing as a primary means of getting things done also means relationships in a nonprofit are more important than positions on the organizational chart. In a command-and-control future, the loud personality in a management position could often be counted on to get more than his or her share of things done. In a shaping and influencing future, the loud personality is more likely to be ignored.

Persuasion is more important than command, and political ability is as important as technical knowledge.

From Employees to Employee/Consultants

In keeping with the shift to flatter, less hierarchical organizational work styles, the common model of employment in nonprofits is shifting as well. In an industrial age nonprofit, people were hired to fill slots. The value of any single direct service worker lay in his or her ability to perform a specific job description. There were relatively fewer distinctions among workers. The relationship between the nonprofit and the employee was proscribed and, at least implicitly, had no natural end point.

Today's nonprofits, in step with employees and various socioeconomic realities, have had to change those expectations. Whereas the labor force in the industrial economy tended to be composed of large numbers of the same type of position, the labor force today is more highly articulated, with greater specialization, more degreed professionals, and a greater diversity ranging from highly educated to less well educated. In areas such as health and human services, there has been enough time spent in developing distinct service models that one and perhaps two generations of employees now have enough long-term service that they can be just as valuable as degreed professionals. There is greater specialization in the workforce generally—professional human resource management only began to gather momentum as an accepted practice in the last three or four decades—and modern nonprofit executives truly see their employees as having inherent value rather than just being the right people at the right time to fill prefabricated slots.

This employee-as-consultant model also has produced many other characteristics. Consultant types do not expect long-term employment arrangements: whether today's nonprofit employees want them or not, factors such as increased mobility and the sheer variety of job choices tend to make today's employees look more like consultants on three- or four-year assignments. Nonprofits for their part cannot afford and do not want the long-term liabilities that come with an implicit expectation of long-term employment tenures. And a younger generation of nonprofit employees are more demanding of their employment situations, either out of a desire to have more personal time or because they have overwhelming personal demands.

All of this means that the nonprofit work force has changed dramatically in recent decades and will continue to do so. This has implications for everything from how easy it is to start up new programs to the benefit plan choices the nonprofit employer decides to offer. The details for each organization will differ, but these overall themes will remain the same.

From Square Footage to Megabytes

It used to be that a building was essential to doing business in the nonprofit sector, and in many cases the unofficial rule was the bigger, the better. This was because site-based services were the norm: to get most kinds of nonprofit services in the industrial era you had to go to the nonprofit's site. This is most evident in universities and hospitals, but just as evident in things like YMCAs and special education residential schools.

There were very practical reasons for this situation. Transportation in most parts of the country was difficult for the first half of the twentieth century, at least until the interstate system began to take hold. People in general were not as mobile as now, and the primary identification tended to be with one's neighborhood or town. So, it made sense that community-oriented organizations staked their claim in real estate.

The building also served a secondary purpose as a statement: *we have arrived*, it said. We are rich enough or wily enough or we work hard enough to be able to afford this building, and you'd better pay attention. This was a nice PR statement as well as something of a statement of fact—not every organization had a building it could call its own, especially as the numbers of nonprofits began multiplying. The for-profit sector took exactly the same approach. One need only look at Detroit's massive auto factories or Pittsburgh's steel plants or the sprawling textile mills of the northeast to see that square footage was an integral part of the production process. It did not hurt either sector that real estate went through several bursts of rapid appreciation during that time.

But something subtle happened over the past two or three decades. The building that was such a prize began to be a drain. Organizational energy that should have gone into programs and services got diverted into haggling with contractors, repairing the roof, and pursuing special zoning approvals for expansion. Moreover, all those bricks and mortar started to cost a lot in out-of-pocket dollars that could have gone to more productive uses. For

THE BOYS & GIRLS CLUBS MODEL FOR GROWTH: CLUBHOUSES WITHOUT THE CAPITAL CAMPAIGN

Even some old and venerable service models can be tweaked to be less reliant on fixed sites. During the late 1990s and into the current century, Boys & Girls Clubs of America put up some 300 new clubs every year. The fastest growing segment? Clubs on Native American reservations, at public schools, in public housing, and on military bases—all locations where someone else owned the buildings and fledgling clubs could concentrate on programs instead of spending years raising money for a building.

those organizations that weren't into the ownership game before real estate started appreciating, getting in proved a more daunting task.

The trend away from site-based services was hastened by the rise of automation. Faster computer networks, improved broadband access, and the general rise of the Internet as an integral part of doing business all reduced some of the rationale for a fixed site. But an equally important part was the development of alternative service models. Outreach programs in the 1970s and later were an explicit rejection of the idea that nonprofits had to have a building in order to offer services. Today, the nonprofit that does not need a large or fixed site for its operations is positioned to enjoy a distinct strategic advantage. In fact, many of the new models of nonprofit services have little to do with unique pieces of real estate: look to the newer advocacy organizations, or youth groups like City Year to see how irrelevant a fixed site can be.

Today the ability to acquire and manage real estate is less important than the ability to acquire and manage information. A digital footprint is more crucial to manage nonprofits' ability to manage than is a fixed site. The terms of that technological capacity varies from organization to organization, but the infrastructure that can get information into the organization, process it, and then get it out again is the new equivalent of bricks and mortar.

From Social Elite Fundraising to Cognitive Elite Fundraising

In years past the monied class tended to have gotten that way from the luck of the parental draw. There was an elite in our society, and it tended to iden-tify and reproduce itself via institutions with names like Phillips Andover and Yale and Smith Barney and the Met. Very East Coast-y and closed, and the governing principle was to stay that way by keeping things within the family, metaphorically speaking. Either you were the factory owner or the owner's offspring or you worked in the factory.

Fundraising in this world was not all that difficult, as long as you were part of it. Fundraising if you were not part of it was mainly a matter of identifying the key players and trying to get as close to them as an outsider would be allowed to do. Persistence and a certain demeanor paid off, and luck helped too.

In the seventies a number of factors began to break down these com-fortable divisions and to create the best educated class of young people the country had ever seen. It helped a lot that universities and colleges had learned how to be very skillful and efficient at picking cognitively strong future students, and that the social elite could not monopolize the cogni-tive skills bank completely. Social trends toward more inclusion and less class rigidity helped as well.

As the economy moved more toward services and away from manufac-turing, that first batch of educated workers fit right in. Some did more than that and created companies that soared in the new economy, bring-ing them huge newfound wealth. In turn, their companies created another round of similar entrepreneurs, and all those companies employed fellow cognitive achievers. Today, what used to be known as the white collar workforce has expanded way beyond its initial dimensions to encompass a large percentage of workers in most areas.

This swelling of the cognitive elite and the accompanying improvement in the standard of living has placed wealth available for donations in more hands. The Internet boom in the late 1990s and the great wealth transfer as the baby boomers' parents pass their wealth onto their now middle-aged children has boosted prospects too. The result is that fundraising is no longer the exclusive purview of the gentry but an undertaking avail-able to ordinary affluent Americans as well. It may still be the province of clublike networks, but the dimensions are larger and the pitch is more cognitive-based. Much has been written about the new donors, and we will not attempt to add to that here. The essential point is that their wealth came from a different base, they are acting differently in their charitable endeavors, and the strategically well-positioned nonprofit will take that into consideration.

From Growth to Productivity

During much of the industrial economy, growth was an imperative for all organizations, including nonprofits. The middle part of the twentieth century saw impressive growth trajectories for many nonprofits, especially the national household name federations, partly to keep up with the booming postwar demand and partly because domestic energies made the time right for growth. In that future, numbers were all-important because reach was important.

A growth imperative changes things inside an organization. When sheer volume is the target and the future provides the resources, organizations are excused from performing what in other times might be tougher tasks. Losses are easier to hide because there are always new dollars that can cover them, problem employees can be more readily shifted to new parts of the entity when they wear out their welcome, and there's a general sense of excitement and forward motion.

Conversely, when growth is no longer as important and no longer as easy to achieve, the focus turns inward. This is what has happened with the majority of nonprofits in recent years. It is often superficially interpreted as a concern with cost control, but it is really broader than that, instead being an effort to rework the economic structure. That's when productivity becomes a more important goal than growth. It is the way that health care providers have had to respond to managed care and the other changes in their industry, and it is what is just beginning to affect higher education.

The term "lack of growth" is also sometimes a euphemism for a stagnant or declining field, which drives a focus on productivity just as surely as does an economic downturn. The fact is that many of the fields in which nonprofits are active are "mature industries," meaning that the growth curve has leveled off. Hospitals are part of a mature industry, and so are allied services such as mental health and skilled nursing. Many social services are mature in this same sense as well, having reached a point where growth is not an option, and the larger struggle is just to hang on to what has been achieved.

In this kind of setting, the important type of growth is growth in productivity. Driving productivity gains internally can create the same degree of change as growth will create, but for different reasons: cost cutbacks, constant retooling of processes, increased use of technology, and mergers and alliances are all ways of changing to adapt to the demands for more productivity. In a productivity-driven future, growth in the sense of more-of-the-same is no longer possible, and this sets the stage for mergers and restructurings.

From Standalone Nonprofits to Integrated Delivery Systems

Remember the original advertising logo for the IBM PC when it first came out? It was Charlie Chaplin's Little Tramp, a lovable warm and fuzzy little guy who duck-walked his way across television screens whenever IBM advertised its brand-new personal computer. The icon served a purpose because it softened the hard edges and blurred the scariness (for many) of this new device. After all, before the IBM PC the best-known computer for most people was HAL, the menacing computer from *2001: A Space Odyssey*. The species needed a publicity makeover, and the Little Tramp helped soften and make accessible something that could easily have been alien and ominous.

Ironically, for all his lovable qualities, The Little Tramp was in his own way not a break with the past. Because, above all else, The Little Tramp was every bit the rugged individualist, just as much a solo player as the television cowboy of a previous generation. It did not take computer makers and users long to figure out that the real breakthrough was not the power of the personal computer alone but the power of many personal computers linked together. There is a reason why IBM eventually adopted the *M.A.S.H.* team from the television series as its new logo—it was arguably the best-known team in America, and IBM needed to show that computers are best when they play well together.

In symbolic terms this migration from individual computer to networked computers parallels what is happening in nonprofit service delivery as more and more nonprofits find that they must work closely with others to get their work done. The iconic standalone nonprofit is as much a thing of the past as is the lonesome cowboy riding the range. This means that nonprofits expecting to execute a strategic position will need to build collaboration muscle into their execution plans.

From Innovation in Programming to Innovation in Management

To understand this shift, which has been well under way for several years now, it is necessary to go all the way back to the middle of the last century. This was a time of remarkable expansion in all phases of American society, not the least of which were several grand experiments in social welfare such as Medicaid, Medicare, and the supplemental amendments to the Social Security system. These were some of the most innovative steps of their time, and they were based on the contributions of the government and the nonprofit sector's best brains.

It was a time when new programs and program models seemed to be created every week. Foundations helped things along by willingly funding new models that had promise: it was assumed, with justification, that some arm of government would eventually pick up successful program models.

As a result, most of the energy and resources available for innovation in the nonprofit sector went straight into programming. From a historic perspective, this direction made sense. Management considerations are secondary when the underlying objective is to create society-wide change while experimenting with new models at the same time. And it worked. The shared spirit of innovation carried throughout the sixties and seventies and into the eighties.

Note that we are talking about where the bulk of innovative energies go in the sector, not where any innovation at all was occurring. There are so many nonprofit organizations and so many people involved that innovation is going to occur in any era in most aspects of delivering services. The point is that different types of innovation occur at different times. What happened in most of the second half of the twentieth century was that the critical mass of leadership energy was directed at program innovation.

All that began to change during the last two decades. Federal cutbacks initiated during the Reagan years—plus the decision to channel federal awards to nonprofits through state governments rather than directly to the nonprofits or through local cities and towns—began to jack up the pressure for new ways to manage existing resources.

The recessions of the mid-1980s and early 1990s upped the pressure. The early stages of a preference for innovation in management over program could be seen as nonprofits' desire to add a "grant writer" or someone skilled in some aspect of fundraising. Later it would be a focus on finding someone to be a human resources professional, and later still it would be information technology.

Innovation did not occur just in the positions hired. In the health care world the innovation energy shifted into cost control with the popularization of managed care, capitated payments, and health maintenance organizations. The arts world was one of the first to innovate in management practices by creating mergers, albeit somewhat reluctantly. Privatization of government services to nonprofits is another example of management-based innovation. All this time there were unquestionably innovations going on in program services, but the real momentum and urgency for innovation could be found in management. This trend continues today and gives every indication that it will continue long into the future.

FEDERAL CUTBACKS LESS IMPORTANT THAN CHANGING RESPONSIBILITY

Although the effect of the Reagan era cutbacks in social services was well documented, the larger impact was the switch from large-scale direct federal involvement with nonprofits to large-scale direct *state* involvement. This meant that organizations had to refocus their activity from the federal bureaucrat to the state bureaucrat. While putting decision making a bit closer to the front lines, this change also meant that states assumed more of a management role. Subtly, expectations began to shift from the federal government to state governments when community-based programs sought new monies, wanted rule changes, and looked for overall direction.

From Strategic Planning to Strategic Positioning

Finally, there has been a gradual shift from strategic planning as it was originally practiced in the postwar years to a more subtle yet more powerful emphasis on what we call strategic positioning. Strategic planning is generally held to have roots in the military, making its way into American business practices beginning in the mid-nineteenth century. By the middle part of the 1960s it had been embraced by corporate America, and the term was comfortably on its way to icon status. But something happened en route.

Gradually, strategic planning became more like planning and less like strategy. Any finished product that has to be packaged in three ring binders is a planning document, not a strategy. Strategic thinking came to be the province of planning types and middle managers for whom bulk, not insight, was the major goal. Nonprofit organizations, which were relatively slow to adopt strategic planning in the first place, began doing so at just about the time that this creeping bureaucratization started to take over the practice.

The result is that, for many nonprofits, strategic planning became largely a collection of recipe cards and formulas. This trivialized the process and made the inherent difficulty of such an organization-wide process seem largely a matter of filling out the right forms.

The result is that organizations and their leaders feel unsatisfied with much of their strategy planning experience, or that the product does not produce the gains desired.

Still, many organizations have positive outcomes. We feel that this is because they are "deviating" from traditional practice by developing a more durable, practical strategy defined in terms of external and internal realities such as the nature of the need or demand for their services, the competition, effective program models, organizational strengths, and people to carry out the strategy—in short, a strategic position. Organizations that aim to achieve or maintain a strategic position—or some equivalent concept—are finding that it is a more workable way to make the critical distinction between the plans necessary to carry out a strategy and the plans necessary to execute it.

A strategic position is an approach to the strategic task, not an unvarying set of steps. The dual goals of strategic positioning, whether articulated as such or not, are to create a long-lasting view of the desired future and to differentiate this view from the detailed, management-based effort needed to achieve it. Think of strategic positioning as a great deal of shared thinking synthesized into a relatively small amount of intellectual gray matter, supported by the skeleton, muscle, and tissue of the working body. Strategic positioning is in keeping with the demands of carrying out nonprofit business in the twentieth century—a lean, flexible, and powerful way of moving an organizational agenda forward in an uncertain and constantly changing future.

THE PARAMETERS OF A FUTURE SCAN

For many people, staring at the future is a difficult task. A figurative look outside the front door brings a swirling, senseless mass of energy that has no obvious form or meaning. For those more comfortable with administrative details and routine procedures, the act is frustrating and of questionable usefulness. Even for those comfortable with ambiguities, the task can be intimidating.

The solution is to break the chore down into manageable parts. This "future" we have been referring to is really the business conditions that exist outside of the organization's day-to-day control. Whatever can be controlled, at least on a day-by-day basis, is more likely going to be the subject of operations, not strategy. The typical nonprofit organization can study its future through a handful of lenses:

- The demand for one's services
- Geography
- Users and potential users of one's service
- Competitors
- Funders (and regulators)
- Labor force
- Special assets, if any

These lenses are useful categories only. While groups can place the vast majority of their strategic material in one of these baskets, the purpose of suggesting them is to provide a framework for scanning, not a rigid system of categorization. The best way to use these categories is to concentrate on the ones most pertinent to each individual organization. For example, in

USE MICRO-PLANNING

Future scanning is a good place to use micro-planning, our term for individual or very small-team-based research and documentation. By assigning responsibility for preparing scan sheets for each of the seven elements of future scanning to one or two people, an organization creates broad-based knowledge and wide buy-in for the process itself. Those individuals become in-house experts who can speak to the topic's nuances and offer deeper insights into the material than can be communicated in writing.

some nonprofit situations there are no direct competitors or alternatives owing to situations like rural locations or governmental regulations. So, the attention in those cases would go mainly to indirect competitors or alternatives. Special assets may not be very relevant in a given case, and regulators may not even exist as a consideration.

With the understanding that strategic positioners should prioritize these categories for their own institutions, we will take each one in turn and try to suggest ways of examining it to derive the maximum amount of insight and self-education.

The Demand for Your Service

Since most nonprofits are responding to some sort of community need—often a dysfunction—it is critical for the organization as a whole to learn everything it can about it. Oddly, this is a problem. One reason that the future scan of community need can be a problem is because it is such an unusual assignment. Most nonprofit board members and managers come on the scene well after the big thinking has already been done. In these circumstances, it is only natural to settle in and try to make things work rather than reexamining the larger context in which the organization got started.

When some people try to do future scans of something as abstract as community need, they tend to equate the need with their clients or with the programs and services they provide. Instead of thinking broadly about the larger community's need in the context of the agency's mission, they

**WILLOWS' END SCAN SHEET:
COMMUNITY NEED—DEMENTIA**

Trends
- About 3 percent of men and women 65 to 74 suffer from dementia.
- After 65, this percentage doubles with every decade of life.
- Women are more likely to be caregivers than men (58 percent to 48 percent).
- One third to one half of caregivers reported a significant impact on their lives.
- The over-85 population is the fastest growing group in America.
- The baby boomer generation will swell the aging population (65 or older) beginning around 2012.
- The baby boomer generation will have a life expectancy in the 66–71 year range.
- The elder population, which was 13 percent of the total population in 2000, will be 21 percent of the population in 2040.
- Until about 30 years ago, the only caregiving alternative for those suffering from dementia was a nursing home.
- In the 1999 *Olmstead v. L.C.* case, the U.S. Supreme Court ruled that unjustified institutionalization is a form of discrimination, fueling community-based care.
- On average, states spend about 35 percent of their Medicaid budgets on long-term care.

Implications for Willows' End
- Demand for services to older adults with dementia will grow.
- The current model of nursing home-heavy care is not sustainable, and there will be a need for alternatives.
- The aging boomer generation will demand and get more services outside of institutions.
- Willows' End will have many opportunities in the coming 10–15 years to either grow in size or increase the range of its services.
- The next two decades in elder care are likely to be characterized by heavy demand for Willows' End's services and short supply of alternatives

will focus on the clients as the definition of need. Or, they may regard the existence of the organization's programs and services as obvious evidence of the need. The result is that they can never get to the starting point.

Part of good management consists of fitting the right people's skills with the right demands, and that is true here as well. The easiest way to get some good work on this first part of the future scan is to enlist the right kind of thinkers. For this task one needs broader thinkers, not technical types. Once the group understands the nature of this task, the right thinkers will usually self-select themselves to do it.

Community need changes constantly. This may seem so self-evident that it borders on the trivial, but it is a real problem if community needs change faster than the organization can keep up (the smaller the geographic focus, the more likely this will happen). This is all the more reason for scanning community need as part of the planning process. Also, needs do not always get expressed straightforwardly. The school criticized for low standardized test scores may need increased parental involvement as a prelude to score improvement, but that will not always be clear.

Geography

The default starting point for all future scanning should be what is going on nationally. Chances are that what is happening locally is not all that different from what is happening in other localities. It is a rarity when there is a significant difference. In any case, collecting information from comparable areas and from national perspectives puts local affairs in context. Done right, it can even suggest patterns and trends that will play out locally.

National research is meant to expand the bounds, so draw a big circle and explore it. Census data is essential in most cases and can now be obtained electronically. The big market Sunday paper magazines are often good for an occasional timely article in your subject area, as are the national news magazines. Pundits count for more than one might imagine—after all, the point of scanning the future is to begin to guess at what is going to happen, and talking heads are as good at that as anyone.

Demographics are vastly underappreciated as drivers of change. If you can get past the dry presentations of many demographers there's a payoff to be had. The beauty of demographics is that most changes unfold in slow motion. A sustained period of increased newborns will mean a spike in youthful crimes about 18 years after it starts. Increased obesity in children will lead to an increase in type II diabetes. A wealthier older generation will mean increased philanthropy and so on. What's more, one can often draw a straight line between national demographic changes and the same changes locally. What's happening nationally will often tell you what's happening locally.

That said, most nonprofit management is local. This is not as much of a paradox as it may seem. Nonprofits usually arise in response to local conditions, and local conditions ordinarily shape service-providing entities in their own dimensions. Neighborhoods and towns do not create multinational corporations; they create grassroots organizations. Even when those grassroots organizations grow to a large scale they still tend to be large versions of local entities, never really losing their local flavor.

As a consequence, organizations like the headquarters of national nonprofit systems, which are expected to have a countrywide view, are usually composed of lots of locally oriented chapters or affiliates. This tends to make them less than the sum of their parts, because while they may collectively represent 500 million dollars worth of programming, it comes in 500 locally oriented parts. The usual economics of scale do not apply.

Here's another angle on the geography question. Is yours a local organization with a national reputation or a truly national organization? Universities or hospitals or museums may have a national reputation and a national (or international) sensibility, but that is not the same thing as a national geographic range. There are some true single-entity national organizations in the nonprofit sector—groups like Oxfam America or Share Our Strength or The Nature Conservancy are close to being one-of-a-kind nonprofits— but for the most part it is neither easy nor desirable to cover the entire country with a single nonprofit entity.

PERSON-TO-PERSON RESEARCH

Personal professional perspectives lend invaluable depth and richness to a research project. For a list of good sources for personal perspectives, see the Appendix B.

The hard part about framing your geography may be figuring out exactly what "local" means for your organization. In dealing with this question, you are really trying to figure out what "local" means to everyone else, especially your funders and clients.

Geographic boundaries are important in a primordial way. They are often the first way that strangers have of placing a nonprofit in a familiar context—as a name, The Los Angeles International Airport says just about everything you need to know about where the entity is located. Still, most nonprofits do not incorporate cues about geography in their name. For those that do, everyone understands that names do not necessarily tell the whole story and, therefore, may not be very useful for planning purposes. So, there need to be other ways of defining geographic bounds. The ones that follow are for suggestive purposes only. They are not necessarily exclusive of each other and are meant to offer different ways of framing the bounds of one's area of concentration.

Land Mass The geographic boundaries that are the simplest, cleanest, and most powerful for all parties are the ones determined by land mass—islands, maps, rivers, canyons. These are the natural borders of one's defined area. They are also fairly rare as agreed-upon lines of demarcation, and not terribly reliable unless they also happen to coincide with some of the other styles described below.

CROSSING THE LINE

Beware the insidious yet ironclad boundaries posed by geography. We were in an organization's lobby one day when a staff member dramatically signed out as absent for the following day, throwing the pencil down and complaining that she was "going over the line" for a training session. The receptionist commiserated with her, and wished her luck. "The line" in this case was the modest-sized river—comfortably crossed by a high sturdy bridge—that made her two-community locale an island in name only. Crossing that line was an important psychic event, not an ordeal, because it meant leaving the confines of the island and all the comforts it represented.

Municipal Borders The most common land-mass-based borders are municipal lines drawn on a map by governmental units. Of all the means of geographic definition, these give the greatest illusion of clarity. When demand for services links with funding for services, municipal borders are good sources of clarity. The problem is that they are, in behavioral terms, almost completely unreliable. Human behavior has virtually no regard for municipal borders, which means that your future scan has to be set wide enough to encompass the direct and indirect impacts generated by possible developments far away from your seeming borders.

Service Area A practical way of thinking about geographic range is by what we call service areas. To determine your current service area, put the zip codes of all your clients on a map. The area that encompasses 65–70 percent of your entire client population is your primary service area. Those using your services who live beyond this range probably do so with some vague sense of being outsiders, and your own service delivery mechanisms likely reinforce that. It takes them longer to get to you, or they need special arrangements to bridge the gap, or they are more likely to cancel, and so on.

It is possible for your primary service area to have a dual nature. One nursing home sponsored by a statewide fraternal organization drew about 65 percent of its patients from within 10 miles of the facility. But the home's high visibility within the fraternal group drew referrals from different areas of the state because of its fraternal ties and familiar culture. Many if not most universities show the same kind of pattern.

Girl Scouts USA, the national office of the Girl Scout movement, classifies its local councils as being one of four types of service areas: urban, high density, emerging, and low density. These categories not only determine the national contacts for the local councils, they also help guide resource allocation policies. For instance, low-density councils tend to be located in rural and exurban areas, where transportation is difficult, communication limited, population growth slow or stagnant, yet market share is reasonably high. These councils need very different kinds of attention than the inner city areas where market share is lowest.

Socioeconomic Geography is also, to some extent, a code word for socioeconomic distinctions. In urban areas, socioeconomic boundaries are

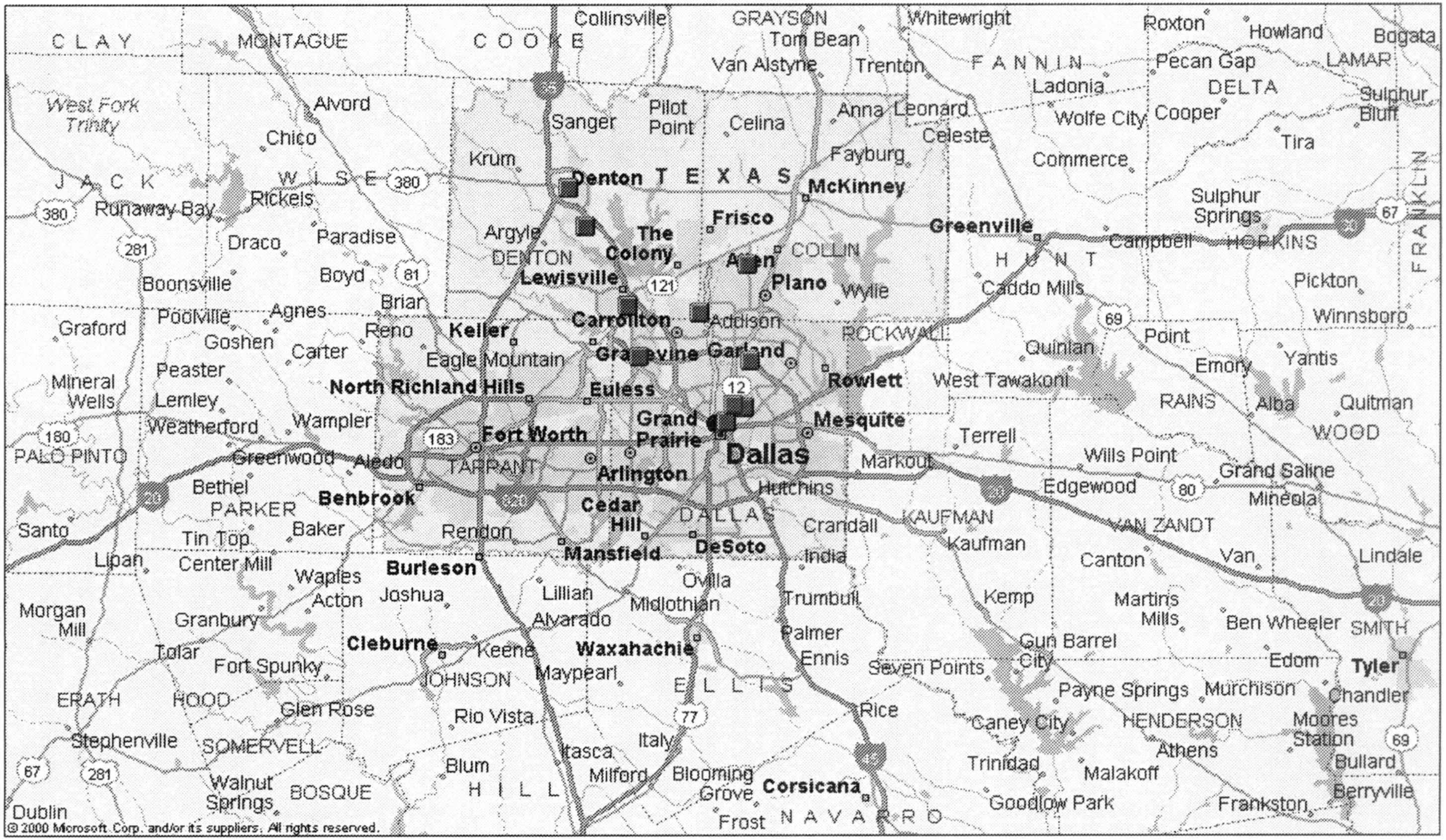

EXHIBIT 5.1 **Productive ZIP Codes for Adult Volunteers**

more important than municipal ones, and they should be analyzed accordingly. They are also more fluid than administrative boundaries, so be ready to adjust the bounds of your scan. Socioeconomic boundaries also are more influenced by factors two and three steps removed from the service area, such as when a major population shift in one part of the area cascades down into other neighborhoods formerly untouched by population changes.

In the early part of the new century, mapping software became highly popular with strategic planners and those concerned with marketing and fundraising. These programs, especially when combined with relevant databases, are enormously powerful analytical tools. But an entrepreneurial nonprofit does not have to invest in high-end software to get workable results. Exhibit 5.1 was produced using a spreadsheet and a popular commercial trip-planning software package—the spreadsheet software is standard on many computers, and the trip-planning software package retailed for less than $40.

What this map shows is the most productive zip codes for adult volunteers in a youth mentoring program in Dallas. It was useful in the agency's planning because it clearly revealed two important patterns. First, it confirmed that the most fertile areas for volunteers, marked by squares, were in the more affluent suburbs, which workers had long assumed but no one had studied. Second, it suggested an intriguing pattern. The office, shown by a dot, was on the north side of town along a secondary commuter route. Most volunteers were from north of the city where they would be most likely to see the building regularly, and where it would be easy for them to attend meetings and meet their mentees. This insight emphasized the importance of being located in a volunteer-friendly area—and it confirmed the lack of activity south and southwest of the city toward Arlington, where a similar mentoring program was located (the two agencies eventually merged to capitalize on their strengths).

Geography As Set by Funders Often a nonprofit's implied geography is sketched, intentionally or not, by funders. Community foundations, for instance, effectively suggest geographic bounds just by their names. Government funders draw lines on maps easily, as when mental health planners designed catchment areas in the sixties and seventies. Look at Exhibit 5.2, which shows the city of Buffalo, New York, and surrounding areas as divided

WILLOWS' END SCAN SHEET: GEOGRAPHY

Trends
- The Willows neighborhood is a roughly 2.5 square mile area in the northeast quadrant of the city and is easily the most rapidly changing neighborhood in the city. It is named not after a tree but for a device used in the production of wool, which used to be processed in the neighborhood until the mid-1950s.
- Willows' End lies in the northern portion of the neighborhood, bounded on two sides by the ocean and on the other two sides by Route 112.
- The seven old textile mill buildings in Willows' End have been either torn down or rehabilitated. The last of the buildings is to be converted to mixed income housing within two years.
- The former coast guard station in Willows' End will be fully developed within 18 months and will include high-end condominiums, small shops, and a marina.
- Public transportation serving The Willows is limited to a single bus line.
- A recent poll of Willows residents put traffic control as their number one priority by a wide margin.
- The Willows' End Assisted Living property is a former textile mill sitting on 3.2 acres with an ocean view from many of its rooms. It is permanently deeded to the nonprofit corporation with oversight from the state attorney general.

Implications
- WEAL is limited in the growth it can accommodate on its present site.
- Employees' most consistent complaint is the time and difficulty they encounter in leaving WEAL, having to rely on limited public transportation, friends, or the facility's single small bus.
- Traffic in Willows' End will increase measurably within two years.
- The present character of the neighborhood will change dramatically within 5–10 years as the planned housing units come on line.

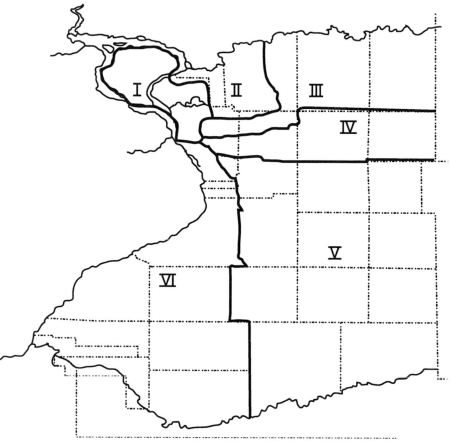

EXHIBIT 5.2   Sample Catchment Map

by mental health planners five decades ago. The city itself is at the center of all the hand-drawn intersecting areas, a pie wedge strategy designed to give the six catchment areas a more or less comparable cross-section of inner city and suburban populations. In the end, it never worked out that way, of course. The main institutions in some catchment areas concentrated on serving a regionwide population, while others retreated to a portion of the catchment area and left the remainder to other institutions from other catchment areas. But for the first few years, these were the boundaries that controlled everything.

Media Markets The most obscure but sometimes the most powerful way to define one's geography is through media markets. Media markets are truly the epitome of boundaries drawn by others. Media markets are generally arrived at by measuring the reach of an area's major electronic media outlets. In the Nielsen ratings methodology, there are approximately 210 media markets in this country, ranging from New York City to Glendive, Montana (for a list, see Appendix E). Media markets are a particularly good way for local chapters of national organizations to approach their markets, especially if they are the only one in the market. The brand development done on a national scale should make awareness in the local media market a lot easier to achieve.

What makes media markets so powerful as boundary-setters is that they obliterate the more common and easier-to-understand land mass markers. Since most nonprofits still define their service area by reference to some sort of land mass or municipal boundary, media markets represent a threat. Most often, that threat is simply ignored because the implications of organizing according to media markets are too confusing.

Transportation Zones Just as there are media markets, there are established transportation routes, or zones. These can be local or national in nature, and they are the general routes that people and goods most often take to get from one place to another. Lewis and Clark were trying to establish a kind of transportation zone many years ago, and the Panama Canal was created to cut short a notoriously long and dangerous transportation zone.

What do transportation zones have to do with nonprofit organizations? Whenever people move along established transportation routes they bring their plusses and minuses with them. Virtually all organizations are affected by transportation zones in one way or another, but few realize it. Yet they can be extremely powerful determinants of behavior.

In India, for example, AIDS initially spread rapidly along a north–south axis because those were the established trucking routes and drivers using those routes visited prostitutes all along the way. The northeastern route out of New York City is well known to college students going home or back to school. Drug traffickers know it as an aid in diversifying their markets. This is why unique drugs or blends from the Port of New York can often be traced first to New Haven, then to Hartford, Connecticut, and then to Springfield and Holyoke, Massachusetts—all are dense population centers along those routes. Coastal fishing ports are often centers of high drug usage because fishing boats going in and out are natural carriers of contraband. Community hospitals arose in part because transportation systems were much less robust during the early and middle part of the last century.

These are some of the strategic implications of transportation zones. Your organization may or may not be directly affected by them, but it is worth considering whether they should be a part of your future analysis.

TO CHANGE IT OR NOT

It is easy to get trapped by geography-based boundaries. The neighborhood focus that seemed like such a good idea early on turns out to be hopelessly quaint when the neighborhood changes character. Or success leads far beyond the boundaries of the initial geography until the nonprofit feels pot-bound by its original name and focus. When these kinds of things happen, it is time to reconsider those once-comfortable geographic boundaries.

The primary difficulty with changing one's geographic reach is that it can be difficult to remember that one usually has a flexible geographic reach in the first place. Because the name of the city is in the agency's title, or because the socioeconomics of the original geography are so comfortable, it is easy to take the borders as unchangeable.

Deciding to change the organization's geographic boundaries is rightfully the task of the planning process itself, but people in the early stage of the planning process will hopefully have an inkling that this may be necessary. If that's the case, try to set the geographic boundaries for research a notch or two bigger than the current ones so that they will accommodate any eventual change.

All nonprofits are geographically bound, in one way or another. Even the national organization has a clear-cut purview that just happens to be the entire country. The real question for most nonprofits is how explicit its geographic range will be. It is wise to be clear about this, because the geographical boundaries you observe send a powerful message to others.

> ## IT IS AN ELEPHANT, AND IT IS BIG.
> ## AND BRICK-COLORED. AND DONATED.

One youth group many years ago received a wonderful gift—a building. And what a building! It was built in the first part of the twentieth century for a fraternal organization, and it had something for every kid—a gym, a swimming pool, two (!) bowling alleys, classrooms, and much more.

There were two problems with this building. First, it was expensive to maintain (there was a reason why the fraternal order ended up donating it!). More important, it was located on a street corner across from a hospital and near a business district. There were restaurants nearby, a print shop, retail stores—but no kids. The kids and their families had left a long time ago, moving a half mile or more away when all those institutions began taking over the neighborhood. At that point, the youth group needed to buy vans and improvise ways to get the kids into the building. Playing fleet manager and public transportation authority was not a good use of their time and resources, but it was necessary because they were locked into a physical area in the most powerful of ways.

Competitors

From the inside, one of the best-understood secrets of the nonprofit world is that it is insanely competitive. Not competitive in the Hollywood sense of lizard moguls with slicked back hair and nano-morals, and not competitive in the way that professional athletes compete, but competitive nonetheless. The fact that the competitiveness is masked by kind words and warm embraces at conferences only makes the reality that much more jarring. Culturally, most nonprofits would rather not think of themselves as having competitors or even as being particularly competitive, preferring instead to emphasize collaboration and focusing on the good of the whole. To the extent that this reflects a strong and consistent organizational philosophy it is laudable. But more often it is a desire to politely evade reality.

Nonprofits compete for money. Everyone understands that. Foundation staffs routinely complain that they are besieged by requests for grants from far more organizations than they can possibly fund. But nonprofits also compete for staff, especially for bilingual staff or staff literate in a particular culture. They compete for board members, for media attention, and for bragging rights the same as other proud teams would do.

Competition is usually misunderstood by the world at large as being largely about besting the other players. In truth, competition between organizations is only partly about what the other organizations are doing. Mostly it is about looking inside one's own organization and figuring out how to best position it so as to satisfy one's market. In turn, that means figuring out how to match the organization's strengths with what the future is calling for. This is a time-consuming undertaking, and it is why many executives are so focused on improving their own operations that they spend less time thinking about competitors than they probably should. Nonprofit competition is also misunderstood in a similar way, and sometimes it is overlooked entirely (the average person would be shocked to learn exactly how competitive some of their favorite nonprofits are).

To compete effectively one has to understand who else is doing the same thing. In planning jargon this is called a competitor analysis, and it begins with a cold, clear-eyed look at external competitive realities. But analyzing the competition is not just a matter of opening the window and pointing the binoculars outside. To be useful, a competitor analysis has to involve disciplined, analytical work carried out as part of a coherent model. Here are some elements of the analysis.

Direct Competition Direct competitors are the easiest to understand because they are the easiest to spot. They have signs and buildings and

---

SURVEY TIPS

If you are inclined to create your own survey of external parties for a planning process, do two things to improve your chances for a high response: 1) make it simple, and 2) give each respondent a small reward for responding. The most frequent benefit for surveys of other organizations is a summary of your results. Remember—if you are interested in it, they probably are too.

brand names and staff, and they tend to look a lot like the organization doing the planning. Their leaders show up in the same meetings, they pursue the same foundations for grants, and sometimes they even join the same collaborations.

Direct competitors are the easiest to assess because almost everyone in the organization knows who they are. The fundamental question to ask in identifying direct competitors is: Who could take away your revenue? Any group that has that capability has to be considered a direct competitor.

In its simplest form a competitor analysis is a list of organizations' names. How much further one goes is largely a matter of style, time, and resources. For some practical tips on how to research direct competitors, see Appendix G.

WILLOWS' END SCAN SHEET: COMPETITORS

Trends
- Assisted living facilities in this state are generally regarded as having been overbuilt, with the industry on the verge of a shakeout.
- In this state, for-profit assisted living companies outnumber nonprofits 4:1. For-profits have grown rapidly and have much better access to capital for further expansion.
- The general geographic area in which WEAL is located is unquestionably overbedded.
- However, the density of land usage, the island-like location of the city and Willows' End in particular, and the fact that most of the surrounding "old-money" towns typically refuse to permit congregate living of any kind, gives WEAL some measure of protection.
- WEAL has been approached to sell the company to for-profit chains on numerous occasions.
- Internal surveys have indicated that WEAL's chief competitive weakness is the perception that the facility is somehow for "low income" residents, as opposed to its competitors, which are seen as being for higher-income individuals.
- In the same survey, respondents expressed a strong preference for the WEAL "local-angle" story over that of most competitors.

- At least three WEAL senior managers have gained national recognition for their work in the senior care field.
- WEAL has numerous indirect competitors, including home health care, nursing homes, hospitals—and potential pharmaceutical advances that will keep seniors living independently longer or without needing assistance with daily activities.

Implications
- WEAL must constantly monitor the competitive landscape. Beyond direct competitors, the potent mixture of baby boomer retirements, Medicaid cost overruns, and a growing cultural predisposition against end-of-life arrangements that take seniors out of their homes for any reasons could create unexpected sources of competition for the organization.
- WEAL should assume that there will be recurring opportunities to sell to for-profit chains in the near future, and it should have a firm policy for how to deal with such overtures.
- WEAL must maintain its local identity while staying at least even with the capabilities and features offered by the for-profit chains.
- WEAL leadership needs to remain actively engaged in senior care thought leadership both for marketing purposes and to protect the organization's strategic position.

All competitor analyses are limited by the fact that the researchers are inescapably external parties. No matter how much quantitative information you get on an organization, and no matter how much your results seem consistent with perceived reality, it is still not possible to assess things like organizational culture, managers' true operational effectiveness, and various intangible leadership resources.

In the end, the only real solution is to be suitably humble about your analysis. A competitor analysis can only be expected to give broad information about this part of one's strategic position, and in truth there is a point beyond which effort devoted to competitor analysis is better put toward operational improvements. Where that point lies is up to each organization, but earlier is better than later.

Competition from For-Profits Competition from for-profit companies is really a form of direct competition, but it is so important in some parts of the country that it deserves separate attention. Nonprofits and for-profits have long competed to provide certain services. Home care was a natural opportunity for for-profits when visiting nurse associations left parts of the market open. Day care is another classic area that has seen significant for-profit encroachment, as are nursing homes and assisted living.

The conventional view of this kind of competition is that for-profit companies have an incentive to keep costs down, have more efficient administrative systems, and are run by better managers. While any one of these things may or may not be true on an individual basis, this explanation does not go deep enough.

True competition is not rooted in the tax code. It has far more to do with the way the competitors are organized and with the way they approach various economic and management challenges. Look deeper into the areas where for-profits have succeeded in taking market share from nonprofits and you will see a more important distinction between competitors.

Prototypers versus Industrializers We call this distinction the prototypers versus industrializers difference. Organizations generally take one of the two approaches. In the industrializer approach, the organization specializes in one or a small number of services and produces large quantities of the same kind of service every day. Museums are industrializers, as are hospitals and information and referral agencies.

The other type of nonprofit is the prototyper, which has one or a small number of programs that are unique, potentially complex, and constantly changing. In this model, the one program is the entire range of corporate activity, and most of the policies and procedures governing it are self-generated and easily modified. Advocacy organizations, for instance, are prototypers, because they are typically small groups whose agenda, tactics, and even personnel must frequently change to keep up with the changing future.

Here's the difference in everyday terms. The church that runs a spaghetti supper once a year is a prototyper, because it has to reinvent (or "remember") how to do it each year. A homeless shelter is an industrializer because it has to mount the same service in the same way each day.

The details of operations may change frequently in both models, but the methodology must stay largely unchanged in the industrializer or else chaos will take over.

When a need arises that nonprofits attempt to meet, everyone runs a prototyper at first. In the early days of the AIDS epidemic, no one knew the nature of the disease, its prevalence, or its likely course for either individuals or society. The models for coping with it had to be developed or modified from other models, so for a while everyone was experimenting. As those in the field learned what worked and what did not work, it became possible to codify the experiences, share them with others, and develop program models and standards of service delivery. In short, they succeeded.

This is the trajectory of many services in the nonprofit sector. With success comes demands for more service, which can now be met more efficiently because less time has to be spent figuring out how to provide it. When demand continues to escalate and the nonprofits serving the demand grow along with it, many of them eventually notice that they have evolved from small, seat-of-the-pants operators to established solution-providers. In our terms, they have moved from prototyper to industrializer.

Nonprofits are good at identifying dysfunction such as disease, obstacles to cultural access, or lack of education, and then coming up with ways to deal with them. For-profits, on the other hand, are not often paid to do that kind of work. They function best with proven ideas that can be brought to scale quickly. When a response to dysfunction can use a proven idea to develop large-scale enterprises and provide room for a profit, the for-profit sector will usually get interested, because the for-profit industry is all about building factories, literal and figurative. This is why the nonprofit sector developed home care but for-profits built it into a huge industry. It is why day care for middle and upper class people is overwhelmingly provided by for-profits, and, conversely, it is why large-scale institutions like hospitals are regarded as for-profits by the average person. Industrial-strength production is so much the norm for the for-profit world that anything that looks like it is regarded as a for-profit operation.

The real competition in the nonprofit sector today, therefore is, not between nonprofits and for-profits; it is between industrializers and prototypers. Those nonprofits that have learned how to become industrializers are every bit as much a competitive threat to the prototypers as the for-profits. Industrializers and prototypers have very different strategic positions.

Indirect Competition The really tough part about competitor analysis is recognizing indirect competition (the second really tough part is knowing what to do about it). Indirect competition can take many forms, but once again you can start with the assumption that this kind of competition comes from any source that can cause one's revenue to be shifted away or cut altogether.

Funder-Based Surprisingly, the most virulent form of indirect competition in the nonprofit world comes from funders themselves. Donors' and governmental officials' relatively short attention spans are well documented and can pose a threat by shifting away or dissolving revenues completely, but here we mean conscious, deliberate decisions made by funders.

In New York state, as in many other industrialized states, for example, state government itself was for many years a substantial and oversized competitor to the very system of nonprofit disability service providers that it helped spawn. It did this by retaining many of its large institutions, while developing a network of smaller community-based alternatives. While those large institutions were always theoretical direct competition, the more insidious form of competition was the quiet pressure for funding, personnel, and legislative attention that the institutions exerted.

Indirect competition in the cultural sector is especially vicious. Symphonic music halls and theaters are essentially delivery formats that thrived when they were among only a few options. As alternatives proliferated with the advent of recorded music those venues became less necessary. For a modern insight into a similar dilemma, talk candidly with a symphony executive. The incessant cutting of music and art education in the public school system over the past years has undercut an entire generation of future arts lovers. Most symphony executives wonder where they will get the large numbers of donors and patrons they need in the next decade or two. That's truly "funder-based" indirect competition.

Donor Preferences It may be hard to see, but donors can be a source of competition for the very programs they fund. Remember, our definition of competition is any entity that can take your revenue away. Funders can exercise their power to take away—or to not renew—funding for programs. This almost makes them direct competition, but to be generous we will call it indirect.

Funders have an understandable appetite for the latest thing. Given many funders need to raise money from an equally fickle body of donors, this is not surprising. It means that recipients must constantly monitor funders' tastes, a practice which grant writers know how to do instinctively after a grant cycle or two. The significance for planning is that a funder's desire to cut funding for an established program can be the most definitive form of indirect competition imaginable.

Technology-Based Technology is a prime example of indirect competition, though perhaps less so in the nonprofit sector because of its distaste for innovations that eliminate employees. Still, technology is a formidable indirect competitor. Consider programs that deal with illness. Many years ago the March of Dimes got exactly what it wished for—the elimination of polio. It nearly resulted in the elimination of the organization, until they refocused on birth defects, multiple afflictions not likely to go away as the result of a single technological innovation.

Project what would happen should mental illness be definitively linked to a series of genetic abnormalities as a result of the mapping of the human genome. Or consider the strategic implications for methadone providers if it were found to be possible to manage heroin addicts through implanted microchips. These sweeping possibilities will not happen any time soon, of course, and so it is for good reason that they are well off most nonprofits' radar screens. But they serve to illustrate the kind of thinking that planners need to do to be ready for unexpected technology-based indirect competition.

Families In the health and human services, families are worthy indirect competitors. This sounds crass since many experts strongly support the idea of families providing care for their members who need it, and since in fact the practice of institutional surrogate care is historically in its infancy, having only arisen with the industrial revolution. Nevertheless, strategic positioning is about anticipating future developments, and whether family care is socially desirable or not, it can be a real threat to certain types of nonprofit-provided care (strategic positioning could also be about anticipating the rise of family care and finding a way to facilitate it instead of competing with it: competition breeds collaboration,) as we'll see shortly.

Referral Sources In certain areas, an organization that sends along new clients may be a future competitor. As governmental entities' budgets shrink, some are finding that they still need to maintain a referral and monitoring system and that the best way to do this is to convert key existing service providers into combination managers/providers. This is similar to, though not the same as, management services organizations. The difference is that these providers are contracted to be "supermanagers" who refer and monitor as well as provide services. That there is a very real potential for conflict of interest in this role is obvious—so obvious, in fact, that these arrangements may actually be harbingers of eventual future consolidations. Those receiving referrals in these systems should be mindful of the possibility that today's referral source could eventually become tomorrow's merger partner.

TO COLLABORATE, COMPETE

Competition breeds collaboration? What could be more counterintuitive? Yet that's exactly what happens. Consider the realities of other industries. Real estate salespeople are a notoriously competitive bunch. The good ones develop a nose for new listings and know how to persuade and cajole sellers to list their houses with them because if they can sell the house as well as list it they get a larger commission. They hustle to get potential buyers in the door, and they work hard to make the deals happen. Yet real estate agents developed multiple listing services years ago to rapidly communicate houses for sale, and a region's brokers will not hesitate to attend other firms' brokers-only open houses because they know that it is in their interest to learn about new properties on the market. Competition gives way to collaboration when it comes to communicating market information.

Or consider the airline industry. Airlines spend millions of dollars on advertising and do not hesitate to tout their on-time ratings or the fact that they have an inch more seat room. Yet if an airline mistakenly strands a passenger and cannot accommodate the traveler's schedule, it will quickly send that person across the terminal to a competitor airline to jump on one of its flights at no cost to the traveler. Why? Because the airline that helps the passenger will some day mistakenly strand one of its own passengers and then it will be the one needing the assist. To maintain their competitive advantages they must collaborate.

No entity exists in a vacuum, a fact brought home regularly to managers who must face their institution's limits on a daily basis. Just to get the job done they often need to find pathways outside their organization. Ironically, however, for nonprofits the absence of profit as a primary institutional motive tends to reduce the pressure to collaborate in any systemic way.

The case for collaboration among nonprofits has not been as strong because of this absence of external pressure. But in recent years the competitive future has intensified, and this helps prompt some serious thinking about the go-it-alone mentality. It is not an accident that foundations have emphasized collaboration in recent years. As that competition increases, so will the need for collaboration.

COLLABORATION USUALLY BEGINS IN THE BACK ROOM

No participant in a competitive industry wants to compromise their brand in any way, which argues against collaboration that's visible to the consumer. For nonprofits, this plays out in a similar way, though the currency of their realm tends to be regarded as the mission, not the brand. Still, it is the same idea—the mission is the point of highest pride, and the thing least desirable for what is perceived as the risks of collaboration. That's why collaboration involving back room services—accounting, information technology, and purchasing, among others—is more acceptable.

Saving money through this type of collaboration is nice but not primary. The bigger payoff may be improved skills and better institutional capacities. United Ways (UWs) learned this principle when many of them got together to create technological tools to handle pledge processing. YMCAs have been doing similar kinds of things, and many smaller local alliances have quietly formed in recent years to explore and implement collaborative back room activities.

Back room or administrative collaboration also has the distinct advantage of not disrupting direct services. There are few more sensitive pressure points in a nonprofit organization than the staff, models, systems, and processes used in delivering direct services. For a variety of reasons, most of those systems and processes are homegrown. In addition, the majority of people involved in delivering services directly to the consumer are proud of what they accomplish each day. That combination of pride and highly individualized services makes it extremely difficult to do joint programming of any kind—why would anybody involved in such a situation willingly take apart what they have worked so hard to build just to make it more compatible with another organization? There has to be a powerful incentive to make this even vaguely possible: beginning collaboration in the back room postpones or eliminates this difficult proposition.

BACK ROOM COLLABORATION DEMANDS STANDARDIZATION

Administrative collaboration is an attractive goal for its possible savings and its more likely capacity building. But administrative collaboration without standardization is like a sailboat without a rudder. There will be lots of action but no particular direction and even less accomplishment.

Take computer systems as an example. A good deal of the work involved in creating a local area network for an individual nonprofit consists of making sure that the networked computers, printers, and other devices can communicate with each other. In turn, stitching two or more local networks together in a wide area network involves a similar focus. All the parts need to be able to exchange data quickly and without mistakes. Without standard protocols and accepted ways of setting up the devices, they simply would not work.

Yet, like programs, technological solutions tend to be homegrown or at least highly individualistic. This organization uses fairly sophisticated accounting software but relies on simplistic spreadsheets to track donations sought and received, while that organization has invested heavily in

STANDARDIZATION ALSO DEMANDS OVERHEAD

As collaboration demands efforts to standardize, standardization demands overhead resources. First, organizations have to have a large enough management staff to have developed reliable systems in the first place. Then, those same staffs have to be free to spend some time—probably a considerable amount of time—doing the hard work of bringing their systems together. This is one of the reasons why small nonprofits have such a difficult time collaborating: they simply do not usually have the overhead resources.

programmatic software that few others have, though they also use common word processing programs and the same version of Windows as all their peers. The problem arises when they try to align their practices: Whose choices will prevail? Even if there is a clear benefit to all in collaborating around technology, it will be months or even years before all systems are standardized enough to allow them to work together.

Collaboration takes time, money, and effort, and it usually involves standardizing at some point along the way. Nonprofits traditionally do not feel strong internal pressure to collaborate—no organization does—until the competitive future demands it. When that pressure achieves a critical mass, the results tend to unfold in a predictable way. The principles above might not be natural laws, but for nonprofit organizations they are close to it.

Users and Potential Users of the Service

The people who need the services offered by nonprofits are called consumers. Or users. Or patients. Or students. Or participants. Or . . . you can see the strategic problem here. The demand for services comes in many forms, with many connotations, qualities, and demographic baggage. Specifying the exact demand for service can be a complex undertaking.

One way to clear the confusion is to recognize that all these terms refer to people after they have been identified, in one way or another, as needing the service *that a particular organization offers*. That means that there has already been some cementing of labels, and that can be dangerous to creative strategic positioning.

The place to start is with the admittedly amorphous concept of need. But what truly constitutes need? Not only is it an amorphous concept, but it is also subject to massive distortion. The biggest confusion is when organizations look out at the future and see a need—*for the service they offer!* This is not shocking, but it tends to stop honest inquiry before it ever gets started. People do not come stamped with a label pronouncing their need for a specific service. In fact, determining what service an individual needs, if he or she is not clear about it in the beginning, is usually a blend of ideology, coincidence, practical realities, and personal styles.

Terminology is important but somewhat misleading in this area. Nonprofit planners in years past have often referred to what they call "needs analysis." It may be a bit misleading to speak of the "demand" for service when not all users could be described as demanding anything of the sort. Teenagers do not demand to be in probation programs, and seniors do not demand to be in nursing homes. So "demand" is a bit of a technical term here that may or may not have to do with users' desires.

There are two reasons why we will use the term demand rather than need. First, the concept of need seems a bit self-centered and entitled. Further, in cases where the user does not agree that he or she needs something it is presumptuous. Demand admittedly is not much better, except that we are trying to remove the focus from anything referring to innate user characteristics and focus instead on the circumstances, however they arose.

The second reason is that managing demand is a fundamental task for all managers of all services; to talk about managing need is presumptuous and hard to fathom. The concept of managing demand is foreign to many managers, nonprofit or otherwise. There's an implicit sense of limitations in the concept, and so, although untrue, the whole idea of voluntarily limiting services for many nonprofit managers is off-putting. Still, managing demand is one of the most important aspects of strategic positioning. Overstimulating demand can be catastrophic. One of the first cracks in the perceived telecommunications juggernaut of the late 1990s was when several new online retailers were completely unable to keep up with peak-time Christmas season demands, and gifts arrived late or not at all. Understimulating demand can be equally catastrophic, for different but obvious reasons.

Demand for service is really the beginning of the justification for the existence of any nonprofit organization. As stated previously, most nonprofits are created to respond to a perceived need in the larger society, often a social dysfunction or a void in the marketplace. This is not the same thing as the nonprofit's mission, or its programs. In fact, assessing the demand for a particular service is one of the things most nonprofits do not do well.

For-profit organizations call this market research. Who are one's potential customers? What do they need? How do they need it? Under what circumstances will they be willing to pay for what they need, and how much would they be willing to pay? These are the questions that classic market research attempts to answer.

Market research is imprecise, expensive, and not always reliable. It is also an up-front cost that has to be paid for at a time when there is uncertainty about whether the results will even be useful. All these things make it an awkward fit for nonprofits, which do not typically start out with a big investment that they can spend partly on determining whether they should exist or not. Fortunately, nonprofits do not generally have to make that investment. Others do it for them.

Nonprofits typically operate on the basis of a three-way transaction between the consumer of the service, the supplier, and the funder. For many for-profits, the funder and supplier are usually the same thing. In a three-way transaction model, the consumer of the service does not have as much influence on the transaction as does the funder. If the government or a foundation says that there is money available for a service, the market research is essentially done and both parties can move on to figure out how to provide it.

This market-defining role of foundations and government is a hidden subsidy for nonprofit organizations. It means that market research can consist of little more than being able to read the handwriting on the wall. It also means that nonprofits can confuse need with the program or service designed to meet that need. Society does not necessarily need ivy-covered brick buildings to educate young adults, it needs young adults to be taught how to think and learn and work constructively with others. The form that the response to this need has taken in the past may have involved ivy-covered brick buildings, but that model was simply the response to a complicated set of factors shaping the way the need was met.

To properly shape a strategic position, a nonprofit must dig beneath historic accidents and understand the nature of the demand for its services. It also needs to do this without spending undue amounts of time or money on what could be redundant market research. Most thoughtful nonprofit managers and staffs already understand the need for the service they provide, at least on some level. It is hard to work in a popular museum or a busy preschool and not have some thoughts about the nature of demand. But it is this familiarity that is precisely the problem. Gauging demand from that perspective is like being a dozen miles downstream from a big dam. The sluice gates could open or close and turn that part of the river into a raging torrent or a trickle. Without knowing what's happening upstream the change would seem to be sudden and unexplained. Strategic thinkers need perspective on the demand for services.

Being clear about the demand for an organization's services is a multi-step process. While we will not pretend that the steps are like a recipe card, followed in the same order for all organizations, there are some more or less consistent elements that one must incorporate. To put the concepts of analyzing demand for service into a realistic framework, we will use the Make-A-Wish (MAW) organization, analyzing its strategy in the following sequence:

- Defining the irreducible demand to be met
- Defining the population to be served
- Establishing the feeder system—define demand
- Identifying behavioral considerations affecting demand

DEFINING THE IRREDUCIBLE DEMAND

The initial act of what would become the Make-A-Wish system occurred in Phoenix, Arizona, over 20 years ago when a local boy with a serious illness expressed a desire to be a policeman for a day. Spontaneously, the community arranged for him to be granted his wish with much fanfare, including a special proclamation appointing him a temporary "policeman" along with a small parade in his honor. A local television station picked up the story, the national media ran it shortly thereafter, and suddenly this small group of volunteers realized their gesture had identified an archetypal situation. The work of forming similar chapters and then a national organization began quickly thereafter.

The central demand for service in Make-A-Wish is rooted in the social and psychological needs related to life-threatening or terminal illnesses. This is the condition giving rise to the opportunity to grant wishes. There are extensive medical lists and definitions of life-threatening and terminal illnesses, and often there are studies available that show how often these illnesses arise (their incidence), and how widespread they are (their prevalence). But Make-A-Wish has a primary strategic task even at this early stage in that it has to define exactly what constitutes a life-threatening or terminal illness. It turns out that this is not as easy as it may seem.

Defining disease in this way is subject to many nuances and complexities.

DEMAND IS EXTERNALLY DETERMINED

Demand always comes from outside the organization, and it is not always neatly identified. The difference between nonprofits of the twentieth century and those of the twenty-first is that today's organizations will have to get better at recognizing the core demand for their services because the government is no longer going to articulate it and most foundations will prefer to hear applicants' interpretation of it.

For instance, both cancer and the flu can be life-threatening and even terminal under certain circumstances, so one positioning task is to find ways of differentiating between them. A second, more difficult chore is keeping the definitions current. For example, when Make-A-Wish first began, the illnesses classified under the heading of leukemia were largely fatal. Since then, medical knowledge and treatment has progressed so fast that experts no longer consider childhood leukemia potentially terminal until the second time it appears. This means that the Make-A-Wish system must keep its strategic and operational integrity by constantly staying on top of the best medical research.

DEFINING THE POPULATION TO BE SERVED

Since the population is already substantially determined by the nature of the irreducible demand, theoretically, the organization could have chosen any age groups suffering from life-threatening or terminal illnesses. The poignant juxtaposition of children and serious illnesses was a powerful combination. But even here there are thorny issues to be addressed, the first of which is the perennial question of when childhood ends and adulthood begins (for Make-A-Wish the answer is age 18). At the other end of the age spectrum, MAW has to determine how young its participants can be. Is the objective to give a child a pleasant experience no matter what the age, or does MAW leadership desire a certain level of comprehension? The minimum age for a wish is the product of this debate.

ESTABLISHING THE FEEDER OR REFERRAL SYSTEM

How do the users reach your organization? Every service system needs one or more feeder systems. For professional baseball, it is colleges and the minor league teams; for medical schools it is undergraduate programs; and so on. This feeder system has to do many things, including disseminating word of the availability of the service and passing judgment on initial applicants or preapplicants. In the Make-a-Wish system, there are four major referral types: parents of ill children, social workers, nurses, and physicians. Physicians also serve as a filtering device, since no wish can be granted without written physician approval. Part of managing demand in this future consists of establishing the right relationships with these four groups. Another part implies working with the physicians to make sure that they understand the current definitions of life-threatening illness.

IDENTIFYING BEHAVIORAL CONSIDERATIONS AFFECTING DEMAND

If estimating demand were just a matter of totaling up the incidence and prevalence of qualifying diseases, it would be tricky but manageable to simply calculate how many people diagnosed with what diseases were in the eligible age groupings at any one time. But every organization supplying a service must also account for users' behavioral choices, and in the Make-A-Wish system the choices are particularly complicated. Most important, parents of potentially eligible children may or may not have heard of the service. They may or may not understand what it entails, and they may or may not know that it is free. They may be in such a state of denial that to even consider applying for a wish may seem to them to be equivalent to admitting that their beloved child is seriously ill. There may be cultural obstacles (the original Make-A-Wish logo had to be changed because it was inappropriate in at least one foreign culture), or parents may feel that they can afford to fund a child's wish themselves. And acute episodes of life-threatening illnesses can occur at any time, canceling plane trips or scuttling carefully planned visits with celebrities.

Referral sources' behavior can also affect demand. Make-A-Wish is a social model of service, while physicians operate in a medical model.

THE FRAGILITY OF A DEMAND FOR SERVICE

The nature of a community need, or demand for service, is a fragile thing. The YouthBuild system is a national movement with 110 affiliates around the country. Each affiliate involves young people earning their graduate equivalency diploma (GED), while also learning construction skills by helping to build affordable housing for homeless and low-income people.

This is a brilliant marriage of two parallel needs—youths' need for positive involvement in their community and communities' need for assistance in rehabilitating the housing stock. The model worked brilliantly throughout the 1990s. But one local affiliate found that by the beginning of the twenty-first century half of the equation no longer was applicable. All of those marginal buildings that many city governments had found themselves reluctantly controlling were being rehabilitated not just by YouthBuild and other similar organizations but by owners and real estate speculators, who found that there was good money to be made in sprucing up distressed properties.

After a while, the affiliate realized, the supply of houses in need of attention was dwindling. The private market had moved in and done on a widespread scale what YouthBuild was attempting to do one by one—a classic case of for-profits industrializing a process that nonprofits were trying to do as prototypes. This was obviously good for the community, but for YouthBuild it challenged a fundamental part of their service model. Suddenly, the community need had disappeared.

But there was a positive side to this changing picture of need. While the private sector had filled the need to renovate much of the housing stock, and while the overall attractiveness of carpentry skills in a saturated market had declined slightly, now there was a need to learn how to manage all those properties that had been rehabilitated. A decline in one need often gives rise to another.

Physicians trained in a classic medical model are unlikely to give credence to much of anything outside their service model, or they may simply not have enough time to provide the kind of care that would lead to applying for a wish. This is the reason why physicians typically refer a very small percentage of potential wish children, while parents and social workers, unencumbered by medical training or economics, are more likely to make a referral. Yet it is the physicians, clustered in long-term institutions like hospitals and medical practices, that are the easiest marketing targets for a Make-A-Wish chapter because they are far more identifiable and accessible than the small number of parents whose children might someday be stricken or social workers who might work with them.

A strategic positioning exercise is a good time to rethink what "everyone knows" about the demand for services. After years of doing things a certain way most staff members, including professionals, may be blinded by what they think they know about the need for their services. In truth what has happened is that their focus has narrowed. Instead of being broadly knowledgeable about why and how people come to them for service they have thought themselves into a box. This is why it is useful to have people on a planning committee who are not thoroughly knowledgeable about the services the nonprofit offers—they will not accept all those preexisting barriers to clear thinking.

Funders

Funders and regulators also help shape a nonprofit's future. Funders are important because the nonprofit sector, to the extent that it is part of a larger public policy framework, is part of the classic make-or-buy calculation that all organizations must face. Governmental entities that wish to provide services can either provide them themselves ("make") or choose to purchase them from the private sector, including nonprofits ("buy"). In the

THE NONPROFIT MULTIPLIER EFFECT

The national income tax was instituted in 1912, and the first provision for a tax deduction was put into place seven years later. This was not a mindless altruistic move on the government's part: some economists estimate that for every dollar the government foregoes in tax revenue, it gets approximately $1.30 worth of services from the nonprofit sector.

nonprofit world, the decision by a government to "buy" as opposed to supply or "make" its own services is known as privatization.

The reasons for turning to the nonprofit sector as a supplier of services are multiple and include things such as lower costs, better quality, greater flexibility in program design, and less direct political influence in service delivery. Governmental funders also supply a kind of de facto needs assessment, as noted previously. The fact that a governmental entity determines that a need exists and that it is willing to pay for services to address it dramatically lowers the cost and risk of undertaking a new service.

Governmental funders rarely offer lucrative opportunities to the nonprofit sector over time. Generally they can take advantage of their market position as the largest purchaser to drive down costs and turn services into a commodity market, thereby forcing recipient nonprofits to compete on price rather than the quality of service. What the government dollar can provide is a base for stable if largely breakeven services. So, the attractiveness of government funding is that it will not make you rich, but it will help cover your costs and allow you to make some money on other funders' programs.

Private funders such as federated fundraising organizations, foundations and corporations, on the other hand, offer almost totally the reverse opportunity. Whereas they usually have no serious mechanisms to enforce commodity purchasing, they do have cyclical programming. This is mostly because any effort to raise funds in the open fundraising market has to be connected to some kind of popular cause, and popular causes tend to have short shelf lives. Moreover, the way that funders give out their dollars is every bit as important as the purpose they give them for.

Consider the various stages of United Way fundraising in this country. Many years ago, United Way funding was given to whole agencies. The next evolution in United Way philosophy was to give funding not to whole agencies but to individual programs that those same agencies ran. The third step in the evolution was to attempt to fund outcomes, or results. The fourth and current step, still very much evolving, is to position United Ways as community builders.

Let's look at the ways each of these approaches might influence the strategic position of nonprofit organizations receiving United Way funds. Exhibit 5.3 shows the four United Way approaches along with an effective

UW approach	NPO strategic response	NPO marketing tasks	Key NPO administrative tasks
Funds whole agencies	Board-to-board CEO to CEO	Develop strong political relationships, create attractive market presence	PR, limited fiscal reporting
Funds programs of agencies	Board-to-board CEO to CEO Managers to managers	Create attractive program footprint: be prepared to juggle sponsored programs	Cost accounting down to program level; PR at same level; support program "brands"
Funds outcomes	CEO to UW board	Create or adopt persuasive metrics	Develop tracking systems beyond fiscal
Builds communities	CEO to UW board	Define community; establish value	Broaden research and tracking capacities

EXHIBIT 5.3   Four United Way Approaches

strategic response on the part of a nonprofit funding recipient (or possible recipient), the marketing-related activities the organization would have to undertake, and the administrative demands they would have to fulfill to succeed in each approach.

In the classic UW approach of funding whole agencies, the nonprofit has to nurture two key relationships—their board of directors versus the UW board, and their CEO versus the UW CEO. This is largely a political imperative. Since there is essentially a single funding decision—does the UW fund this organization?—it is in the interest of the nonprofit to make a negative answer unthinkable. The organization has to have an attractive market presence and, preferably, a strong overall brand name. Financial reporting is not as important as long as financial results are neutral or positive. This is one of the reasons why classic UW funding recipients such as the Red Cross, the Scouting organizations, and Boys & Girls Clubs were so strong when almost all UW funding was agency-based. At base this is a strong defensive strategy. It is hard for the UW to muster a case to do anything other than roll over last year's funding and decide whether and how much to increase it by.

When United Ways fund programs of agencies, the strategic position and related tasks change. Now, each program must stand on its own, which fragments the appeal to the UW. Board-to-board connections are still important, as are CEO to CEO ones, but now program managers may be called upon to take more of a leadership role in seeking or defending funding for their program. Each program has to be attractive in its own right, and the nonprofit has to be able to cycle unfavorable programs out of UW funding and replace them with more favorable programs. This means that individual programs must develop local "brand names" to ensure continued attention and attribution of value. The administrative chore is to be able to do fiscal reporting, especially of costs, at the program level.

Funding outcomes change the nonprofit's strategic position with respect to the United Way in another fashion. In this approach, which can become fairly technical, the nonprofit board's role is liable to be diminished, relying instead on its CEO and possibly individual program managers to be fluent in persuading the UW board of the effectiveness of their programs. Those nonprofits that can find or create a persuasive set of metrics may very well win a larger stake: Who has the time to challenge them? And internal administrative systems must be strengthened to track more than just dollars coming in and dollars flowing out.

Finally, the new approach of UW as community-builder is changing the dynamic yet again. The nonprofit CEO is likely to remain as a key link to the UW board because making the case for the agency's importance in building community will take more knowledge and sophistication than most nonprofit board members can develop in their limited roles. Until the functional definition of building community becomes widely accepted, the nonprofit will have to develop its own argument for how it builds community and be persuasive about how it brings value. It will not hurt to spend some time on pure research, either, since everyone still has much to learn about what it means to build a community, and to be able to track at least some indicators will be very impressive.

To be sure, these are only possible responses to UW funding approaches, and in any case there are many other funding sources out there. The takeaway point is that funders are a major part of the strategic future and should be researched and studied carefully.

Labor Force

For the vast majority of nonprofits, personnel cost is their single largest expense, usually accounting for as much as 60–80 percent of all dollars spent. For that reason, the quantity and value of the labor asset has a lot to say about how effective the organization can be. In recent years, managers have paid a lot of attention to this area because labor shortages have forced them to do so. While it is important to have at least a broad understanding of labor trends in your region—and the Department of Labor's website and regular reports can help you get this—it is also wise to be very clear about how your particular labor force, present and future, is likely to behave.

THE TWO-TIERED LABOR MARKET

Start with a look around your organization. If yours is like most, you have two distinct labor forces. The larger one is characterized by low wages, high turnover, and possibly steadily declining job satisfaction. These are the people from whom you hope to get two or three good years. To replace them, you are resigned to having to run year-round recruitment campaigns. The second labor force is very different. It tends to be composed of the executive director, credentialed employees, a handful of senior managers, and/or long-term highly committed employees scattered throughout the organization.

The two-tiered labor force is your future, whether you run a large hospital or a small land conservation agency. There are many implications of the two-tiered labor force, the most important of which is that you need to track two very different labor markets. For the largest number of employees, the labor market will tend to be lower-paid, lower-skilled workers with an ability to work with people. Chances are they will live within 5 to 10 miles of the employment site or on a major public transportation route. The best will be committed to the mission of the organization, though not so strongly that they would be unlikely to do anything else for a living. This labor force will probably be quite diverse both ethnically and in personal circumstances. It is not a long-term group of employees.

The second labor market is much smaller, and consists of highly committed employees. They will sometimes have specialized educational credentials, and often they worked in the field at a similar organization before joining yours. They may in fact have joined your organization hoping for a long-term situation: even if they did not, they may turn into long-term employees if you treat them right. In the best of cases, these second tier employees grew out of the first tier as they added education and experience. They are the long-term, dependable core of your labor force.

OTHER ASPECTS TO TRACK

The baby boomer generation has changed everything it touched, and employment practices are no exception. The front end of the boomer generation, generally described as having been born around 1947, will begin reaching retirement age starting in 2009. The boomers' lack of savings for retirement is well documented; look for twin waves of retirements and new part-time workers to begin around that time.

The Sesame Street generation, now in their late twenties to early forties, started out just as idealistic in their own way as their boomer counterparts. They will soon begin moving into executive positions and begin formally redefining work-life balance rules.

What few nonprofit workers will continue to be is unionized. This will happen not for ideological reasons—nonprofit workers and many managers tend to be predisposed to traditional union ideology—but because the economics mitigate against it. Unions cannot afford to draw much from each low-paid member. Assuming $300 per year in dues, a fully unionized employee base of 50 would only produce $15,000 in yearly dues. This kind of money will barely support a fraction of a union staff member and is rarely enough to justify the effort expended to organize the group.

Our personal experience is that in the current generation of twenty-somethings, the most strongly drawn to nonprofit work tend to be much more open to entrepreneurial nonprofit management styles and much more willing to try to maintain consistency between their values and the organizations where they work. This could be a potent force in future years as they add experience to that orientation.

Finally, all employers are having to take on more of a role in training their workforce, including a remedial function. Employers have to fill in some gaps in their employees' education in addition to offering the usual technical and on-the-job training for organization-specific functions.

Technology

Technology touches everything in today's world, but nonprofits have traditionally had an uneasy relationship with it. Not only do the fields where most nonprofits are active tend to be unrelated to technology, nonprofits' people-first culture works against anything that could be seen as replacing human workers. Also, nonprofits' difficulty in gaining capital funds from donors and the easier task of getting monies for operations makes it that much less likely that nonprofits will favor technological solutions.

Still, technology has made its way into nonprofit operations. Its first beachhead was the back room functions like accounting, but the explosion in Internet commerce began to penetrate programmatic areas as well. Increased connectivity holds special promise for nonprofits who have always had a philosophical commitment to collaboration

Where nonprofit technology will have its greatest impact is in transforming those things that formerly were just good practice into things of strategic importance. Take Guidestar.org, for example. This simple website has made the corporate finances of every nonprofit public charity in the country transparent by posting each year's crop of IRS 990s, the nonprofit tax form, on the World Wide Web. Such a simple act lays open for public inspection in a standardized format the way each nonprofit raises its money, keeps it, and spends it. In turn, nonprofit CFOs have realized that they must now file this form with the very real expectation that it could be read by donors, regulators, newspaper reporters, and casual Internet surfers.

Technology has dramatically changed the philanthropic world as well. Donor-advised funds, by themselves innovative ways of raising money, have been almost inextricably linked to technological changes in banking and recordkeeping. The ability to control charitable donations with pinpoint accuracy gives real immediacy and strength to donor-advised funds.

Technology is also mostly responsible for what we have called flash philanthropy, the near-instant mobilization to raise funds seen within weeks of 9/11 and again during the aftermath of hurricanes Katrina and Wilma. Such success on the fundraising side put enormous and unexpected attention on the disbursement side, and many charities stumbled in trying to respond fast enough and fully enough. There is far less latitude for slow disbursements in the new world of flash philanthropy. Celebrity fundraisers have no patience with chin-stroking, months-long, agonizingly extended decision-making processes about where the money goes. These are people governed by Nielsen ratings, box office revenues, and audience share statistics, and the public will expect the same of the charities for whom they so visibly raise money. Flash philanthropy's high visibility causes will demand high visibility responses, and these conditions change the rules.

Finally, in the future information on reaching charities providing social services may take its place alongside traffic reports in its ordinariness. This is because in 2000 the federal government approved the use of 211 as a dialing exchange for information and referral to social services. This puts these three digits on the same level as 911 for emergencies, 611 for telephone service, and 511 for traffic reports. Because the government's action only authorized the use of the dialing exchange without providing any funds for implementation, its adoption has been and will continue to be slow and patchy, but eventually this innovation could have a major impact on all organizations offering such services.

RECIPE CARD   HOW TO CARRY OUT A FUTURE SCAN

Steps for Conducting a Future Scan
Assign One Individual the Responsibility for Researching Each of the Seven External Strategic Factors (Need, Users, Competitors, Etc.)
Ask one person or a subcommittee to take responsibility for researching one theme. Depending on the size and complexity of the organization, that person or group might or might not need to have his or her own subcommittee to carry out this task (in very large organizations, this process is infinitely scalable). Use one of the templates in the Appendix F for each Theme.

Remember that this form is just a communication device. Tell the participants that it is not enough just to identify fact patterns. The key is to project those trends forward. Happily, most future factors develop in slow motion, especially for those in the field. In the early 1990s, the Internet seemed like new news to many, but to people working in information technology it had been old news for decades. The same thing happens with many federal policies and governmental changes, and most social changes too. It usually takes time for major factors to develop, giving even casual observers plenty of time to identify them.

*Answer the So What? Question—The Implications of the Themes
for Your Organization*
These planners' real contribution to the process is to answer the "so
what?" question. That's the point of the section titled "Implications."
Again, using no more than a handful of bullet points, explain to
someone who has not had the benefit of doing all that research what
implications it has for your organization. This is an opinion, of
course. No one knows for sure what the implications of any aspect of
the future will be for any organization. But that's okay—this is meant
to be a thought-provoking exercise, more about raising good questions than about providing good answers at this point.

Produce a Briefing Book for Each Theme
Do not worry; this is just for reference purposes. Have the responsible individual and/or committee produce a collection of documents
(files on a CD, etc.) that were the raw material for the information
captured on the template. Make these available as desired by other
members of the overall planning group.

Brief the Whole Group on Each Theme
This session could be held in advance of the strategic positioning
session, or as an introduction to it if the planning is to be done all
at the same time (such as a single retreat). Again, the purpose is to
communicate information and to provoke thinking and discussion.

Scan for Internal Strengths

T his is the point when, in a conventional strategic planning process, you are supposed to do a S.W.O.T. analysis that identifies your Strengths, Weaknesses, Opportunities, and Threats. It is supposed to unfold nicely, with careful, deliberate attention to each of these things in turn. At the end, you have a rounded, symmetrical idea of the good and the bad about your organization.

Forget the S.W.O.T. analysis. It does more harm than good. We know this is strategic planning heresy. But we will back it up.

BUILDING THE FOUNDATION

Let's approach the question in this way. In doing strategic positioning, you are trying to build a foundation. Would you be better off to build a foundation on weakness or on strength?

We thought so.

Few strategic concepts have taken hold quite so thoroughly as the S.W.O.T. model of strategic planning. It offers an appealingly balanced approach—identify your strengths and weaknesses, and be aware of your threats and opportunities. But in practice it does not deliver. In fact, it tends to divert attention to unproductive areas and reinforce some already problematic tendencies.

It is easy for traditional strategic planning efforts to be more tactical than strategic. Strategy is about what your organization is planning to be: work plans deal with the things you are going to do to get there. Long-term strategy planning is the responsibility of the board and senior managers;

regular work planning and all operational matters are the province of senior managers and their staffs.

Herein lies one of the problems. The Weakness aspect of S.W.O.T. analyses indirectly encourages micromanaging by boards and senior managers because weaknesses are almost always operational in nature. The organization may lack adequate information technology capability, or its human resource function may be woefully inferior, or it may not be capable of innovative programming. But what role does that knowledge really play in formulating strategy? These are operational concerns that should be dealt with in the context of what is needed to fulfill the strategy, not as a determinant of it.

Weaknesses are the currency of the manager, not the leader. Do you know what an entrepreneurial nonprofit executive does upon encountering a weakness in her organization? She works around it! She finds a different way to get things done in spite of the weakness, at least in the short term, and if it is a major weakness that stands in the way of the overall strategy she does whatever is necessary to help her managers turn it into a strength.

There's another dynamic at work here. Those of us closest to an organization tend to see its warts and blemishes with alarming clarity. Focusing much time and energy on weaknesses tends to satisfy only the doomsayers and take away some of that mental energy everyone needs to focus on the future. It also endorses organizational navel-gazing at the precise time when attention should be directed outward. This is why Strengths in the S.W.O.T. approach are so crucial to good planning. Strategies can only be built on strengths, not weakness.

No need to chin-stroke over Weaknesses, because the messages from the future will point out positive directions to take. At most, Weaknesses really amount to omissions—gaps in internal resources or structure that will have to be addressed operationally in order to accomplish the strategy. Strengths and Opportunities get top billing. Weaknesses and Threats should be secondary.

Subtly, the Weakness/Threat axis can undermine commitment and energy. It may sound strange, but a surplus of analysis in a strategy-formulating future can actually be bad. Sure, there's a need for analytical thinking and clear-eyed assessment. But an unspoken objective of a strategic planning session is to get all participants on board with the strategy and the thinking that lies behind it. Most likely, the process itself will represent the high water mark of hope and energy, so to give substantial air time to the doubters can cripple the process from the beginning. Moreover, concentrating overly long on one's weaknesses may cement a culture of vulnerability and uncertainty.

This is where Threats from the old S.W.O.T. model will be found. But let's be honest about what that term means. In most cases, "Threats" is just another word for competitors, and competitors are nothing more than organizations that can threaten the resources that might otherwise have gone to your organization. And you have already covered competitors in the work you did before this point.

Opportunities also do not exist in the future like apples on a tree. Opportunities only exist in the interaction between what the future demands and what you can provide. We will deal with this matter in the next section.

Yet another dynamic related to the focus on weakness is rooted in human nature. No matter how rational and balanced the S.W.O.T. model may seem to be, it defies common sense to expect that any staff members whose compensation or reputation are linked to a weak area will be happy to explore that weakness publicly and honestly. The more a weakness is relevant to a strategy, the greater will be the incentive for the responsible manager to minimize it—or worse.

THE ALTERNATIVE— STRENGTH-BASED PLANNING

In place of the S.W.O.T. analysis, we'd like to suggest something we call strength-based planning. In comparison, strength-based planning is a simpler, more elegant way to identify and build on organizational positives. Strength-based planning starts with clear-eyed self-analysis and builds a full picture of the organization as a uniquely well-qualified entity capable of solving societal problems.

The framework for strength-based scanning looks a lot like the framework for future scanning. This should not be a surprise, since future forces exert so much pressure on internal operations. Inventorying your organization's strengths helps you to think about the interaction with your future in a systematic way.

Take programs, for example. Many currently successful and highly regarded programs offered by nonprofit organizations have now been around for decades. They are typically well established in their communities and have a strong brand name. At the same time, those program models are constantly evolving to keep up with changing demands.

The Girl Scout movement, known the world over for its troop-based activities, now serves as many as 15 percent of its membership in non-troop activities. Boys & Girls Clubs of America are moving in a similar direction as they move into nontraditional areas like Native American reservations and military bases, and as the demand for lengthened after-school activities has grown with two-wage-earner families. YMCAs, which initially helped move young men into the industrial economy of the cities in part by offering a clean, safe place to live, have moved away from providing residential services.

Each of these cases illustrates the incremental nature of change in something as fundamental as program models. And each happened in direct response to an explicit demand from the future when one or more affiliates began to see its traditional strength becoming misaligned with future demands and started looking for different ways to use that strength.

What we will do in this section is to show how to identify strength wherever it exists and how to set up a planning and strategic thinking process that will lead naturally to better correlation between future demands and internal strengths.

What Is a Strength?

What constitutes a strength for an organization? For these purposes, we define a strength as equal parts systems, people, formalized knowledge (such as policies and procedures), and dedicated resources. A strength has to result in the production of some sort of verifiable outcome—a product, a definable service, a desired condition, and so on. A strength is not something that only one person knows how to do, and it is not the capability of the staff to do hard work or the cheeriness of the workforce.

Here is another way to gauge a strength. To be a true organizational strength, something needs to have a definite value. So, think about strengths as those capabilities that, under different circumstances, could be sold in the open market. If it were to be carved out and offered to the general public, would they value it?

The Enemy of Strength Scanning

Anytime an organization sets out to scan its own strengths it risks confronting a formidable enemy: self-puffery. When a group of ordinary mortals attempts to give itself what amounts to a report card, the temptation for individuals to engage in a little bit of self-promotion will be irresistible. Department heads will skew the discussion toward the strengths they already feel their group possesses. Functional leaders such as HR folks, CFOs, and IT specialists will feel compelled to present their function as a tower of strength for the entire organization. Glowing reviews are handed out with alarming thoroughness: the board, the staff, the programs, the volunteers, even the consumers all belong at the top of the scale.

In this out-of-control world, no one is left behind, and absolutely everyone exceeds the minimums. And CEOs—well, the CEO who cannot go on and on about their organization's dozens and dozens of strengths is just not in the right job. So, the group as a whole will experience Garrison Keillor's Lake Woebegon Effect, the community where all the children are slightly above average.

The fact that this is nonsense does not seem to enter most promoters' minds. It takes a lot of hard work over a number of years to develop most organizational strengths, and they are not evenly distributed over the entity. Further, strengths are fragile too. What works well during one period may stop working well just a little while later.

Here's the irony: *everyone knows what your organization's strengths are anyway*. Your competitors know it. Your funders know it. Your consumers definitely know it. Your task is to find a way to listen to all those parties.

THE PRINCIPLES OF STRENGTH-BASED INTERNAL SCANNING

Start scanning an organization's internal strengths with some general principles. Set the ground rules by insisting on adherence to this handful of principles, and the process will go a lot more smoothly.

Fact-Based

Make all scanning fact-based. Facts are independently established pieces of information that reasonable people can agree upon. Frequency of repetition, sincerity of message, and decibel level do not make facts. If the internal scan does not establish a fact base with which planners can work, the strategy will not be implementable.

No Recriminations

In the process of scanning for strengths, it is critical to set the right tone. There could be a tendency to spin off into recriminations for weaknesses rather than identification of strengths. Strength scanning should be free of accusations and grudges for past failures.

True Strength Is Replicable

If it can walk out the door at 5 PM, strength is of no systematic use to the organization. Talented individuals are necessary, and their contribution to the organization should be valued, but they alone do not constitute an organizational strength.

Group Opinion Counts for More Than Individual Opinion

In seeking strengths, a group is always a better filter than any individual. Just as true organizational strength is not found in individuals, neither should the assessment of what constitutes a strength be the province of any one individual. Groups cleanse opinion.

ASSESS YOUR NEED

Assessing the demand for your organization's services is a bit different from assessing the nature of demand in the future, principally because you can be so focused on a narrow range of data without worrying about missing something and because it is likely that you will already have some data on hand to analyze. Start with descriptive information first, then move to the analytical and interpretive.

The easiest place to begin is demographics. Who uses your services, where do they come from, how old are they, what are their ages and genders?

SIMPLIFY YOUR ANALYSES
WITH THE RULE OF 7

Most human beings are not programmed to be able to digest large amounts of data at one time. Most spreadsheet users can generate endless variations on the same analysis with little effort. This is a prescription for glassy-eyed stares. Try to cover no more than about seven variables in a single analysis. For example, household income, family size, ethnicity, numbers of dependents, and highest education level make a nice package of variables to analyze key socioeconomics in many situations. Any other data field might be helpful, but the effect of including it could actually overwhelm casual readers with facts they will not remember anyway.

Sociological information is probably important, as is economic. It is also hard to come by. For that matter, it is entirely possible that you will not have much data at all (if so, it is time to start collecting some).

Next up is multiple years' worth of data to allow you to spot trends. This is what we mean by the analytical stage. We can specify no all-purpose analyses that every organization should perform, but chances are that you already know some that will work for you. Analyses do not have to be complicated to be useful. In fact, for many of your planners simpler will be better.

Data can be described and analyzed endlessly and still not convey much useful information. It needs to go one step further and provide insight. This is the *so what?* factor. What does it imply that household income is staying flat while educational attainment is dropping and dependents increasing? Even an untutored observer would wince at the obvious implications of economic decline that this scenario paints, but interpretation will add meaning to it. In this case, interpretation might go beyond stating the obvious to drawing a parallel with what happened in other areas that have experienced the same thing. An interpretation might try to estimate when the downward trend will reverse, or what it will imply for changing needs.

Interpretation as we have described it here is necessarily subjective, and that is okay. This is not an interpretation meant for the general public or to support a lawsuit. Academic interpretation and litigation support activities are expected to follow standard protocols and are constrained in their ability to make projections, estimates, and educated guesses. If you can find interpretations of your data that rise to this level, or if you have access to people who can produce such material, grab it. Otherwise, remember that this is for your organization's use and that it is meant to help aid everyone's understanding. Be as rigorous as possible in making interpretations, but do not be afraid to make them. Perfection is the enemy of many things, including decision making, and part of strategic positioning is decision making.

UNDERSTAND YOUR PROGRAMS

One of the most remarkable, if somewhat disconcerting aspects of preparing for a strategic positioning project is discovering how little that some insiders really know about the organization. To some extent, this is predictable, since people tend to focus most intensely on the bounds of what they do every day. In large organizations, it is even more understandable because of the sheer scale involved. We once asked the public relations officer of a large, newly merged nonprofit hospital chain for a simple list of the locations of all their hospitals, clinics, administrative offices, programs, and affiliated operations. "I wish we had one," she sighed. "It has been 18 months, and we still do not have a single reliable list of everything we own."

A program is nothing more than an artificial construct—a theoretical overlay placed upon reality that is used to manage mission-based services. Ideally, there is something about the way the pieces of a program fit together that allows its managers and staff to deliver broadly predictable services to the same type of consumers at different times. Various elements of a program such as a physical location and specific staff may or may not correspond neatly to a program. A single site or one person can be part of many different programs all at once, or they could be solely dedicated to a single program. So, programs are a bit like holograms that can move right through each other without changing anything about the other. This is why programs can be so difficult to grasp for everyone who does not work in them. The group of insiders least likely to understand are, unfortunately, some of the most important—board members.

> **LISTS WORK**
>
> Board members of medium to large organizations like lists. Yes, lists.
> How many of them do you think really understand the full program-
> matic and geographic breadth of their organization's service offerings?
> And how many do you think are willing to admit that they do not?
> Do not underestimate the power of simple lists of services or pro-
> grams. But downplay it so as not to embarrass anyone.

Before trying to compose their strategic position, all planners must have at least a rudimentary idea of the programs offered by their organization. For small or uncomplicated entities, this is not much of a problem, but for all others it can be. The solution is to set the level of description high enough that it encompasses the vast majority of programs comfortably. Usually this means creating categories of programming—a workable number in the 3–7 range is best. Board members and even staff people might be embarrassed if they work for an organization so large that they do not know every program offered, but at a large-scale institution that is really not surprising. How many people who work for a Wal-Mart know the locations of more than a handful of nearby Wal-Marts?

Core Competencies Might Help

A good way to grasp the strengths of programming is to study the core competencies of the programs. The concept of core competencies was developed by Prahald and Hamel a few years ago and is a powerful strategic tool. Briefly, the idea is to identify the organizational abilities systemized by an entity so as to be able to deliver programs, products, and services, which are really the next level up from core competencies.

Core competencies are not resident in individuals, and they are not entirely mechanical things like software or assembly lines. At first blush they sound like what we described above as a strength, but they are actually more complex. A core competence lies in the interaction of replaceable staff with well developed service protocols and perhaps identifiable equipment. A well developed core competence will have a substantial institutional base of knowledge behind it. For example, Sony's ability to develop the Walkman many years ago was due to its core competence not just in consumer electronics—which a number of companies had mastered—but in miniaturization, which no one else could match.

When one looks at nonprofit organizations in search of core competencies, some surprisingly standard ones emerge. Youth mentoring programs are essentially brokers, for instance, because they bring together two different parties—kids and mentors—with complementary needs and then try to make sure the match works. At the heart of assisted living programs is the same hospitality competence as in the hotel industry—at a minimum, keep people safe and comfortable around the clock. Children's athletic programs are not about sports but about managing child development (it may be child development disguised as fun, but it is still child development. It is when adults interpret programs as competitive sports that problems arise). Four months out of each year, when they run their campaigns, United Way organizations turn into operations that look a lot like banks.

All but the very largest nonprofits have only one or at most a handful of really important core competencies. For example, any advocacy organization really only needs to be able to do one thing well—gather and manage information. Some of that information may be called lobbying, some of it may be called publishing a newsletter, but one way or another the job is still about information management. A core competence that means anything takes a long time to develop and a lot of human resources to maintain. In this respect, organizations are a bit like human beings. It takes so much time, effort, and energy to become a good physician, for instance, that one rarely finds a good physician who is also a great opera singer. There are just as surely limits to an organization's capabilities as there are to an individual's.

There are also secondary competencies in most organizations. These tend to be in support-related areas such as administrative systems, technology management, or property management services. Large nonprofits are particularly good at developing support-related secondary competencies because they have to be, and because it is easy to develop effectively scaled operations when even the support services are large in absolute terms.

On the other hand, it is actually quite difficult to develop additional mission-related core competencies. Hospital managements, for instance, tend to be quite good at running hospitals but not at running ancillary services. Many hospitals found this out in the 1990s when they diversified into services like nursing homes, only to discover that the practices that work well in hospitals are disastrous in a skilled nursing setting. This is why some for-profit nursing home management companies grew rapidly. They were able to do the day-to-day nursing home management tasks of the larger hospital on a management contract basis, thereby freeing the hospital to concentrate its own resources on the core competence it was already geared up to perform.

There is another reason for scanning for secondary competencies. Since many of them tend to be rather generic support-type services, it is at least theoretically possible that a generic core competence could be turned into a revenue source. For example, one hospital realized that its in-house printing department had become as sophisticated as any small print shop in the community, so they set about to make it a revenue-producing operation. And every nonprofit with a large building that rents out portions on the open market is in effect acting as a property management firm.

Service Models

Every service-providing entity has a service model. The lunch truck driver has a simple service model—pick up prepared foods, go to work sites, and exchange the items for money. Art museums have a different service model. They establish a physical site with things that people would like to see, and create reasons for them to want to go there. Universities have a well known service model, as do hospitals.

There may seem to be an infinite number of service models in the non-profit sector, but for the most part that is because it is easy to tweak a basic model slightly. In fact, those tweaks usually come about to some degree for marketing reasons—it is best to stand out from the crowd when it comes to attracting funds, volunteers, and consumers. This is one of the reasons so many nonprofits consider themselves to be innovative. What they are really saying is that they have found one or more ways to adjust their service model to seem different from comparable organizations. Or, they have taken a basic service model and created ways to execute it that are different from others.

Fundamental changes in a nonprofit service model are extremely difficult.

That is because there is no funding for true research and development in this sector, so there is no formalized way of extracting new approaches from the necessarily hit-or-miss nature of service model innovation. Foundations might be expected to play this role, but the cultural inclination in foundations to be conservative in handing out funds tends to limit the impact they might have in this area.

For profit organizations tend to talk in terms of business model, which is similar to the idea of a service model except that the explicit intent of a business model is to make money. By contrast, a nonprofit service model is about how the organization gets funds to deliver a service that fulfills its charitable mission. Implicit in a for-profit's business model is its value proposition, the idea that it can justify its presence in the stream of commerce by the fact that it adds something to that stream that would not otherwise have been there or would not have been there in the same way. Nonprofits must offer value too. What makes it difficult to track a nonprofit's value is that the consumer is not always the funder, and so value may accrue to two different parties. Nevertheless, value must be there, or in the long run the organization will face extinction.

Analyze your service model for the value it purports to add. The temptation will be to assume that your entity adds value, but that is not always the case. The prime strategic challenge to the United Way system is that the marketplace is beginning to devalue its service. Why? Initially, the United Way's model positioned it at the intersection of two powerful forces: large numbers of charitably inclined employees and the only common administrative infrastructure (employers' payroll systems), which was large enough and sophisticated enough to facilitate charitable donations. Another part of the model was that the United Way served those donors by doing the research and recipient management that none of them could do alone. Finally, it offered charities a collaborative way to raise more money than each could raise individually.

The initial United Way model began to break up when three things happened. First, the number of charities grew far beyond the United Way's ability to fundraise for them. Both a cause and effect of this development was that the government emerged as a much bigger funder of social services than the United Way could ever be. This created more competitors for a spot in workplace giving. Second, the workplace as the locus of donations began to fade in importance when those very same new charities started going to donors directly. Third, the rise of personal computing and more widespread business savvy meant that the workplace itself was no longer the only practical option for administering charitable giving.

So, the fading of the original United Way model was the result of a complex interaction of factors. But look more closely at that model. What really held it together for so long was its monopolistic quality. United Way's value for many years lay in the fact that it was the only real presence in workplace giving and community-based service funding. It began to lose its strategic position when threatened on all sides of the fundraising transaction—by government, empowered donors, and efficiency-seeking companies on the funding side, and by new alternatives to United Way agencies on the service side. This is one reason why so many United Ways now fund a disproportionate number of small organizations. Larger entities have developed their own fundraising capability and do not feel they need the United Way, while companies and donors have many other alternatives. This is also the reason why, during the first decade of the new century, the United Way system has been moving to reposition itself not just as a fundraiser but as a dominant force in building local communities.

UNDERSTAND YOUR STRENGTH WITH YOUR CONSUMERS

Your users choose your organization for a reason. Know what it is. It could be as simple as geography. How many people choose their bank, dry cleaner, car dealer, hair dresser, and even their doctor at least partly on the basis of geographic convenience? Or the determining factor could be reputation. Never underestimate the power of a brand name, especially in nonprofit services. For many nonprofits, the determining factor may be far simpler—they are the only one of their kind for miles around. Or some kind of authority simply assigns consumers to a given organization. Many health care organizations of today got their start in some form of a catchment area system, in which consumers living within district boundaries drawn by a government entity were assigned to a specific service provider.

That which largely determines who uses your service is your strength.

In the catchment area system the service provider has no strength, at least at the beginning. Strength in consumer matters lies in the ability to reliably meet needs. If the primary needs being met are the funding or referring entity's, strength in the consumer base will be relatively weak.

QUICK, DEFINE "CONSUMER"

Here's what might be a stumper for you. What's your definition of consumer? It probably has something to do with a person (or perhaps an organization) that receives some sort of service from your organization. But go beyond that. Is a consumer someone who has a single experience with your organization? Is it someone who gets only a particular kind of service? Is there a time aspect to the definition? Do you attempt to be all-encompassing in your definition, or more narrow? What's the implication of your choice?

Many youth-serving organizations are wrestling with the definition of a consumer. Girl Scouts USA defines a consumer as a girl of a certain age who is a member of a troop or the equivalent formal unit. But in recent years many girls in regions not heavily served have participated in one-time-only events. Should these girls be counted as members? How about girls who are not troop members and who attend a week of Girl Scout camp? Two weeks? A full summer?

There are significant implications to this movement's definition of a consumer. Size always matters, and troops can bump up their numbers by carrying out many one-time events. But is that really in the spirit of Girl Scouting? On the other hand, if the idea is to have a positive developmental impact on girls, who's to say whether a single event for one girl might not have more of an impact than a full year of organized troop meetings? And if attending one-time events are enough to make a girl a member, does that say anything about the core model of Girl Scouting?

Or take Boys & Girls Clubs of America, a federation that faces many of the same issues. As with any club, there is an implication that attendance is not mandatory. Yet veteran club managers usually feel that sustained attendance is necessary to increase the chances that a given club will have a positive impact on kids. At the same time, they often find it necessary to do one-time events or time-limited programming. And they cannot discount the possibility of having a big impact on a kid who only attends a single

WILLOWS' END SCAN SHEET: USERS OF THE SERVICE

Trends
- The average age of all residents is 74, up from 71 five years ago.
- The average number of activities of daily living with which residents need help is 2.4, up from 2.1 five years ago.
- Approximately 65 percent of all residents come from within 8 miles of the location.
- Indoor falls among residents have increased from a monthly average of 5.1 to 6.0. No correlation can be found to explain this rise, except the increasing average age of residents.
- Emergency hospital admissions among residents have held steady at 1.3 per month.
- The average length of stay among residents is 2.2 years; 5 years ago it was 1.15 years.

Implications for Willows' End
- Residents are aging in place.
- As residents age in place, they become more frail and need more attention to activities of daily living. This leads to more demand on staff time and more complex patterns of caregiving.
- Staff appear to be meeting the increased care needs, as evidenced by the lack of increase in emergency hospitalizations.
- As the average length of stay increases, fewer new residents will enter. This will likely strengthen the bonds between existing residents, enhancing the sense of community.
- Over time, the staff should adapt to a higher-level of caregiving.
- A higher level of care giving must be accompanied by economic adjustments if Willows' End is to maintain fiscal viability.

session. So, should these one-timers be considered members too? What about those who pay the nominal yearly "fee"? And what, exactly, does it mean to be a club member? These are all difficult yet absolutely fundamental questions, and they pivot around the central question of how BGCA is going to define a member.

ANALYZE THE ELEMENTS
OF YOUR USER BASE

Understanding the elements of your consumers' demand is like the internal equivalent of market research. Unlike with traditional market research, you do not need to find out if there is a demand for your service, or what it might look like: you already know there is. Most of the work is almost purely a matter of pattern recognition. While pattern recognition in a large amount of data is far easier with today's powerful computers, technological prowess really only gives one speed and sophistication. The real chore is to figure out what elements of one's user data will give the most insights. It is not easy to spell out where to look in a way that will work for all nonprofits, but here are a few factors that will usually yield some decent information.

Number of Users

The sheer numbers of people using your services tells you something. Headcount almost always drives things like revenue, visibility, numbers of employees, and so on. It is one metric that almost everyone can understand, and it is relatively easy to track. Moreover, numbers of customers is a presumed indicator of a successful product or service.

Mix of Users

Just as important as, if not more important than, the number of users is the mixture. A good mixture of users is extremely valuable and can make the difference between fiscal health and marginal performance. Mix of users is not just a matter of numbers. Health care providers that serve large numbers of Medicare patients are in some ways uninterested in those numbers alone because it is typically very difficult to break even on Medicare payments. They are more interested in the number of patients with private or non–Medicare insurance-based coverage, because this is where they make their profits and get monies that are not restricted as to use by government policymakers.

There are many elements that go into user mix, and they will likely vary tremendously by the type of nonprofit seeking to do the measurement. In most charter schools, the mix of learning capacities of entering students is one of the most critical measures of future success not only for educational reasons but also because payment is often tied to an average of the costs to educate a student from the referring community, so either very gifted or very slow students will draw disproportionately on the organization's resources. User mix can include a myriad of other items as well, all of them determined by the unique nature of every organization. In-patient health care facilities know that they must maintain a careful mix of patients requiring extensive clinical care and those requiring average clinical care but above-average attention for behavioral reasons.

Impact on Users

Impact on consumers is fast becoming the holy grail of measurement in the nonprofit sector. United Way organizations were perhaps the first to attempt in a widespread manner to measure impact of programs on consumers rather than simply financial inputs and outputs. Other organizations have been wrestling with the same question in their own ways.

The stakes are high. From a macro perspective, many developments in the nonprofit sector in recent decades have involved the question of impact in some way. The questioning of results of classic government-funded social service programs that began brewing in the 1970s culminated with the Reagan "revolution" of the 1980s when programs were cut substantially. At the heart of the defenders' failure was not just an unfavorable political calculus but the inability to demonstrate the programs' worth for consumers. Some of the new venture capitalists' hands-on style of the late 1990s and early twenty-first century was driven by a lack of faith in old models' effectiveness. There can be little doubt that if there were reams of statistical proof of programs' effectiveness, these new entrants would have behaved quite differently.

A lot of smart people have been doing a lot of smart things to document the impact of their programs, yet few organizations would claim to have figured it out. The reason for this is complex and worthy of a long analysis—some other time. For our purposes, there is a reasonable way to measure impact on users of the service: consumer surveys. Few things can energize a strategic positioning project more than honest-to-goodness consumer feedback.

One national federation conducted such a survey of its members prior

WHY BRAND NAMES ARE SO IMPORTANT

The nonprofit world offers a bewildering complexity of services and options for most users of most kinds of services. How is a user—or a donor—to know which service is effective and which is not? Until widely accepted and independently applied standards are available in fields where nonprofits are active, we suggest that most users and funders will resort to a simple alternative—the brand name. In effect, outsiders will say "do not ask me to measure it myself; that is why I'm picking the brand name provider. I may not be able to figure out how to measure impact, but I'm willing to trust that these people know."

This will not change the absence of an accepted yardstick; it just focuses the pressure to develop one on strong nonprofit brand names, national or local. And a good faith effort to measure effectiveness in the context of a trusted service provider may be the best we are going to be able to offer for the foreseeable future.

to reworking its strategy. For the first time, it asked its members what they wanted most from the national headquarters, and the answer was resounding: money. Of course, the national headquarters did not have a lot of money to give out—member dues were a large part of its revenue, after all—but the response caused all parties to think about their relationship.

What emerged from the dialog was that the members did not truly expect money to flow from national, but rather that there were certain things— like insurance-purchasing programs and capital-borrowing initiatives— that the national office could do to facilitate the easier flow of capital and cash to members. Eventually, the national office took the message to heart and restructured itself, renaming itself a "service center" rather than a "headquarters."

Do Our Services Work?

Here's a dare that is not for the faint of heart. Ask your collective selves these questions: Do our services really work? How do we know? What are we accomplishing for the people we elect to serve? These are potentially explosive questions if approached honestly, but a bit of humility never hurt anybody.

There is a tendency, especially among board members, to feel that the services their organizations provide are of the utmost in importance, exceeded only by their quality. That may or may not be true, but it ought not be an article of faith. Especially in the health and social services, there is a rich history of treatments and approaches that, when seen in the cold light of elapsed time, do not seem very helpful after all and may appear odd or even inhuman. There was a time when lobotomies and hydrotherapy seemed like the height of sophisticated, humane treatment in the mental health world. And we quickly found out that hospitals, which were intended to heal the sick, were also hotbeds of infectious diseases.

Sometimes giving is also a form of taking. And if what is taken—things like liberty, personal freedoms, or even health—amounts to more in the long run than what is given, it is time to reevaluate the services. This may be the right time to take up the question.

Check Those Boundaries— What's Your Geographic Strength?

Of all the organizing principles known to human beings, geography is one of the easiest and most durable. Anyone who can read a map can instantly figure out the chosen geographic area of a nonprofit organization. Whether the chosen area is the entire country, a region, a specific city, or even a neighborhood, maps tell the story efficiently. Even so, geography is also one of the slipperiest and most cumbersome of organizing principles. That is why it pays to be very clear about your geographic boundaries as part of a strategic positioning process.

Think about your geography in terms of market coverage and penetration. No matter what size area you are working with, virtually every organization will have strong coverage in some areas and not so strong coverage in others. Nationally, most of the large federated service systems are strong in some or all major urban areas and weak in rural areas. This is so common as to be almost a law of organizational nature. It costs more to service rural communities, and there are fewer resources available to pay for this. Rural areas also find it harder to mount and maintain enough widespread interest in a cause to keep it current in a lot of residents' minds. So, if your area includes cities as well as farms, it is a safe bet that the latter will be less well endowed.

Penetration refers to the degree to which your organization has managed to reach into the full pool of potential consumers. It is a simple enough idea, but a difficult thing to actually measure. Girls Scouts of the USA uses population measurements combined with data from local affiliates to calculate the percentage of certain populations participating in the movement. This allows them to measure the effectiveness of affiliates over time in exceeding or falling short of local averages. It also provides them insight into how they serve entire geographies.

The problem with geographical boundaries is that they are terribly misleading. Not only do they imply that it is possible to tie up one's service area in a tidy package, but pockets of strength can mask pockets of weakness.

Take national name-brand organizations with local affiliates, for instance. Local charters in such organizations are almost always issued according to land mass. During the middle part of the last century, when many of today's systems were just beginning to spread over the entire country, they issued charters for specific land-based regions. This allowed them to claim, with some credibility, that they were a nationwide system. For some such groups this became a point of pride.

But the groups receiving the charters did not necessarily service all areas within their region equally. In fact, most concentrated only on a portion of the total area given to them. Or, they specialized in only one or a small handful of services that they could have offered. The result was an apparently uniform coverage area that in fact was riddled with empty or weak pockets. This is a problem plaguing many national federations right up to the present.

By contrast, if charters were granted not according to land mass but according to services provided, the weak areas of penetration would be clear and it would be easier for noncompeting groups to service the same geographic area. Alternatively, national federations could issue charters with the explicit provision that certain programs be offered uniformly across a service area. The federal government did something like this in the 1960s when the Community Mental Health Center Act made startup funding available for mental health centers as long as they served a distinct geographic area and provided the same set of basic services.

ELECTRONIC STICKPINS

Some popular computerized mapping software programs, once installed on your hard drive, will allow you to create serviceable mapping points. Just feed a list of zip codes into the software and ask it to create visible symbols for each zip code. This simple analysis creates the electronic version of a map with stickpins, and it may tell you far more about your geographic reach. The advent of more sophisticated mapping software from the likes of Google and Microsoft will make this approach even easier.

In some cases geography is a secondary market definer, with another factor being primary. For instance, services to children are often defined according to that population, with the geographic aspect being left either unstated or vague.

Geography is really just another way of talking about one's market. The purpose of assessing one's geographic strength is to force some honest self-examination. The college that calls itself a nationally recognized entity when 95 percent of its students come from within a 50-mile commute is likely to build a bad strategic position if it takes its own assertion about national prominence too seriously. That is why it is essential to be honest about current geography, especially penetration and coverage. Maps do not lie.

Funders: Who Is Willing to Pay?

The informant Deep Throat during the Nixon administration repeatedly told reporters Bob Woodward and Carl Bernstein to "follow the money." That turns out to be good advice for strategic positioners too. Being willing to part with real money is the ultimate test of seriousness in any economy, so an organization's funding sources say something important about who is willing to part with real money in return for what value. Just as important is who might be willing to part with real money in return for your value in the future.

An organization's array of funding sources tells an unmistakable story about who values its work and to what degree. Do not believe your funders' instinctive denials that they do not have enough money, because they have put at least some of what they do have into your organization. What does that tell you? What does it suggest about your strengths? How can you use that information in the future? Analyze your funding sources according to a handful of dimensions: mix of funding, adequacy of funding, and special considerations.

FUNDING MIX

Most nonprofits have at least a handful of funding sources, and they reveal a great deal about an organization. The people and institutions willing to put money into a nonprofit can be read as a proxy for the marketplace. Who believes enough in the mission to trade dollars for value? How much do they believe? And what are the conditions, if any, that they place on their dollars?

Because of the unique nature of the typical nonprofit transaction—a third party such as a government entity or a foundation pays a supplier of a service on behalf of a consumer, who may or may not know anything about that third party's actions—nonprofit funding sources will be either direct or indirect. Indirect sources predominate, with governments and foundations and the like giving the lion's share of revenues to nonprofits. Direct revenues are things like fees, admissions, memberships, and so on. Here's how to decode the messages buried in your funding portrait.

Memberships

To those that do not have membership revenue it looks like unfettered, nongovernmental money that can be used in practically anyway one wants, as long as members at least tacitly approve. To those that do have membership revenue it can look like fickle funds forwarded with the level of enthusiasm reserved for paying taxes by members who do not fully appreciate what the association does for them. Both are right.

Government Funding

This all-encompassing category is monstrously large and can include just about every type of funding mechanism imaginable. Often though, government money is cost-based in some way, meaning that it is great for building a base of funding for core operations, while it generally causes overall losses that have to be made up somewhere.

Interest Income

The prize of fundraisers and nonprofit chiefs, this is income from endowment. Usually unrestricted monies, income from interest on holdings is gravy and normally reliable from year to year except now and then when the market goes down and brings the value of endowments with it, as happened in the early part of the twenty-first century.

Fees for Service (Program Revenue)

Also not a bad source of unrestricted income. The only problem with fees for professional services delivered is if the fees fall short of the costs. This can be caused by overspending, but more often it will happen when revenue just does not materialize to the degree expected, and expenses cannot be adjusted quickly enough to match.

Conferences

Conferences look great, as long as you count only the direct, nonpersonnel expenses. Once you factor in the cost of staff's time to put on that national conference for a few hundred people, the math probably will not look so good. Why? Because, as with memberships, consumers have been conditioned to expect slightly more than they pay for from conferences. Still, conferences have lots of other benefits, so do not discount them—just remember that huge profitability is often not one of them.

Fundraising

In terms of effort, fundraising revenue is located well below the peak of interest income and above the base camp of government funding. Its return on effort puts it a lot closer to heaven, but it still takes some work. Fundraising revenue is also a widely diverse field. The holy grail is planned giving—over the very long term it should represent one of the easiest and highest-margin forms of revenue, but it takes a long time to get rolling, and its effectiveness can be surprisingly difficult to measure.

WHY NONPROFITS CANNOT EASILY DIVERSIFY

Most economic transactions in our society involve many buyers and a few sellers. This is the root of a consumer-based society. But many nonprofits operate in a very different future in which there are many sellers (the nonprofits) and one or just a few buyers (governmental agencies and foundations). This turns traditional economics on its head, rendering many conventions and assumptions meaningless. Most important, in this kind of future, the buyer wields far more clout over an individual seller than is normal because it effectively has consolidated what would usually be the diffuse pattern of many small buyers into a single, much more powerful buyer.

GENERAL CONSIDERATIONS

It is important to consider a few general issues when analyzing your funding mix. First, in case it is not already clear, be sure to understand the dimensions of your primary funder. For-profit company advisers get worried when a single funding source is more than about 10–15 percent of total revenue. That is not a realistic standard in the nonprofit world, where government or foundations often account for 50, 60, or even higher percentages of revenues. Still, the theory is valid. Overreliance on a single funding source, albeit understandable, is always dangerous. If nothing else, planners should understand the percentages.

Private money, including donations and fees for service, is ice cream. It has no restrictions, can show a profit, and often is the easiest kind of money to get, once you get the spigot flowing. If there were a single indicator of financial health, it might be the percentage of revenue the organization gets from private sources. Helpful and necessary as government funding is, its restrictions and bureaucratic demands can stifle an organization.

It is worth mentioning that we are only talking about revenues here, not money that comes in and sticks around. Dollars in the revenue category are, by definition, expected to be spent, but dollars that come in through things like a capital campaign are intended to add to the permanent body of wealth controlled by the nonprofit. Funds intended to be used to provide services tend to be more broadly reflective of what the market considers important, whereas capital funding is more likely to be considered a one-time donation from a smaller base of donors that suggests approval of the organization rather than what it does with its funding.

Finally, most revenue received by a nonprofit is from third parties such as government, foundations, insurers, and individual donors. This simple fact sets up some subtle yet profound dynamics. For one thing, it means that the sources of distinct revenue streams are small in number and large in importance. That is typically a big difference from the for-profit sector. For instance, mid-price-range retail stores rely on having lots of customers engaging in relatively small transactions. Any one of those customers or individual transactions is not all that important because it is the volume that counts.

Most nonprofits have the reverse situation because they are not consumer-oriented and have a relatively small handful of funders. Institutional funders come like watermelons, not grapes. So, each one has to get considerably more attention than they would be likely to get in a small-transaction model of business, customer satisfaction questions aside. There are two advantages to this model. First, institutions like to do business with entities that look like them. Street vendors want to deal with individual buyers, while huge multi-national companies are best when doing business with other huge multi-national companies. Foundations and nonprofits have a lot in common, so it is easier for them to understand each other. It is usually harder for a non-profit, even a small one, to understand and respond to the needs of single individuals, whereas the foundation that is willing to make the investment in some feedback should always find a willing audience in their recipients.

Second, the nonprofit as a recipient can get a great deal out of the direct contact that funders require, to the point where it can act as a replacement for the direct contact that a service provider would ordinarily get from its customers. With the nonprofit's reliance on third parties for funding, it has an imperfect, open feedback loop. The funder provides the resources, the nonprofit provides the services to the user, and the user may or may not ever give information on the service to the funder. For better or worse, funders for nonprofits can act as substitutes for the market's voice. This is the reason that thoughtful large donors willing to take the time can be so valuable to a nonprofit. In a small way, it is part of the reason for the success of social venture funding, offering the knowledge and experience of the funder in place of user feedback.

Funding Adequacy

Let us acknowledge that a nonprofit's funding is never adequate. The mission is always bigger than the resources, or at least it should be. Let us also acknowledge that not every organization always makes the best use of resources available to it. Somewhere between these two poles usually lies the truth.

There are two complementary truisms about funding adequacy in the nonprofit sector. First, funds are rarely adequate to do the job. Second, somehow it usually gets done. In a larger sense, that is one of the sources of value that the nonprofit sector offers. When a government program is inadequately funded it has to go back to the legislative branch and lobby for more money. Nonprofits do not have to do that, so they can be a lot quicker in responding.

Assuming that you have found a way to overcome funding inadequacy, what is it? For some, that is the role of an endowment. Frankly, this is the easy way, and there's not a lot to talk about beyond the amount of money the endowment produces each year and how much of it you want to use to supplement your inadequately funded programs.

However, most nonprofits do not have an endowment and they still manage to get by. How? Here are a few common techniques.

Cross-Subsidies Perhaps the most common way of coping with inadequate funding is to cross-subsidize programs. This means that profits in one program or service offset losses in another. There can be controversy and argumentation about ethics in this area, but it is a fact of life for most nonprofits. The irony is that when for-profit companies do the same thing they are commended for their brilliance.

Profitability Just creating a profit will help ease the inadequate funding crunch. This can be easier to say than to do, of course, but funding inadequacies are not usually uniform and broad-based. Often, it is possible to carve out a little profit in one or two service areas. Even if the profit is not explicitly used to offset losses in one of the programs, it gives some financial breathing room.

Growth Sometimes overlooked, growth is one of the best ways to compensate for inadequate funding. Normally, it takes a year or two for an

ARE YOU ADEQUATELY FUNDED?

Here's a way to judge the adequacy of your overall funding stream. Take all your revenue and subtract anything not directly earned, such as fundraising, interest income, rental payments, and so forth. This is called your operating revenue.

Now calculate your operating expenses by eliminating all expenses connected with the amounts you subtracted above. Practically, this will usually involve subtracting fundraising costs.

Finally, subtract your operating expenses from your operating revenue. Divide the resulting number by your operating revenue. This is your operating margin. It tells you how you would fare if you had no fundraising income and no unearned income. Often, organizations with a small fundraising program will find that it brings in an amount roughly equal to the profit the organization produces each year.

organization to institutionalize a use for the extra funds that growth brings in: the new program may bring enough overhead funding to hire that assistant director of human resources, but the position never actually gets filled until the end of that year. In the meantime, the growth money creates temporarily free-range funding, kind of a yearlong float. That can help take the sting out of inadequate funding.

Cash Surplus Occasionally, a funding source will pump some cash into the organization without expecting it to be used right away. Foundations may allow advance funding on a grant, for example, and some government funders actually run programs that advance cash to nonprofits. Even though in these situations the money usually has to be repaid or spent, for a time it can be another source of financial breathing room. Warning: this only eases the cash flow aspect of funding inadequacy, since the funds eventually have to be used.

Spending Less The time-honored way of coping with inadequate funding is to spend even less than is provided. This is a regressive approach that in the end may actually make the situation worse, but in the short term it is one of the few widely available coping mechanisms.

Special Funding Considerations Scanning for your internal strengths may reveal other advantages that are not immediately apparent. Every funding source has its unique strengths. Foundation grants are generally quite reasonable about spending guidelines, offer good cash flow, and are somewhat lenient about mid-course changes without excessive bureaucracy. Government dollars are notoriously rigid, unforgiving, and slow in coming. But what they do offer is a solid base—once the money starts flowing, it usually keeps coming. More important, it sometimes carries a good share of overhead. So, government funding becomes a good base on which to build, even if individual government grants or contracts are breakeven at best. Consumer dollars, coming in the form of things like fees for service or memberships, are the least restrictive of all and the most flexible in how they can be used. Each form of income also has its negative points, but remember that this is a scan for strengths, not a hunt for problems.

Geography

Geography should be a straightforward assessment. Document your geographic boundaries in a similar manner to the way you examined your external geography. Where are you strong? Where do your users come from? What is the potential market for your mission? The central question to be answered here is whether you want to change your explicit boundaries or not.

One of the biggest changes in the last decade or so in the nonprofit sector has been the blurring of formerly clear-cut boundaries. When community hospitals were a big part of the hospital sector, their community boundaries were clear. When mental health centers were first funded in the early 1960s their "catchment areas" were preestablished as part of the initial funding process. Many national and statewide service systems still divide up their territory according to geographic boundaries. But geography is not necessarily the best way to apportion service areas, and even where it persists as an important way of setting boundaries the clarity may be waning.

The problem you will face at this stage is that board members often come to their seats with geographically defined loyalties. Although this is diminishing somewhat as for-profit businesses themselves expand their geographic reach (bank consolidation in recent years has made strong local banks almost an anomaly), most civic-minded individuals still have a clear geographic identification, and it is critical not to let that kind of attachment have too much influence over the nonprofit's internal assessment. Even if this kind of psychic connection can be put aside, chances are that board members' usefulness will be defined by their contacts and networks, which will be concentrated in a specific geographic area. If there is a match, this works well. If not, a valuable human asset could be wasted.

Boundaries themselves are never sources of strength. They constrict and divide and ultimately weaken. They also may or may not relate to the true nature of the demand for your services. They may very well be necessary as, for example, a way to control wasteful competition between local affiliates of the same national federation, but they bring very little on which one can build. Instead, they encourage silo thinking and unconnected action.

One of the most important boundaries for nonprofits is not geographic at all and is also elusive in its true meaning. It is the term "community-based," used to distinguish services provided in and by the community rather than those provided in and by an institution. It was useful when it was a code word for organizations that were small, innovative, and grassroots in nature, but many of those same organizations have now grown tremendously and some are even larger than the institutions they replaced. So, what does the term "community-based" really mean?

We suggest that the term no longer has any geographic connotations and that it would be wise not to infer any in order to avoid misleading board members, funders, and the public. Instead, it should simply mean that the organization's locus of control is firmly in the voluntary sector, not the public sector. "Community" should mean not a specific municipality or group of municipalities but rather some defined segment of the public as a whole that is intended to be the beneficiary of services provided through and controlled by members of that public as opposed to the government or the for-profit sector.

Labor Force

In the early twentieth century world of scientific management, with its one best way, workers filled slots and it was management's job to figure out how to direct them for maximum productivity. There are some ironies here.

First, with the exception of universities—which are always unusual beasts—few classes of nonprofits ever reached a mass-production style of organization until hospitals began scaling up in the mid-twentieth century. Second, when other classes of nonprofits began reaching mass-production level later

WILLOWS' END SCAN SHEET: LABOR

Trends

- WEAL employees' average age has declined to 29.4 years from a high of 31.2 years five years ago.
- One half of all WEAL employees have some level of post-high-school education.
- A near-majority of WEAL employees are immigrants and/or minorities.
- Industry turnover rate for direct service employees is an average of 55 percent: the Willows' End turnover rate is 45 percent.
- In a recent survey, 65 percent of all employees said they would encourage a friend to work there. The recent employee recruitment bonus given to existing employees who refer a friend has already resulted in two new hires in the first week.
- Approximately 80 percent of all employees take the bus to work.
- WEAL compensation levels for all employees are consistently in the 60th percentile of assisted living facilities in the area.

Implications

- With a somewhat younger and more educated workforce than average, WEAL is better positioned to adapt to residents' changing needs.
- WEAL turnover may suggest a slightly more committed workforce than average.
- WEAL employees may be a significant source for future employee referrals.
- WEAL employees may be more impacted by the growing traffic congestion.
- WEAL employees are less affected than most by the limited public transportation in the future, as long as service levels remain steady.
- The increase in mixed income housing may create an expanded potential labor force for the organization.

in the twentieth century, it was at about the same time that the primary form of organizational structure for for-profits began to shift toward the demands of an information-based economy, not an industrial, production-oriented one. Nonprofits are beginning to follow suit, but slowly.

To analyze your labor force, which is at the heart of mission-based management, use the prototyper-industrializer model described earlier. Following this distinction will make it easier to assess what you have and what you will need in the future. In prototyper nonprofits, the labor force must be highly individualized because the organization is constantly inventing and reinventing itself and the way it responds to external stimuli. People who work in prototyper nonprofits usually are the brain workers of the sector, highly skilled and/or educated and able to invent and reinvent what they do or how they do it with some regularity.

It is, therefore, not an accident that prototyper nonprofit workers will tend to be highly educated and at least somewhat self-directed. Often they will have advanced degrees. In fact, one of the little-understood characteristics of the higher education sector is that the ultimate product of that world, a doctorate holder, is by training and expectation a highly unique individual. Doctoral research is expected to be different and groundbreaking to some degree, and the inevitable logic of the higher education process is to encourage individual effort rather than team or group efforts.

This is one reason why prototyper organizations' employees can seem like a ragged bunch. As smallish organizations, they do not have to deal with the force of cultural conformity created by a large workforce, and the comfortable future can be nurturing. Often prototyper staff talk a lot about program development or innovation, because those are the things that most interest them, not the repetitious act of providing specific, little-changing services. If it seems a bit of a hothouse future, that is because it is. Prototypers are the ultimate incubators. The typical product of the prototyper workforce is ideas and knowledge and information, not services.

By contrast, a nonprofit industrializer will usually have two distinct labor forces, one characterized by low wages, high turnover, and steadily declining staff quality or job satisfaction, and the other composed of people like the executive director, credentialed employees, a handful of senior managers and/or long-term highly committed employees scattered throughout the organization. The first labor tier is composed of the people from whom you hope to get two or three good years. To replace them you are resigned to having to run year-round recruitment campaigns. The second labor tier is the wellspring of organizational continuity. That smaller, second-tier labor force is also unlike any other. In addition to being different from the direct service workers, it is not much like prototypers either. This is because they mostly are managers first of all, users of ideas and knowledge second. In prototyper organizations, there is often little functional difference between the supervisory level of work and the direct service level of work. The organization is frequently not large enough to need a very distinct class of supervisors, and in many cases the real producers would not stand for close supervision anyway because avoiding close supervision is one of the reasons they work in a prototyper organization.

That smaller labor force will have higher salaries, if only because they have typically been around long enough to earn them, and if nonprofits were not so egalitarian in their nature the class would have more and better benefits of other kinds too. The larger labor pool for the most part will not stay around long enough—or bring enough undeniably high value to the organization—to justify such treatment. Proportionately, the situation is not unlike a classic university setting where the students vastly outnumber the professors but will be gone in four or five years.

BENCHMARKS OF STRENGTH— PROTOTYPERS

Scan for strengths in your labor force in part by looking for typical benchmarks. Prototyper organizations often attract people with a notable passion for the cause. They are creative, high-energy types who seem quite willing to put the organization above their personal interests—although, paradoxically, doing that kind of thing fits nicely with their personality types. They feed on the kind of charge that comes from doing something innovative, unusual, or just plain interesting. Since in most prototyper organizations, it just is not possible to do things the same way twice, they find a compatible outlet for their interests.

Another type of person that prototypers attract is someone with a previous career who is ready to shift gears. Yet another type is the person with one or more highly unique accomplishments or experiences, like the hardy soul who spent six months hiking Tibetan mountains or someone who figured out a way to make modern papyrus and runs a wedding invitation business using the material.

What you usually do not see are individuals with deep experience in that field, probably because prototypers may not pay as well, do not know how to use so much experience, or do not value it. Also, visionary founders may not likely have much respect for veterans, or simply do not want to be told how hard it will be to do things the way they want them done. One can see why prototypers prefer these kinds of employees.

By contrast, people aware of or interested in serving large numbers of users in an industrializer setting will not be likely to have patience with the free-wheeling, frenetic, borderline chaotic prototyper culture. They will instead prefer the kind of predictability and reliability that they simply would not get with a new and/or small organization that seems not to have all the right answers and may in fact exult in discovery and ambiguity.

These types of organizations are the nonprofit sector's rough equivalent to breakthrough organizations in the for-profit world. All of that brashness and fresh attitude can lead to incrementally better ways of serving the mission. It will not happen all the time—in fact, most prototypers never really come up with anything innovative that can be passed on—but if it is going to happen at all it will probably be here.

BENCHMARKS OF STRENGTH—INDUSTRIALIZERS

Each industrializer nonprofit's labor force has two different sets of strengths, one for each of the two tiers of workforces. The larger workforce will tend to be a reasonably disciplined service-oriented group that values personal relationships, with each other and often with the users of the service, above all else.

We once worked with a genealogical research institute that employed a core group of research assistants familiar both with the subject matter and with the organization's resources. Their strongest connection, other than with each other, was with the numerous institute members who would periodically call with a technical question. The researchers created a bit of an efficiency problem for the institute because they liked nothing better than to talk for hours on the phone with each member, lovingly tracking down all the information requested and answering all questions. If they had been a support team for, say, a computer manufacturer, they would have been forbidden to spend so much time on relatively few users. Happily for all parties, the economics of their department were not an overriding issue.

Industrializers' main workforce will tend to include most of the middle to lowest paid employees in the organization. Usually, they will be younger employees (except for the part of the boomer generation that is now aging in place in these types of jobs), and everyone understands that they will be transient. This is the main reason for the trend from the employee model to the consulting model discussed earlier. Youthful workers offer numerous intangibles like energy, fresh perspectives, and an open mind, but as most managers know intuitively, this is almost a code phrase for "trainable." This is why most larger industrializers have developed their own training systems. They have no choice, and in any event it allows the employer to shape workers the way they want them to be at a time in their lives when they are most susceptible to it.

Most industrializers' workers do not expect to be in the same job in five years. Even if they did, many nonprofits' revenue streams will not support a large cadre of experienced and well-paid workers anyway. While it is true that such high turnover costs money in the long run, it does at least offer the prospect of constant renewal in the population closest to the users of the service. For many, the job choice is as much a lifestyle-related decision as a career one. The deciding factor tends to be schedule flexibility, or the geographic location of the job, or a sincere fondness for the consumers. Money is decidedly not the chief draw for these people. And while their overall low cost may appeal to the managers, their real value is the sheer potential of having so many people so broadly dedicated to the mission.

That smaller workforce looks very different. Consistency over the long term is perhaps the most differentiating characteristic here. These workers have probably been with the organization for a while, but even if they are relatively new they will almost certainly have done the same kind of thing in another organization. There is a commodity nature to much of what they do because similar jobs in similar organizations tend to demand similar actions, but they are also comfortable in their uniqueness.

These people are typically managers and executives and have made a personal commitment to the field in some way. Getting an advanced degree is an obvious illustration of commitment, but so is persistent success over the years. They are predictably knowledgeable and, by nature as well as experience, they are production-oriented. This means that they have accepted the consumers and their needs, they embrace the program models and services, and they are impatient to put the two together.

This smaller labor pool in an industrializer organization may sound somewhat like a prototypers' workforce, but they are actually far from it. Whereas prototypers often have a joy-of-discovery quality about their work, these individuals are largely beyond that stage. They have seen a great deal, and they are quietly confident about what works and what does not. Conversely when an industrializer organization resists change the source of much of that resistance is usually this group of employees.

THE DIMENSIONS OF THE LABOR FORCE

Taken as a whole, labor is the greatest source of value for a nonprofit organization. That value gets expressed along a number of dimensions. First is the demographics of the work force itself. Age is an obvious dimension because it can be so closely tied to mission and strategy. Young people are often a critical part of an institutional change strategy. They are often idealistic, energetic, and willing to work for low wages. By contrast, few senior service organizations truly prize energetic young people. Neither seniors nor the organizations that serve them tend to value change, and so there can be a fundamental mismatch if young people make up too much of a senior organization's staff.

The workforce's credentials are also a significant dimension of strength. Credentials, whether formal certifications of training and education or just experience, are a reasonably good predictor of success. As with age, however, credentials are best understood in context. Each organization will have at least some level of consensus about what constitutes the most desirable credentials, so a survey of those credentials can help identify the existing pockets of strength.

Monitoring reports can be helpful in determining labor strength too. Where are there typically few vacancies? Which programs and services have the lowest turnover? Which ones have employees with the longest tenure? Finding these answers will suggest pockets of strength. In order to move up, employees in the nonprofit sector often have to move out, going to work for a similar and possibly larger organization. Parts of the nonprofit that have found ways to counteract this tendency know how to offer hope and the promise of continuing advancement and challenge.

Finally, promotional pathways are a good indicator of strength. To gauge any organization's future, find out where its best people are going, because that is where the future lies.

Special Assets

The last object of internal scanning is your assets, especially those that are uniquely necessary to carry out your services. We define the term assets for these purposes as being any tangible or intangible item, which could, at least in theory, be sold to another. Assets, as we define them for these purposes then, have an independent and more or less recognizable value for anyone that owns them.

Narrowly, one can think about special assets as the major nonfinancial items on what is called the balance sheet of an organization. Most commonly these would be land, buildings, equipment, and the value of improvements one makes to them. But special assets can also be intangible things such as a brand name or intellectual property such as patents or protected processes.

What's not a special asset? Staff energy. The loyalty of key managers. A really super board of directors. The reason these are not useful to treat as special assets is because they have no real independent value. Special assets can be acquired or built, and they should have value to another organization—even if one could never imagine transferring the asset.

Many organizations do not have any special assets because they do not need them in order to deliver their service. Other organizations may have assets that are not essential to the services delivered. A building containing administrative operations, for example, is not essential to the effective delivery of those services. Other assets may in fact be unique to the services delivered but not really large enough to have strategic importance.

Why is it necessary to look for these kinds of assets? A familiar theme here—strategies are built on strength, not on weakness. For those programs and services that need (or simply have) some kind of special asset, it is important to recognize it as such. It may help gain or solidify a strategic position, and if it is truly an asset it should always be available if it is needed. This kind of asset may allow the organization to do something that others

WILLOWS' END SCAN SHEET: SPECIAL ASSET—BUILDING

Trends
- Willows' End's largest single asset is its building and the plot of land on which it sits.
- According to public records, the land and buildings owned by WEAL are assessed at $2.1M.
- When the old Willows' End Hospital went out of business, it deeded the building and land to WEAL or its successor organization in perpetuity with the proviso that the property always be used to operate programs for elders.
- The name Willows' End, although it refers to a geographic location, is occasionally interpreted as a commentary on the ultimate fate of residents. However, this is not typically a problem for residents who lived or had ties locally.
- Many residents who came from the neighborhood express pleasure at the building's rebirth, remembering it as an abandoned textile mill that had been an eyesore for years.

Implications for WEAL
- The building is an inherently valuable resource, but WEAL is somewhat limited in how much it can use it other than as a service site because of the deed restrictions. The building is essentially a "trapped endowment."
- The building's status as a locally treasured rehabilitation project gives WEAL a substantial amount of community approval and support.
- As WEAL's geographic source of referrals expands, the misinterpretation of the name could become a problem.
- Rehabilitated older buildings can be difficult to maintain and may be susceptible to unpredictable system failures.

cannot, or it may somehow produce efficiencies in operations. Whatever its value, planners need to recognize it.

The other reason for scanning special assets is to avoid leaving anything unused in the effort to achieve the goals. Nonprofit organizations usually do not have so many assets to throw at a task that they can afford to over-look any. A related risk is that assets will be undervalued, causing planners and managers to underuse them.

YOUNG PEOPLE AS CHANGE AGENTS

When Jerome Miller, a former university social work professor, was appointed commissioner of the Massachusetts Department of Youth Services, he soon became appalled at the conditions in his depart-ment's large "kid jails." In response, he became a reformer.

Miller was able to get the support of key governmental, political, and public leaders, but he still needed large numbers of people to staff new programs and to be a counterweight to institutional staff still wedded to the old methods. He found them in local colleges, universities, and voluntary programs. Putting these eager young recruits to work, he crafted a critical mass of alternative workers as well as a training ground for future leaders—dozens of his volunteers and first-job recruits later became influential leaders in the community-based service movement they helped him create.

In retrospect, it is easy to see how demographics helped Miller succeed. The swelling ranks of baby boomers born in the late forties and early fifties were at that precise moment entering the workforce for the first time with college educations, a social conscience, and a burning desire to change society. This was truly a case of need find-ing necessity.

RECIPE CARD   HOW TO CARRY OUT
AN INTERNAL SCAN

Methods for Ensuring Objective Scanning

Getting a group to do objective internal scanning is not an easy undertaking, but it is essential. Here are some tips for how to increase the chances of objectivity.

First, get the scanning group to buy into the principles of internal scanning listed at the beginning of this section. Better still, have them devise a variation on these principles themselves. Groups that develop their own guidelines are more likely to follow them.

Next, remind everyone (again) to attempt to be objective in their assessments. Point out that a strategy based on a flawed view of one's strengths is only going to fail anyway, potentially dragging the whole organization down with it. At the same time, the reality is that the incentive to exaggerate may be too strong to resist.

Finally, consider the following ways to verify potential strengths.

Independent Verification

The prime method for determining true strengths is to seek independent verification. Sometimes this is practically built in. Accreditation programs, for example, are a form of strength ratification. What's useful about most accreditations is not their simple existence but that they often give nuanced information. Most certifications or accreditations will spell out, often quantitatively, where the organization scored high and where it scored low on the evaluation scale.

Satisfaction Surveys

Another useful measure of strength is consumer satisfaction. The whole concept of explicitly focusing on consumer satisfaction in American business is relatively new, and in nonprofits it is sometimes positively revolutionary. One major university introduced an instructor evaluation system during the 1970s over the opposition of many long-time faculty members. It took two decades, but today the system is a sophisticated, computerized tool widely used by students, administrators, and faculty themselves. And this is not an isolated development.

Consumer satisfaction surveys can be a good tool to support a strategic positioning project because they can be designed and launched on a one-time basis even if they are not routinely employed. They do not have to be complicated—in fact, they should not be—and they have the additional payoff of communicating that the organization cares about how its consumers view its services.

One thing that both complicates and enriches nonprofit consumer satisfaction matters is that the term "consumer" can mean the actual user of the services or the payment source. With third-party funding marbled into the nonprofit world—foundations and governmental entities being two prime examples—the user is not always the consumer. Happily, the problem is easy enough to solve—survey both groups.

External Benchmarks

External benchmarks are another classic way of measuring strengths. There are logistical obstacles here, though. External benchmarks of a nonfinancial nature are hard to come by in the nonprofit sector, or anywhere else. Not only do organizations naturally tend to resist being evaluated by external standards, but usually no one has a financial interest in disseminating benchmarks. Associations are great sources of benchmarks, as are specialized advisors and even governmental entities. For those ambitious enough to do it, it is always possible to create one's own survey instrument. There are now online survey tools that, for a fee, take the headache out of creating one's own survey and then processing the data.

Internal Benchmarks

When properly designed, a system of internal benchmarking can be a good way of identifying patterns and trends. Internal benchmarking is helpful for trendspotting because their homegrown natures make their reliability and replicability outside of the organization questionable. Chances are that nothing developed without explicit use of the definitions, customs, and practices employed by the outside world will be reliable for anything other than narrow internal purposes. Still, if the benchmarks are consistently kept, they can be enormously useful in highlighting trends and patterns within the organization.

Accreditation

Accreditations from an outside body can be useful in two ways. If the accreditation is for the organization as a whole, this can say something about its overall level of achievement. The downside is that organization-wide accreditation does not necessarily say anything about discrete strengths. For this, it may be necessary to dig into the details of the accreditation report, if they exist. If the accreditation is for a single program or service, all the better, because the greater precision will be more meaningful.

Outside Review

One of the most straightforward ways of objectively assessing strengths is to get outsiders to do it. Consultants of all stripes will happily do an internal review of an organization's strengths as preparation for a strategic positioning exercise. Although potentially expensive, if the consultants are selected properly, this route offers perhaps the most independent strength scan possible.

Decide Where to Be

Gearshift time. Deciding where you want the organization to be requires a very different way of thinking, and a different set of skills on the part of the planners, than what has been true to this point. Much of what is done in future and internal scanning is research intended to establish a common set of facts. To do that research, one needs a willingness to go on a kind of journey with no preestablished destination and an ability to recognize important facts and the trends they suggest. If there is not a single answer, at least the range of answers is narrowly defined. The research process is also organized by a single individual or a small team.

Deciding where the organization should be is decidedly not a fact-based exercise. It is more an expression of collective desire than a prediction. To accomplish it, one's orientation to time must shift from a combination of present-day realities and historical facts to the future. The planning work is no longer a matter of discerning what is factual and important: it is a matter of deciding what should be factual at some point in the future. Moreover, it involves a larger group of people, and so it necessarily has to be based on a substantial consensus.

This is a problem. Groups usually prefer to problem-solve with the expectation that there is at least one or more demonstrably correct answers out there somewhere. But that's not the point in this part of strategic positioning. As a collective expression of a desired strategic position, the planning group is not problem-solving, it is imagining. And that imagining should be rooted in reality but not unduly bound by it.

This requires an entirely different, and for most people somewhat unfamiliar, way of thinking. An English researcher named Liam Hudson nearly forty years ago explained it this way. In sciences, mathematics, and standardized testing generally, one must start with facts and move toward the "right" answer: one "converges" on the truth. By contrast, divergent thinking starts with facts, or some other type of stimulus, and moves toward ideas.

Most people seem to be convergent thinkers. More important, the majority of professional jobs require convergent thinking. Engineers, accountants, bookkeepers, and physicians have to be convergent thinkers. Their job is to find and use "correct" ideas. A bridge has to be designed based on the laws of mathematics and physics or else it will not work. A diagnosis has to be correct in order for treatment to succeed. Bookkeeping entries have to be accurate or the organization may get an entirely wrong impression of its fiscal health.

Divergent thinking works in reverse. Divergent thinking starts with a set of facts or some other stimulus (passion for a cause, for example), and asks "what if" and "let's suppose" and "maybe we should." Divergent thinkers seek a wide array of thoughts, options, and inputs, and they often operate in fields where there is clearly no right answer most of the time. Disc jockeys, artists, movie producers, hair stylists, and public relations experts are all examples of people who must use divergent thinking in their jobs. They may have a definitive result they want to obtain—higher ratings for the morning drive show, for example—but they still will get there by divergent thinking.

The two types of thinking are not mutually exclusive. Everyone has to do some of each kind. Convergent versus divergent thinking are best thought of as comfort zones, the types of intellectual activity in which people are most comfortable. Over time, people will gravitate to the kind of thought processes with which they are most comfortable, and this part of the strategic positioning process can be tricky. Many high-income professionals are most comfortable with convergent thinking, so as a result boards often have a disproportionate percentage of these types of thinkers. Many managers in nonprofits tend to be convergent thinkers too, so with a large percentage of convergent thinkers in the pool from which the planning team will be drawn it is inevitable that this step will play to most participants' weaknesses.

Traditional board and executive-level responsibilities also emphasize convergent thinking. Most nonprofit board members and managers come on the scene well after the big thinking has already been done, and the typical work of a board of directors tends to emphasize convergent thinking ("will we be taking too big a risk to start that new program?"). In these circumstances the natural reaction is to settle in and try to make things work rather than reexamining the larger context in which the organization got started or how it could be made more effective.

Deciding where to be in 5–10 years is an inherently divergent-thinking-based task. It is the point when an organization can start to determine its own future. Mariners know that the horizontal line across the rocks on shore is the point where high tides over the years have left their signature. Under normal conditions this is as high as the ocean gets, or the high water mark. The purpose of this part of strategic positioning is to set the organization's own high water mark: What will success look like in the future? Where do you want to be? How high do you want to go?

There is always a considerable amount of ambiguity in this question, and there is no right answer that anyone can discern at the moment it is asked. But there is something else about this divergent thinking task. Not only does it have no correct answers, it also requires a considerable amount of will, a kind of institutional ego that says, "this is the way we want it to be, and this is the way it will be."

This is an underappreciated dimension of strategy. While strategy involves a lot of planning and analysis and choices and decision making, these things are all accessible through old-fashioned business-like, analytical approaches. Yet there is an element of strategy that is inevitably based on some very important intangibles. How else to explain why some organizations choose to implement a strategy that seems at best 50 percent likely to succeed, or that appears to require far more than they can possibly bring to the plan? It seems equal parts organizational confidence, willingness to accept risk, clear-eyed vision, and perhaps just plain luck. It cannot simply be the brilliance of the CEO or the persuasiveness of his or her selling skills. Good strategy setting is an intangible commodity and it is deeply rooted in divergent thinking.

MIND YOUR STRENGTHS, FOCUS ON THE FUTURE

In strategic positioning you build a strategy from the ground up, one piece at a time. Again, good strategies are built on strengths, not weaknesses. By now you have an excellent grasp of both your internal strengths and the trends in your external future, so the task is to use the former to take advantage of the latter.

One very important clarification: while you will rightfully spend most of your time building on your strengths, do not let them become overly constricting. From time to time you may well encounter situations where you do not possess some key organizational strength. It is perfectly acceptable to go ahead and develop your desired strategic position without having the necessary strength, because during implementation it will be management's job to develop or acquire it. Just make sure that the whole strategic position is based on a minimum of yet-to-be-acquired strengths because to do otherwise would be self-deluding. It is hard enough to acquire a single strength, but to try to add several while executing a strategic position for an entire organization is unwise.

Begin with the handful of elements we talked about in the beginning:

- The need for your service

- Your geography

- Your users and potential users of your service

- Competitors or alternatives

- Funders

- Labor force

- Special assets

Your synthesized strategic position will be the sum of your responses to the question "where do you want to be in 5–10 years?" for each of these seven factors. Of course, a good strategic position is not simply a list of responses but rather a synthesized, easy-to-understand statement of where your organization desires to be in the future. Occasionally, it will be possible to sum it all up in a single catchy phrase or sentence, but more likely it will take at least a paragraph or two to explain the ideas. That's okay— thoughtfulness always has a place in strategy—because not all factors will be equally important.

Even though the list of future factors has a pleasing linear quality to it, strategic thinking is not linear. It may be necessary to treat one or more factors superficially or as placeholders, to be revisited when the desired response to other factors is clearer. It may also be necessary to go through two or more series of responses to each factor, with each subsequent response making incremental changes to the one before.

For some organizations there will be little to talk about for some of these factors because they are already exactly where the organization wants them to be. In these cases, it will be management's job to figure out ways to keep them there. As managers design an implementation plan for the desired strategic position they will have to decide how to prioritize their work. It may take a lot less time and effort to acquire or develop an organizational strength for a lower strategic priority than it will to achieve a higher strategic priority, for example, so operational work level may not seem to match strategic priorities.

But we are getting ahead of ourselves. The task for right now is to create the desired strategic position for the next several years for each of these seven factors. To avoid talking in vague generalities we will use Willows' End Assisted Living facility to show how an organization might work its way through each of the factors. Since there are literally thousands of possible answers to the "Where do you want to be?" question, we cannot cover them all. And since WEAL is not real, we can only guess what its planners might decide. So for each factor we will cover some possible answers to the question, working through each one based on the organization's strengths plus a reasonable guess as to the personalities and other intangible qualities of its leadership. We will suggest one of the options as WEAL's choice, keep track of them all, and then create a synthesized statement of its desired strategic position.

THE NEED FOR DEMENTIA SERVICES

Like many organizations, WEAL's discussion about the need for its services is not as simple as it may seem. At this point in its development as an organization, WEAL has many important things in place. It has reliable referral sources, a position in the local market, clinical people who have worked out systems of care and the training for it, and a culture that supports it all. It would be very easy for WEAL planners to conclude that they have a pretty good operation, because in fact they do.

But operating from this assumption could prove to be a strategic error. Right now, WEAL's model treats dementia as a function of age, and everything they do revolves around this central premise. However, there are other forms of dementia as well, such as head injury or organic causes like illness. The behavior of people with these forms of dementia is different from the demographics-influenced behavior of an elderly population, and they have different needs. They get referred to facilities in different ways, and they pose different challenges for day-to-day care as well. For instance WEAL staff, accustomed to caring for age-related dementia patients, would probably have a much harder time caring for a strong, agitated 25-year-old head injury patient.

Naturally, WEAL planners would be likely to accept the implicit age-related focus of their current response to the need for dementia services. In this case, that would probably be just as well. But what if the need for dementia services was changing? What if the nature of dementia itself was changing?

The strategic landscape is cluttered with examples of changing need. When the Make-A-Wish Foundation of America began operations in the 1980s, childhood leukemia was almost always fatal. Since MAW defined its target population as children with a life-threatening or terminal disease, children with the disease fit the profile automatically. By the latter part of

MISSION PEOPLE KNOW . . .

Mission people are the first to know. People who worked in women's programs before and after the 1990s were the first to know that something fundamental had changed in the need for their services. In the early days of shelters, the population was largely social service in nature: clients were seeking ways out of troubled relationships and dysfunctional situations. Then, mental health services came under managed care, institutions began to close, and hospitals stopped caring for mentally ill people via long in-patient stays. Welfare reform changed the rules—literally—for recipients and service providers, and the numbers of incarcerated women grew significantly.

Front-line mission people saw the results quickly. Their consumers began to be former prisoners, often with drug and/or deeply rooted psychological problems. What had been a relatively straightforward picture of need turned into complex situations that demanded a different level of skill and far more clinical demands. The service models had to change to accommodate it.

the next decade, medical advances had rendered most diagnoses of child-hood leukemia as non-life-threatening until the first recurrence, and MAW adjusted their list of qualifying diseases accordingly. The apparent epidemic of type II diabetes among children is another example of dra-matically changing need for services for health care providers. The wide-spread advent of latchkey children is another, and so on.

The ideal is to create a rich, three-dimensional portrait of the need for services. However, many factors work against that. For one thing, defin-ing need is easily influenced by preconceptions and unrecognized self-limitations. The tendency to accept the scope and scale of existing programs as a given, thereby reducing one's potential strategic effective-ness, is just one type of unrecognized self-limitation. There may also be an understandable instinct to define need in terms that will not be over-whelming for the organization.

A few simple techniques can help create a fair and useful portrait of need. First, planners should separate their organization's models of service from their analyses of the need for that service. People do not necessarily need a specific service. Instead, they have a need, which a specific service can fulfill. Planners risk accepting a myopic needs analysis if they allow themselves to define a need for service as a need for their model of service. Society does not need public schools, or hospitals, or museum. What it has is needs that, over time, happened to have been met through these models of service. Models are really nothing more than an accident of history. If something changes in the nature of that need, the service models may have to change too.

Another approach is to discuss need only within the overlay of some sort of boundary, such as geographic area. It is also useful to include a diverse group of people and interests on the planning committee. In particular, consider including mission people. Mission people are the majority of most nonprofit organizations, and they perform the services that the orga-nization is in business to supply. Mission people usually have a different perspective on need that should be heard. People who are enmeshed in WEAL administrative roles and those on the board may not appreciate the subtleties of the need for dementia services. Since mission people come into regular contact with those who need services, they are likely to be the early warning systems of change.

Finally, include questioning, thoughtful types. These types are actually far less common than one might imagine, squinty eyes and a contrarian demeanor often passing for intellectual acuity. To some degree need is an inherently relative term, depending as it does on a mix of context, resources and expectations. People with a true orientation to planning and a nuanced approach to applying the organization's mission may be better equipped to detect subtleties and shape everyone's thinking. Deciding how much one wants to respond to community need is one of the most powerfully shaping decisions one can make.

The Options

WEAL might take a few legitimate but very different approaches to where it wants to be regarding the need for dementia services. It could endorse the status quo; that is, WEAL should serve age-related dementia generally. The advantage of this position is that it puts them directly in line to serve the largest bulk of potential residents, giving them the greatest possible selection and the possibility of the highest utilization rate. This is the simplest and least complicated of the options.

Alternatively, WEAL could decide to focus exclusively on Alzheimer's disease residents. Planners would know that this diagnosis is projected to grow in the future and that the market for surrogate care for people with this type of disease is strong and without many options. The number of Alzheimer's residential care providers in its service area likely will enter into the discussion at this point, but should be dealt with more exclusively later on.

WEAL might also note that there is a growing convergence between the needs of elders with dementia and the needs of people of all ages with developmental disabilities or mental retardation (MR/DD). This is happening on a number of levels in multiple ways. The first generation of people with MR/DD to spend a significant portion of their lives outside of an institution is beginning to reach middle age and beyond. They are aging just like nondisabled people and need the same kind of care. From the service providers' perspective, there is a convergence between the styles of programming and the day-to-day needs of the two populations. This might lead planners to speculate about how they might be able to serve two distinct needs using the same general approaches and program designs.

Or a strong and pervasive sense of mission and a desire to stretch the organization might lead WEAL to observe that head-injury dementia is also a serious area of need. They might realize that the remaining heavy industries in their region continue to produce occasional head injuries for workers and that the presence of two major medical centers in the region tends to attract severe head-injury cases from all over the country. They might see that some head-injury patients bring with them reliable payment for services, such as insurance settlements, and that a young head-injury patient is far more likely to be a longer-term relationship than even many healthy seniors. They could conclude that although head-injury patients can be programmatically more demanding than their present senior population, the need for these services is so pressing as to impel them in this new direction.

The variations on these and other themes are endless, of course. As with most organizations, what will push WEAL in a specific direction is some unpredictable mixture of planners' vision, commitment to the mission, knowledge, and personal energy. In the end, institutional ego in the best sense of the term will determine where WEAL wants to be regarding dementia services in 5–10 years.

For our purposes, let's assume that WEAL decides that it wants to continue its current focus on serving dementia clients generally. The board and staff leadership feels that demand will remain strong in the future and that this direction is entirely consistent with the mission of the organization. There may have been a spirited discussion about the need for Alzheimer's services in particular, but the planning group expressed only cautious interest in targeting any of their resources exclusively to this disorder. This is seed planting. At some point in the future if the question of targeted Alzheimer's services is raised again, the group at least will have a history of considering the question. If circumstances have changed enough by then, that future discussion may elevate the Alzheimer's focus to a newer and more compelling level. For now, WEAL's statement of its desired strategic position regarding its chosen need for services looks like this:

NEED FOR SERVICE

Willows' End Assisted Living will continue providing services to clients aged 60 or older who show a need for assistance in two or more key areas of daily living (such as hygiene, food preparation, dressing, etc.) as a result of non-injury-related dementia.

DESIRED GEOGRAPHIC POSITION

Often for nonprofit organizations, geography is the easiest element of a strategic position to create. Sometimes it is given, such as when a national organization lays out the boundaries for its local affiliates. It can be obvious and hard to surmount, which is the case for island-based or rural nonprofits. Or it can be embedded in the name and the culture and the very heart of the organization.

You will note that none of these situations have the force of law, so one can say that geography is always somewhat negotiable. Practically speaking, though, geographic boundaries usually are accepted because it is easier that way. Enough other things are usually up for discussion that it is simpler to take geographic boundaries out of that mix.

This may not be a good idea. Boundaries are restrictive by nature, and they can inadvertently restrict dreams as easily as they can restrict physical movement. Accepting a geographic area as the explicit bounds of operations in some cases can be an outright handicap. If WEAL insisted on a tightly drawn set of boundaries for its market area, and if that area did not have enough potential service users within it, then the organization would not be able to achieve economic size and would eventually fold. A similar thing would happen if a competitor organization increased its market share within WEAL's geography.

As suggested earlier, geographic boundaries can also be misleading as to both scope and penetration. Simply drawing lines around a land mass does nothing to ensure that all users are served or served adequately within those bounds. Endorsing those boundaries without considering their appropriateness or effectiveness limits the development of a strategic position in a fundamental way.

Once again, the answer is to give some thought to the strategic factor. Is the chosen geography still valid? Does it represent the optimal balance between aspiration and resources? What are the implications of the chosen geography for the strategic position? These are the kinds of questions that will help guarantee that geographic boundaries are not blithely accepted when they ought to be pushed, constricted, or stretched.

The Options

For WEAL, the geography factor is starkly etched into their name. Who outside of the local community knows where to find Willows' End? Who beyond a garment industry historian even knows what a willows is? This is a common situation for nonprofit organizations. To paraphrase ex-Speaker of the House Tip O'Neill, all nonprofit missions begin locally. Even the national-household-name organizations and associations usually began with a single local program that no one ever envisioned would spread across the country. Ordinarily, it is that human impulse to deal with local needs in a local fashion that leads to the creation of a nonprofit organization, and as long as that need and the impulse to respond to it remains local the geographic boundaries will too.

The problem is that the external world does not always cooperate with the arbitrary boundaries we seek to impose on it, the most common example of which being when the demand for a nonprofit's services exceeds the initially envisioned supply, and the nonprofit is "asked" to expand its reach. So, the question of geography for WEAL really is a question of market position in disguise. If it wishes to stay local, its name will be an asset because for assisted living facilities most referrals originate within about a 10-mile radius of the site. If it wishes to expand beyond its current neighborhood, people in the new geography will likely regard the name with puzzlement at best. And unlike the American Association of Retired Persons, which changed its name to AARP, WEAL is, well, a plainly unsatisfying acronym.

On the other hand, brand-name considerations are not the only part of geographic choice. Geographic expansion would almost certainly mean adding a second site, which brings with it numerous operational implications. It would probably mean changing the composition of the board to reflect the new community's strengths and needs, and it would entail financial demands that would have to be met somehow.

WEAL has an additional consideration with geographic implications. The "end" part of its name has unfortunate connotations for an assisted living facility. Those who live in the area are surely quite familiar with Willows' End as a geographic location, so the chances are excellent that they would hear the name as a location rather than associate it with an end point for the living. It does not hurt that the nearby college is a well-known local entity with a similar-sounding name. Even people considering moving there from out of town to be near a relative would probably understand the geographic connotation or possibly accept its legitimacy on the basis of the college's name. But if the organization expanded further than its primary market area, it might very well have to change its name.

Willows' End's Choice

Under the circumstances, WEAL would most likely choose to keep its current geographic focus. Not only is it comfortable at its present scale, but geographic expansion would also elevate its management challenge to a whole new level.

> **GEOGRAPHIC POSITION**
>
> Willows' End will continue to focus on its present geography, reserving the possibility of expanding it at some point in the future if that becomes necessary.

WILLOWS' END'S DESIRED POSITION IN RELATION TO ITS USERS

In part because of its service model, which involves a relatively small, slow-to-change, defined group of users, Willows' End is able to maintain good statistical records. These were the basis for the user analysis in the previous section, and they help managers match services delivered with residents' needs. They serve a doubly powerful purpose for planners.

From these records, Willows' End knows that its residents are aging in place. This is a common trend in newer assisted living programs. Not surprisingly, the amount of assistance they need is also up, as is the incidence of indoor falls. The fact that the increase in falls is unexplained and that emergency hospital admissions are holding steady allows planners to reasonably infer that aging is the primary explanation rather than problems with staffing, resident services, or facility maintenance (perhaps a sophisticated statistical analysis would suggest otherwise, but even if that were practical it would be overkill here). So, the fundamental question is "Where do the planners want to be?" regarding the actual users of their services. This question is different from the first question of where planners want to be with respect to the demand for their services. Willows' End must now decide what it wants its core group of users to look like.

Managing demand is one of the most powerful things that a group can do. The market for services quickly figures out individual providers' preferences for the clients they serve. Consumers, potential consumers, competitors, funders, regulators, casual observers, academics, associations, and potential employees pick up signals about the preferences an organization has for the people it serves. So, managing demand amounts to deliberately sending the market the signals you want it to receive.

To arrive at a user population with the characteristics that fit your particular mix of institutional abilities and resources requires constant attention to a delicate calculus. To go from residents needing an average of 2.1 activities of daily living to 2.4 may not sound like a big jump, but it could mean the difference between the staff feeling stressed out or comfortable. Or it could mean a subtle but profound change in residents' feelings of safety that could eventually translate into a threat to the organization's desired position as a flagship among competitors. Since so many residents have local ties, word of these troubles would leak out quickly, often magnified, and could hurt Willows' End's reputation.

The behavior of WEAL's resident mix suggests that the facility is changing in some critical ways and that key people such as executives and those in admissions will shape the organization's long term future in the next few months. This is why it is necessary to be clear about the particular desired user mix now and to make it part of the strategy rather than being passive about where demand pushes Willows' End.

As before, the choice is up to Willows' End. Within limits, the organization can create its own most desirable user population, with the only variables being its ability to execute and how quickly it can do it.

There are an infinite number of variations in what Willows' End might choose. We will say that the organization desires to maintain roughly its current mix, feeling that to deal with a population that is significantly older would put too much burden on direct service staff. If anything, the newness of the organization means that its policies and procedures are all geared to a somewhat younger population. In turn, this means that its culture would have to change dramatically if it were to seek an older population. A younger population would allow WEAL to keep a fairly full schedule of events, and the medical complications that a younger population entails would be less intrusive.

Of course, managing the resident mix is not a precise undertaking. Willows' End cannot simply announce its desired age and level of care to the public and expect it to happen. So, the way they have to achieve the desired strategic positioning is to work backward from the objective. For instance, if they desire a younger average population while their existing residents are aging, they have to find ways to appeal to new entrants in their mid- to late 60s. Younger potential residents may have more options for a living situation, which means that an assisted living option has to be made more appealing to their needs, while still being feasible for people 10–15 years older.

Still, these are operational considerations for later. For now, we will establish Willows' End's desired strategic position in its user mix to be a younger population with fewer needs than the current average.

COMPETITIVE POSITION

Of all the strategic factors it must address, WEAL's relationship to its competitors is easily the most critical. Much of the for-profit world consists of industrializers, organizations that make money by being able to produce commercially viable quantities of goods or services, and the assisted living service model is very amenable to industrialization. The core competencies necessary to run assisted living include site development and maintenance, food management, and basic health and safety, which are the essence of the hospitality industry. To provide assisted living services, one need only add the competence of serving a disabled population that happens to be elderly. The for-profit sector figured out how to do hospitality services on a large scale very well during the twentieth century once automobiles revolutionized travel, and so doing the same in assisted living services was not much of a stretch.

This hospitality service model mastery, in addition to the need to invest large amounts of capital, made assisted living a natural for the for-profit world in the 1990s. In addition, once the assisted living model grew popular, the market demanded a fairly rapid build-up. Neither the hospitality service model nor raising capital nor rapid growth are things that most

USER POSITION

Willows' End will seek to serve a user population in the mid- to late 60s needing assistance with less than an average of 2.5 activities of daily living.

nonprofits are good at, so much of the nonprofit sector was excluded from the boom. This is why so many of WEAL's direct competitors are for-profit organizations. It is also why WEAL must take its competitive strategic position so seriously. Being a nonprofit in a competitive landscape populated mostly by for-profits is a rare strategic challenge.

STRATEGIC POSITIONS ARE INFINITELY VARIABLE

As a divergent thinking exercise, positioning one's organization vis-à-vis the competition can offer literally endless possibilities. Good competitive positioning comes from creative thinking that takes into consideration all of the realities the institution faces. It also derives from the collective personalities and abilities of the leadership group.

Some for-profit management thinkers maintain that there are only a handful of possible competitive strategies for any organization—market leader versus niche player, for example. But that ignores the richness and complexity of strategy, reducing it to little more than a conceptual on–off switch. In our view there are endless variations of strategy, differences that are subtle or profound and that will play out on a continuum of impact. Good strategic positions should come out of a unique set of realities the way a piece of art emerges from a unique sensibility.

There are no cookie cutter approaches in strategic positioning, especially in establishing a desired competitive position. Even broad frameworks are of limited usefulness because competitive conditions change constantly, especially when the competitors are a mixture of for-profits and nonprofits. Add to that the fact that competitors can also be collaborators, and you have an extraordinary range of possibilities. While competitive realities may limit an entity's options in the short run, they are rarely overwhelming or permanent. In the end, competitive positioning is another one of those areas determined by what we referred to above as institutional ego: Where does WEAL want to be?

The Options

We offer three different strategic positions regarding WEAL's competition. These three options are not the only choices available to WEAL. They may not even be the best or most logical ones. They are simply three possible formulations that a group might develop. Another group of Willows' End leaders at another time would almost certainly come up with something different. Still, one needs to put a stake in the ground somewhere, so we will suggest a handful of possible competitive positions that Willows' End might consider.

One thing that makes Willows' End's positioning task difficult is that, most of the time, people do not care whether an organization like this is a for-profit or a nonprofit. Employees, especially those in mission jobs, may or may not give any thought to the question, and in some sectors those employees and many community members may even wrongly assume that an organization is a nonprofit when in fact it just displays behaviors that make it seem that way. Consumers are more likely to be interested in the nature of the costs and benefits of WEAL versus other choices and not to think about—or understand—the tax status of each provider. In fact, society tends to think about the implications of nonprofit status only when something goes wrong or draws attention to the subject.

Consumers do care about quality. This is where nonprofits can have a real competitive advantage. In a commodity business such as retailing, quality is defined by most consumers primarily as the lowest price, and so Wal-Mart has succeeded handsomely. But in a more complex transaction involving personal services, the definition of quality is much less clear. Providers must do something to shift the center of the user's calculation from price alone. Low-cost providers will always succeed even in a personal services marketplace, of course, but there is room for those who offer more than the lowest price.

We call this strategy the flagship effect, and it is most notable in sectors like Willows' End's that are heavily dominated by for-profits with a minority nonprofit presence (it exists everywhere but is most pronounced in a for-profit dominated marketplace). A flagship is literally the ship designated to carry the flag of the fleet or squadron commander. It is not going to be the best of the bunch on a single dimension but rather will have an overall strategic advantage.

In our terminology, a flagship strategy is not quite the same thing as being the market leader, which is a position that implies some degree of ability to influence the market for services through a combination of sheer size and quality. A nonprofit flagship strategy implies that an organization is one to "keep an eye on" because of its leadership role and ability to serve a distinct slice of the market very well while saying something of importance to all the other service providers.

Interestingly, a flagship strategy chosen by a nonprofit can be compatible with other, for-profit competitors too. In industries dominated by for-profit groups, there can emerge a natural alliance between one or more nonprofit flagships and a segment of the for-profit providers that aspire to the same strategy. Normally, this segment is composed of small chains, often closely held entities whose owners genuinely want to make a statement or create a positive public perception for themselves. They stand out

NONPROFIT STATUS—COMPETITIVE—ADVANTAGE OR NOT?

As traditional markets for nonprofit services have begun to allow for-profit competition, the advantage of the tax designation has waned a bit. In these circumstances, it is worth asking why the status is important.

Some of the answer comes from the diminishing role of government in affairs of interest to nonprofits. Groups purchasing services from other groups naturally tend to prefer working with groups that "look like them." Mom-and-pop shops do not typically sell a lot of goods or services to multinational corporations, and such corporations do not seek out mom-and-pops as suppliers. Government entities, when turning to the private sector for services and solutions, seem to have had a distinct bias toward nonprofit suppliers in many industries such as health care or social services. When government is a buyer, it will tend to look for suppliers that aspire to similar goals such as accountability, transparency, and serving the public good. It is easier that way, and less expensive too since the government buyer does not have to worry as much about putting provisions in place to ensure these qualities.

As efficiency and cost-effectiveness have risen higher on the scale than such process-oriented values, and as government's role has declined overall in many sectors, the nonprofit status has become less inherently important and the door has opened wider for for-profit competitors.

in the field because many for-profits in a crowded market often focus exclusively on simply running their operations at a desired profit level with no regard for trying to influence that market.

Nonprofits have a hidden advantage with a flagship strategy. As much as for-profit providers may want to adopt the same strategy, market forces will work against them. Industrializers always get battered by lower-cost competitors, and over time can become the target for takeovers, particularly if they grow large enough to become publicly held. Usually, it is the founders or early owners of the flagship chain, frequently industry pioneers themselves, who are forced by circumstances to sell (including lucrative buyout deals). The new owners have none of the same motivation and are content to run simply a profitable high-end operation, thus leaving a clearer path for the nonprofit flagship.

A flagship strategy is not an elite-service strategy, although there is ample precedent for it to become one. Visiting nurses associations got their start when conditions in nineteenth-century hospitals were horrendous. Everyone understood the risks in being hospitalized, but the wealthy elites had the resources to do something about it and created what would become today's nonprofit visiting nurse associations. Flagship in this context really just means "they do things right."

To succeed with a flagship strategy, a nonprofit must do much more than simply deliver services. It has to speak to the community of users and offer a clear rationale not only for its services but also for the service model itself. It must be engaged with other providers, and it must be sufficiently respected as to be credible when speaking for that community. Sometimes this is as simple as having a recognizably credible CEO, but ordinarily there is more to it than that. The philosophy of the organization has to be at least generally known and its practices consistent with its stated values.

It is a bit of a paradox that executives of a flagship organization must actually spend as much if not more time with other service providers as with consumers. Staff from the flagship have to be a known commodity to their peers, and this takes time. In cold economic terms, this time expense gets paid for in two ways. First, for-profits must make a profit on their services. Nonprofits have to make a profit too but usually not as much. On the cost side, whereas for-profits will tend to be rather strict about spending within their personnel budget, nonprofits will tend to be overstaffed rather than understaffed. In effect, nonprofits tend to use the surplus that would otherwise go into an owner's pocket to buy more staff time, and it is this time that can be used to establish its strategic position as a flagship organization.

Another common direction for nonprofits to pursue relative to their competitors is as the provider of last resort. In this position, which is nearly the reverse of the flagship, the nonprofit not only accepts but actively seeks out consumers that its competitors cannot or will not serve. Often these are low income and/or extremely difficult consumers. This position has four distinct strategic advantages. The first is that it is in everyone else's best interests to keep the last resort supplier alive and healthy, even if that means advocating on their behalf for special treatment in complex governmental funding futures.

The second strategic advantage is that the last resort provider is some-times the last to be cut, at least by government funders. While not all con-sumers will pass through its doors, those that do are often too hard or too undesirable for the others to handle. The situation is analogous to the intensive care unit in a hospital. Not every consumer will need it, but without it the entire hospital would be severely limited in the types of patients it would get because the larger referral stream would flow in a dif-ferent direction.

The third advantage of this strategic position is the program-related benefits it can bring. A focused population will be attractive to certain pro-fessionals. In seeking out unwanted or unservable program consumers, the organization sets up a situation where it is nearly impossible for mission people to fail. Since no one expects much of these devalued consumers, any progress is remarkable. A certain type of mission person, often profes-sional clinicians, find difficult clients attractive. Progress is measured in increments, so breakthroughs, in the rare times when they occur, are all the more gratifying.

Finally, this strategic position with respect to one's competitors can give a powerful synergy by aligning strategy with consumers with the labor force. This is a strong—and fairly rare—statement. There is something appealing about such focus. Everyone in the organization can feel it, and it makes strategy implementation much easier.

A third competitive position is to explicitly position WEAL in collabo-ration with a local referral source. This is what nursing homes do when they work closely with a hospital, or what art schools do when they work with museums. It is a very legitimate strategy in general but could be difficult for Willows' End, since assisted living is not necessarily a logical stop on an established pathway.

Positioning one's self against competitors in the nonprofit sector is different from in the for-profit sector. While leaders owe their organizations a duty of loyalty and the personal energy to differentiate it from similar nonprofits, there is a practical limit to competitiveness in the sector. Competitiveness can at some point actually have negative effects, draining resources and time from mission work.

A creative way for Willows' End to forge a collaborative relationship, strange as it may sound, is to get together with the nearby college. Higher education nonprofits now offer many related programs and services, and one of them is assisted living. In many ways it is a natural relationship. Both program models depend on having an attractive campus, basic hospitality services, and some level of ability to serve a defined resident population. But what makes a lot of strategic sense for colleges is that their fundraising depends in part on having a loyal alumni base that identifies with the college as a lifelong brand. What better way for a committed alumnus to round out a successful life trajectory than to live in conjunction with the institution where they experienced such positive life changes? Especially if that new experience offers free classes, access to libraries and learning resources, and access to stimulating professors and researchers. The advantage to WEAL would be that they would presumably enjoy a strong, almost competition-proof referral stream.

Physical proximity may work adequately here because of the distance between the two locations, but a potentially serious complication in the positioning is that the college would almost certainly require that WEAL take on its name. There could be wrinkles in negotiating the financial aspects of the relationship too, so the idea is not without flaws. Still, the essential strategy of positioning one's organization closely—in a market sense—to another, usually larger organization can be wise.

Willows' End's Choice

We will guess that WEAL would choose a flagship strategy as their desired competitive position. Given their commitment to the mission, their apparent leadership energy, and their advantages as a local nonprofit, this would be a reasonable choice. Communities like Willows' End will happily

COMPETITIVE POSITION

Willows' End Assisted Living will strive to be a flagship organization in its service area by modeling an attractive alternative to traditional medical-based care for the elderly, while leading the local dialog about how best to provide for the needs of a growing elderly population.

support a flagship. Of course, this must not just be an attempt to manipulate perception, it has to be rooted in fact.

This strategic position is well suited to an organization with Willows' End's characteristics, especially the relative newness of the service model and the gathering demographic push toward assisted living that the boomer generation is likely to provide. They will not only be providing a service but trying to change minds as well. The real impact of assisted living on the average person is that it demonstrates a new mindset for care of the elderly. Whereas nursing homes and hospitals implicitly regard old age as a medical condition, assisted living treats it as a social situation. By achieving its desired competitive position, Willows' End will live this message, provide a needed service, offer hope, and shape minds.

FUNDER STRATEGIC POSITION

Willows' End, like all nonprofits, has a double puzzle to solve in securing revenue for its services. On the one hand, it provides services in return for a fee, a standard commercial transaction. On the other, it can—and, according to the terms of its exemption from taxes it must—raise a certain amount of its funds from the general public.

In theory, WEAL has unlimited options for its strategic position relative to funders. In practice, however, they are more limited than it might seem. Willows' End has an unusual profile compared to many nonprofits in that it raises so much of its revenue from private payers yet it also needs to have a philanthropic presence. Willows' End's task, therefore, is to position itself with respect to two distinct funding sources: private payers and donors.

Private Payers

Unlike government funding in which there is usually a single payer with more or less uniform practices, private pay arrangements can be as varied as the number of payers. As a relatively new service model, assisted living does not have the advantage of being widely understood and accepted among the general public, some of whom still see an assisted living facility as a nursing home without medical uniforms. So, the group of residents tends to be a patchwork by-product of a wide range of payment plans.

What seems like a financial problem, however, turns out to be just as much a cultural and behavioral one. The gracious assisted living facility in an affluent section of town will utterly reject a resident who clearly comes from a poverty culture, and in a similar fashion the matronly resident from the suburbs will never adjust to life in an urban facility. This is why many site-based organizations serving diametrically opposed populations use different sites.

Willows' End must decide how it wants to position itself for its private paying residents. Unlike medical model elder-service programs like nursing homes and hospitals, assisted living is neither an entitlement nor a government-funded program. As a result, providers must explicitly target those who can afford to pay for its services. This will bother those who feel that a nonprofit public charity should concentrate only on those who cannot afford to pay for services, but Willows' End has no choice if it is to survive. It simply must target elders affluent enough to pay for its services.

This is a bigger population than one might think. Some quick math . . . let's say an assisted living facility costs $3,500 per month, with incidentals of $1,000. As of the early part of the twenty-first century, a member of the generation old enough to enter assisted living typically had a monthly pension and Social Security. If those two sources of revenue provided only $2,500 per month of income, the shortfall would be $2,000. For elders that owned a home, a national average sale price might be in the neighborhood of $175,000. If the individual had no other source of income—and ignoring the earning power of the proceeds from the sale of the house—he or she should be able to afford at least seven years in a facility. The typical stay in such a long-term care facility is 2–3 years.

Willows' End, in short, will need to target the middle class senior and his or her family as its payer base. The typical resident will have a moderate net worth of somewhere over $250,000 but not so high that the senior will have expectations of luxury that Willows' End cannot meet. They will live locally or have a local tie such as a grown child or sibling, and they will probably be single.

Note that Willows' End has relatively little latitude in targeting its payer base. It can choose exactly who to target (for example, people living within 5 miles or 10 miles) but not the profile. This relative inflexibility is in stark contrast to most of the other strategic elements.

Donated Revenue

Having a strong private pay base can be a disadvantage to an organization if philanthropic entities and individual donors tend to see the institution as self-supporting and needing only to raise fees if it needs more resources. This dynamic is another reason for choosing a flagship strategy, as it might offer donors an extra reason for supporting an organization that is not just providing services but trying to model excellence in a new service model.

Nonprofits that serve a traditional middle-class consumer market have the same dilemma. Nursing homes and colleges are classic examples. Nursing homes typically get the bulk of their revenues from Medicaid and Medicare, but the real differentiation occurs in residents who pay privately. Although Medicare traditionally pays actual cost or less, nursing homes seek Medicare patients because they are the front door for residents who might eventually become private payers when their Medicare benefits run out. Once individuals switch to paying out of their own pockets a different, higher fee scale applies. In higher education, colleges and universities often get a significant portion of their revenue from privately paying students, but they must still find donors and government entities to cover other parts of the overall cost.

But there is a more profound reason why WEAL has philanthropic limitations. Fundraising campaigns are based on hope. In return for a donor's dollars, the organization offers some hope of betterment in the human condition. Examine the major fundraising causes over the years, and you will see the theme of hope stand out. Grand hope leads to grand fundraising. Cancer is a major fundraising cause because we never stop hoping that we can eradicate or at least control the disease. When the late actor Christopher Reeve was paralyzed he was able to raise large amounts of funding for paralysis research by explicitly offering the hope of finding a way to reverse the condition. Youth causes and education are powerful fundraisers because, almost by definition, they offer hope.

When hope fades, so does fundraising. When there is no hope there is little reason to give, or there is reason to give only a little. While youth causes offer hope, programs for youthful offenders offer little hope. Intractable disease with no known cure offers no hope. On a different level, if donors feel that a nonprofit cannot handle funds properly or cannot deliver on its promises, they lose hope and stop giving.

The hope Willows' End can offer is modest, and so its fundraising will be of the same kind. It cannot promise an end to old age or a groundbreaking approach to dealing with seniors' needs, so rather than offer such grand hope, WEAL must offer little visions of hope. It has to build a case for targeted donations offering targeted visions of hope that have nothing to do with the bulk of its activities.

Colleges do this on a different scale by emphasizing capital giving or by arrangements like endowing chairs. Donors are asked to think not about the large volume of money-for-education transactions that take place at the heart of the institution—these are plainly self-interested economic arrangements that inspire little hope—but instead to consider the hope implicit in the new research and public impact that a single professor's future work might offer.

Willows' End could use two appealing assets in fundraising. One is the small operational costs that are visible to the public. The facility van, for example, could be an object of fundraising ("This van sponsored by Local Auto Dealer" on the side). Or local donors could support a volunteer program, or an internship in which students partner with one or more residents for an entire school year. The organization should also partner with the local senior centers and any other senior organizations in order to become a standard part of the senior living fabric in the local towns.

The other asset Willows' End could use in strategically positioning itself with its donor base is its building. It is a truism that casual observers equate a pleasing building with a quality program and since WEAL has such a nice physical setting it should use it. To do this, it might allow community groups to use its facilities free of charge or at low cost, including the dining rooms. When Willows' End staff participate on committees and the like, they could offer use of the facility for routine meetings. Establishing one's building as a friendly, accessible gathering place helps cement the organization's reputation as an integral and respected part of the local community—and, therefore, as a suitable recipient of donations. We will elaborate further on this point in a later section.

Funding sources are a fairly constricted area in which Willows' End can carve out a sound strategic position. Its options are largely bounded by the realities of its service market. Still, the organization has distinct choices it must make. We will summarize those likely choices as follows:

FUNDER POSITIONING

Willows' End Assisted Living will target middle-class homeowners within its service area as the bulk of its revenue base and will seek donations from local philanthropists for small-scale, highly visible projects.

Labor Strategic Position

For service provider organizations like Willows' End that spend so much of their resources on labor-related costs, having an effective strategic position in the labor market is essential. Most managers in this situation realize this imperative now, at least unconsciously, but it was not always that way. In the 1970s, when many nonprofits began providing a variety of services, the migration of the baby boomer generation from school to workforce was well under way and the idea of working in a nonprofit organization dedicated to public service enjoyed a kind of halo effect.

As a consequence, there was what seemed to be an endless supply of fresh-faced young workers eager to do good. It helped that the Peace Corps was in its prime and the general notion of community service was favorably accepted. This was good since nonprofits used a large amount of labor to deliver services. In fact, one might even speculate to what degree supply drove demand—that is, to what degree did the massive numbers of young people entering the workforce help shape the choice of government to provide the very services for which they were hired? The linkage is not perfect, but there would seem to be one.

In any event, many nonprofit managers got used to the hyper charged labor flow and had little incentive to design services any other way. An already labor-intensive industry became even more so. Later on, in the late 1980s and 1990s when much of American industry was embracing computer technology, capital-short nonprofits lagged behind.

But the real determinant of labor needs in nonprofits is the intense orientation to personal relationships that attracts many of the workers and consumers to the sector. Most nonprofits are relationship organizations, especially smaller ones. They exist to provide some sort of structured relationship (called services to consumers), and they often do so through a different set of structured relationships (called staff). In some cases former consumers later become paid staff, such as in institutions ranging from substance abuse programs to youth service groups to universities.

These ingredients all create a powerful demand for large numbers of the right kind of people that must be satisfied. When two thirds to three quarters of an organization's spending goes toward personnel, the composition of the labor force is the single most critical driver of everything from finances to organizational culture.

For many years, organizations like Willows' End have had to perform a delicate balancing act. Wages to direct service workers, never high to begin with, are further squeezed when whole segments of an industry become commodity-like or subject to funder leverage to keep costs down. With downward pressure on compensation, as in many industries, nonprofits have had to trade off something in return for access to large enough labor pools.

What they typically traded off was quality. Those apple-cheeked young workers of the 1970s with BAs and higher became BAs and holders of two-year certificates in the 1980s. From there the hurdle became a high school education, with anything beyond that a bonus. For some during the hard labor markets of the late 1990s the standard became considerably lower.

Each time, there was a step-down in quality in order to keep the pay levels competitive in an adequately sized labor pool. Midway through the first decade of the twenty-first century many nonprofit employers have achieved an uneasy balance out of which it is hard to imagine a pathway. Nonprofits that need a large number of low or semiskilled workers are now in a more or less permanently reactive position to the labor marketplace.

This is where Willows' End finds itself. Paying at the lower end of the hourly scale, the facility still has to recruit enough workers to provide basic services and to sustain a cordial and supportive atmosphere for the residents. That means that WEAL has to find the right mix of personalities, with their skill-sets being secondary. Whatever technical skill is needed may have to be taught on the job.

In this kind of future, other factors can become more important than compensation levels. In addition to the quality of interpersonal relationships, there are numerous other factors that are likely to determine workers' job satisfaction. These would include: unspoken signals of support or neglect from the administration, supervisors' attitude toward personal needs, the personalities of the residents, nature of recognition and acceptance on the job, the attractiveness of the physical setting, the organization's reputation in the community, and employee benefits. Since the pay rates for this commodity labor market are likely to vary only slightly from employer to employer, their effect on morale of minor fluctuations in these "little things" is greatly amplified. Willows' End needs to stay on top of these factors.

Another characteristic of Willows' End's mission jobs is that they are mostly professional dead ends. This is largely because of the lack of a hierarchical production model such as in nursing homes and hospitals. There is always the very real possibility that a motivated paraprofessional in one of these settings could become a certified nursing assistant, a nurse, a therapist, or even a physician. Support and management jobs are also relatively plentiful. By contrast, WEAL does not need highly trained medical professionals or a large management group, but it does need a rather large, solid core of caring individuals supported by a few professionals.

Finally, it is a fact of the labor market that Willows' End will have to do a fair amount of staff training. Many nonprofit industrializers recognize that they need to provide everything from remedial education to on-the-job training for large numbers of staff members. This is a cost of doing business as surely as is maintaining a site or investing in computer systems. Intuitively, managers know that a way to avoid some of this cost is to find workers who already know the material, and who are already predisposed to caring relationships with vulnerable elders.

Willows' End's Choices

As with many strategic factors, Willows' End has a limitless range of choices. Unlike with the other factors, strategically positioning in the labor market is more the sum of many small decisions rather than a single one. Choices here are not as mutually exclusive as in some other areas. Moreover, labor demographics and other characteristics can change rapidly. For instance, all it would take to dent the WEAL labor pool is for a nearby hospital or a large home care organization to expand. Conversely, a major bankruptcy or closure in a similar organization could flood the market with potential candidates.

Different employers prize different characteristics of their labor forces.

We can assume that Willows' End values longevity most, because residents in any form of congregate care feel safer and more nurtured when their caregivers are consistent over time. If this is, in fact, a valid objective from the managers' perspective, they will pay attention to how everything related to the labor force either encourages longevity or discourages it.

This type of labor market can be found in any large town or small city. It is relatively static, and it tends not to move rapidly from employer to employer unless there is a reason. Willows' End must create an optimal strategic position in the regional labor market. Here are some of the elements that they might consider, and how they might position themselves most advantageously against them.

Location

Most low-end workers will live within a few miles of the workplace. Willows' End has a disadvantage with respect to its location, since it is located at an end point, not a crossroads or a way station. Staff who make up most of this kind of mission work force also gravitate to direct routes to work. WEAL staff have to find their way to a facility that, as a destination location, is neither. This is a modest competitive disadvantage, so managers have to offset it by excelling in other elements of attractiveness to labor.

Willows' End planners might institute a shuttle service as a free benefit to overcome its geographic disadvantage. Or it could have an overlarge parking lot so that employees who did bring their cars would not have to pay for parking or risk other unpleasantness from street or commercial garage parking. Of course, that would encourage workers from further away, creating the kind of mobile workforce that might undercut the planners' desire to have long-term staff.

The Female Workforce

The Willows' End labor market is predominantly female, as is typical of caring organizations. Most mission workers can be presumed to have had at least one previous similar position, including aid jobs such as home health aide or raising children. Assuming that its most desired worker is a physically fit woman in her thirties or forties, Willows' End could target settings and situations where such women are most likely to be found. For example, it might sponsor athletic teams for kids in first or second grade, on the assumption that that would be the first age when stay-at-home moms first start looking to rejoin the workforce. Willows' End should never try to position itself with higher-end middle class sources of potential workers such as health clubs, country clubs, or trendy restaurants. If it were to advertise for workers, it would probably prefer the local paper or radio station.

Willows' End's objective should be to position itself as an attractive option for the present or future caregiver. Their approach would be similar to the way automobile manufacturers advertise. One cannot expect to buy a new car every year, but a successful stream of advertising and market positioning is designed to give a brand top-of-mind presence when it is time to make the big decision.

Natural Networks

Naturally occurring social networks are another source of strategic labor advantage. The best networks are the ones rooted in a formal but loose structure such as churches or fraternal organizations. One fast-growing nonprofit tapped into the Sunday school teachers of a nearby church. Starting with one churchgoer, each time they needed a new staff member the word went out to the Sunday school faculty and a fresh candidate appeared.

Naturally occurring networks have the advantage of offering a kind of prescreening, since members will not long tolerate deviant behavior that does not offer some kind of value. But they can also be homogenizing forces that evolve into exclusionary cliques, a sure detriment to hopes of diversity. Conversely, ethnic diversity is served, at least superficially, when a place like Willows' End can attract immigrant community members.

For its mission workforce goal of stability, Willows' End would probably not be well served to court students at the local college. Today's college students are not usually tomorrow's assisted living workers, and if they are they would almost certainly enter at a higher or credentialed level. Even if they are occasionally future mission workers, they too represent a transient workforce.

WORKFORCE STRATEGIC POSITION

Willows' End will position itself as the caregiver employer of choice for women who live within a 5–10 mile radius of the facility.

SPECIAL ASSET STRATEGIC POSITION:
THE WILLOWS' END BUILDING

Finally, some organizations have a special asset that is somehow central to their overall strategic position. Again, the term asset in this case means something tangible that could, at least theoretically, be sold at a quantifiable market value. By our definition, the staff's reputation for providing quality services is not an asset, nor is the presence of a beloved father figure in a specialty field. Planners need to be especially careful not to define intangibles or small common things as special assets, or their process will go off track quickly. A special asset could be an institution's campus, its investment portfolio, a patent, a brand name, or anything similar.

Most organizations do not have special assets of any kind, because they do not need them. Sometimes special assets are collected almost incidentally. Many times they lie dormant, if only because no one has taken the time to figure out how to use them. As likely, the assets are dormant because the organization has started to take them for granted and does not see them with the fresh eyes of outsiders anymore. For instance, one summer camp organization in Vermont faced a minor financial crisis before realizing that their lakeside property was not valuable just in a hypothetical "What if-we-sold-it?" way but as an affirmative source of income. Melding their unusually highly educated management and counselor workforce with the well-preserved rustic property, they began running weeklong future workshops and special study groups.

Willows' End has an inherently special asset in its building. With its historic significance and ruggedly beautiful features, the building has clear market value. Still, that kind of value is trapped and cannot really be used except as a source of collateral for bank loans. What makes the building so valuable as a source of strategic position is that it has a claim on the imagination of the locals. Some locals in their target consumer age demographic will remember it as a functioning factory, while others will remember it as a blight that was transformed into a vision. All will see it as a proud building being put to a creative new use.

Willows' End's Choices

Deriving strategic advantage from their building will require a concerted effort and a bit of creativity. First and foremost, they must maintain it well,

PUT ON A HAPPY FAÇADE

There is no escaping the power of place. Higher education institutions at the beginning of the twenty-first century are experimenting with—and in some cases embracing—online learning. But more than one small college with a robust online program has encountered the same problem: even with sophisticated online students who rarely visit campus, nothing symbolizes learning better than a stately brick library building with the Greek revival columns and sweeping staircase entrance. "If we go all the way down to one building," says one president of a small college, "that's the one we have to keep. We need it for our website."

never once letting it slip into disrepair. Regularly investing in its appearance and working systems is as important as repairing it immediately.

If it qualifies, the building might be listed on the register of historic places (caution: there are often major restrictions that accompany this designation). At a minimum, there should be ample pictorial documentation of the building's history in the public places. This has the effect of interweaving the stories of the current residents with real-life history.

But the most powerful way to use the building would be to make it a gathering place for the community. Managers could deliberately seek out other elder service organizations in the community and offer the use of their meeting rooms. If there is a fundraising march, say for the local Alzheimer's Association chapter, the Willows' End parking lot might be a good starting point.

These kinds of uses are natural outgrowths of the need for staff to participate in local committees, speak out on behalf of elder causes, and initiate community dialogs about elder-service matters. Offering the use of one's facility is always welcomed, but it can be two-dimensional if it is essentially a cost-free room rental.

One way to characterize how Willows' End should use its building derives from the changes that another community staple is going through—the library. Once simply a repository for books and a quiet place to read and contemplate, the traditional library is being permanently reshaped by information technology, declining government funding and changing behavior patterns of readers. In response, some librarian leaders are advocating a repositioning of the traditional library not just as a physical place with stacks of books but as a learning commons, a kind of community crossroads for learners of all ages.

This could be a useful metaphor for how Willows' End melds its special asset positioning with its other strategic positions. If the organization is to play a central role in its community's effort to cope with a growing elder population, and if all concerned are humble enough to admit that they do not have all the answers, then the Willows' End facility could play both a symbolic and real role in furthering that collective learning. This would be a service to the community of the highest order.

SPECIAL ASSET POSITION

Willows' End will use its facility as a special asset to position itself at the crossroads of community learning about care for the elderly.

SUMMARY OF DESIRED STRATEGIC POSITION

On its simplest level, Willows' End's desired strategic position is the sum of its various parts:

- Willows' End Assisted Living will continue seeking to provide services to clients aged 60 or older who show a need for assistance in two or more key areas of daily living (such as hygiene, food preparation, dressing, etc.) as a result of non-injury-related dementia.

- Willows' End will seek to serve a user population in the mid to late 60s needing assistance with less than an average of 2.5 activities of daily living.

- Willows' End will continue to focus on its present geography, reserving the possibility of expanding it at some point in the future if that becomes necessary.

- Willows' End Assisted Living will strive to be a flagship organization in its service area by modeling an attractive alternative to traditional medical-based care for the elderly.

- Willows' End Assisted Living will target middle class homeowners within its service area as the bulk of its revenue base, and will seek donations from local philanthropists for small-scale, highly visible projects.

- Willows' End will position itself as the caregiver employer of choice for women who live within a 5–10 mile radius of the facility.

- Willows' End will use its facility as a special asset to position itself at the crossroads of community learning about care for the elderly.

As is, this is a serviceable list of desired strategic positions that could easily be translated into plans for implementation. Still, it lacks an overarching framework that can be readily understood and endorsed by the many people who were not at the table for its development. Since a large part of the usefulness of a strategy is to communicate with exactly that internal population, it would be helpful to devise a simpler way of describing Willows' End's desired strategy.

As a wordsmithing task, this should largely be the function of one or two people particularly gifted in crafting clear and simple language. They should strive for an economy of words that will convey some of the excitement and sense of direction that planners felt as they went through the process. This is a classic divergent thinking assignment that should be undertaken with maximum creativity. The idea is to touch on as many of the seven aspects of their overall positioning as possible, while communicating an understandable and compelling message.

We may be setting the bar too high for Willows' End, but here are a few ways for them to approach the challenge:

- Willows' End will be the flagship provider of assisted living services and the caregiver employer of choice.

- Willows' End will be the most respected gateway to non-medical residential services in the region.

- Willows' End will fill the gap between home care and a nursing home for elders in the community.

Whatever the phrasing, once the short statement of desired strategic position is complete it needs to be introduced to the entire organization. This should not be a perfunctory introduction because it is the point of the entire process. To understand why, go back to the framework presented in section 3. After mission, strategy is the second natural point of control in a nonprofit organization.

For most people who work in a nonprofit, the mission statement is probably a bit of a nice-sounding but vague document, whereas a well crafted statement of a desired strategic position can offer a practical vision for all employees and stakeholders. It becomes compelling when it shows a path to a desirable future and offers a way to make everyone a part of it. In the first statement, even if someone did not know at first what a flagship was, it sounds positive. And who would not want to work for the caregiver employer of choice?

Once the statement is complete and accepted by the original group of planners, their work is done. They have determined the "what" of the organization's strategy. Now comes the "how."

RECIPE CARD   HOW TO DEVISE A STATEMENT OF DESIRED STRATEGIC POSITION

Plan What to Do

Now it is time to implement.

This section may seem familiar to many with experience in traditional strategic planning because it resembles what many people regard as strategy. It is not strategy. This final phase is about execution, and planning for it will look a lot different and last a lot longer than developing the overall strategic position. It is properly the work of the management and executive staff. Except for individuals with a unique skill set it should not involve board members at all. In some ways it is nothing more than the ongoing responsibility of management. If the work of the executive is to help the organization cope with change, and strategic positioning is the embodiment of change, then management's role is to cope with the complexities that that change entails in order to carry out the strategy.

Consider a few basic principles of this stage. First, good strategic positions always entail change, the only real question is how much. For some organizations, the desired strategic position may be very close to the strategic position the organization already occupies. In that case, devising and implementing a work plan will consist largely of activities designed to support and extend the existing position. But there will always be changes in operations because no matter what strategic position is chosen, changes in the future will have direct implications that managers must handle.

Especially in a large organization, senior staff must operate in good faith and attempt to execute the strategic position that they (hopefully) helped develop. The wheels will come off very quickly in any organization that is executing a strategy substantially different from the one that the board thought it had set in motion. This is far more common than many realize. It can stem from sources ranging from a simple misunderstanding to CEO arrogance, and it is guaranteed to confuse and divide an organization.

Finally, a good strategic position is practically useless without a good implementation plan to go with it. The desired strategic position is by design a highly conceptual product intended to provide guidance to managers. The work plan that gets crafted at this stage is the tool that turns the concepts into reality.

Break Down the Strategic Position
The first step is to break the strategic position down into its component pieces in order to decide which ones need to be part of the implementation plan. To illustrate, we will repeat the components of Willows' End's strategic position:

1. Willows' End Assisted Living will continue seeking to provide services to clients aged 60 or older who show a need for assistance in two or more key areas of daily living (such as hygiene, food preparation, dressing, etc.) as a result of non-injury-related dementia.
2. Willows' End will seek to serve a user population in the mid- to late 60s needing assistance with less than an average of 2.5 activities of daily living.
3. Willows' End will continue to focus on its present geography, reserving the possibility of expanding it at some point in the future if that becomes necessary.
4. Willows' End Assisted Living will strive to be a flagship organization in its service area by modeling an attractive alternative to traditional medical-based care for the elderly.
5. Willows' End Assisted Living will target middle class residents/homeowners within its service area as the bulk of its revenue base and will seek donations from local philanthropists for small-scale, highly visible projects.

6. Willows' End will position itself as the caregiver employer of choice for women who live within a 5–10 mile radius of the facility.
7. Willows' End will use its facility as a special asset to position itself at the crossroads of community learning about care for the elderly.

Not all of these individual components of the desired strategic position need to be implemented in a systematic, large-scale way. For example, the geographic strategic position is simply an endorsement of the status quo. The need-related strategic position is also essentially a continuation of what they are already doing, and the consumer-related strategic position is largely a self-reminder to monitor consumers' needs that should not require extensive implementation energies. Those can be handled without a formal work plan.

The rest of the components of the desired strategic position will require significant implementation and some degree of change. Some fit together quite well and can be consolidated into a single component. Striving to be the flagship organization and the desired positioning as a physical and symbolic crossroads of community learning go together naturally. Focusing on local middle class area homeowners and targeting local philanthropists are really just two sides of the same revenue coin. We will approach the components with these associations in mind. So, the seven components above become three:

1. Be the flagship organization of its kind by modeling an attractive alternative to traditional medical-based care for the elderly and using the facility to become the crossroads of community learning about care for the elderly
2. Be the local caregiver employer of choice
3. Focus on middle class area homeowners as the preferred service user and target local philanthropists for small, high visibility grants

With a little wordsmithing, it is possible to boil these three components into the single statement of desired strategic position with which we began the book:

To be a flagship elder service organization at the crossroads of community learning about care for the elderly.

A flagship is pretty much what it sounds like—the ship that carries the flag of the fleet's leader. From a tactical perspective, it is an important vessel, perhaps the most important of all because it connotes leadership. But it is also symbolically important, and it is in that context that we in non-naval settings have appropriated it. At the risk of pushing the metaphor too hard, we could say that flagships have a few vital characteristics:

- People pay extra attention to flagships.
- They have tremendous symbolic importance.
- They signal a certain kind of power.

It is easy to translate these concepts into a nonprofit caregiving future. Flagship service providers are those relatively rare organizations that industry insiders look to as pacesetters. They seem to have achieved a balance between satisfying consumers and helping staff feel fulfilled and respected. Moreover, they somehow manage to lead the dialog around what constitutes best practices. Notice we said "lead" the dialog. Flagships do not try to dominate the best practices dialog because they know that no one can.

Service provider flagship status can be temporary. It takes a fair amount of skill, dedication, and maybe a little luck to put together an operation that can be considered a flagship, and it does not take much to change that. Moreover, in the for-profit world, companies do not necessarily aspire to flagship status. It may not be more profitable, and in fact it may well be less profitable in a competitive market, so the typical owner is willing simply to put out a creditable product in return for a reasonable profit. There is little incentive for the average for-profit to reach any higher, except for one thing—ego gratification, no small motivation especially in a field where few companies stand out.

We do not use ego in a pejorative way here. The importance of a driven owner or CEO in creating any kind of standout operation is hard to overestimate. This is why a sale or takeover in the for-profit world usually ends flagship status unless the old team is kept on. It can also happen that way in the nonprofit sector, but abrupt transitions are not as typical, and so it may be a bit easier to create a flagship in the nonprofit space.

What can make it a bit easier for nonprofits to achieve and maintain flagship status is a relentless focus on mission in a way that inspires and motivates everyone connected with the organization. In many ways this is the heart of what it means, on a day-to-day basis, to be a nonprofit organization. Without the distraction of profitability as the number one goal—or the tension of what happens to a for-profit for whom profitability is not its number one goal—the nonprofit is freer to concentrate on the services themselves.

Also appreciate what being the caregiver employer of choice

implies. This objective goes beyond some organizations' knee-jerk "people are our most valuable asset" philosophy. It is actually a fairly clear-eyed, economics-driven determination to do the right thing philosophically and the smart thing financially. The same is true for the revenue component of the strategic position. These are fundamental business decisions.

A moment of truth here. No organization can pay attention to more than a handful of objectives. For most groups, it is a stunning victory if the top two priorities get serious, sustained attention. We are lucky that Willows' End's desired strategic position can be reduced to three priorities, although even if an organization has several more it may be worth developing them all. Why? Because what we are really doing here is establishing primary objectives for the organization along with those that are either secondary or will take a longer time to implement. As the top priorities are achieved or become less important, others will arise to take their place. This is a long range plan, after all.

We also acknowledge that it is hard to artificially isolate one or more components of Willows' End's strategic position since they are so interconnected. Still, one needs to do it so that the right tasks can be assigned to the right people. Sometimes the silos that everyone complains about are the very things that make it possible to get things done. We will take these as the three components of the desired strategic position that Willows' End's leaders must plan for in order to achieve their overall strategic position.

(Re)organize the Board of Directors

To understand the logic steps in implementation, refer to the nonprofit management framework in Section 3 of this book (Exhibit 3.1). It is reproduced again here for convenience.

An organization's strategy flows from its mission. In turn, organizational structure flows from strategy. In this framework, structure means both the corporate structure and the way the various task groups such as board and staff organize themselves. Once a strategic position has been established, the primary governing principle behind matters of structure at all levels should be to align intraorganizational strengths and interests as much in support of that strategic position as possible. Reorganizing is a powerful step that many managers overlook—until there's trouble. Reorganizations, in fact, sometimes seem to be inextricably linked to trouble and therefore they are likely to be profoundly reactive and defensive in nature. The

EXHIBIT 7.1   **Formal Control Points in a Nonprofit Organization**

logic of strategic positioning implementation is that reorganizing is done affirmatively, in support of a what is presumed to be a widely desired future. And there is no better place to start than at the top, with the board of directors.

With the various components of Willows' End's strategic position in place, managers can now go about creating a work plan for what they will do to achieve that position. For suggestions on the mechanics of the work plan development process itself, continue reading this recipe card section. Here, we will concentrate on the substance of the plan.

Let's start off with some candor. The average nonprofit board meeting is a snore. The typical agenda looks like this:

    I. Welcome
    II. Approval of minutes from previous meeting
    III. Report
    IV. Report
    V. Report
    VI. Report
    VII. Update
    VIII. Report

IX. Update

X. Report

XI. Next meeting

XII. Adjourn

Who would want to attend a meeting structured like this? Anyone with an ounce of talent and a pinch of energy would be brain dead by the time number six rolled around. The real message of an agenda like this is that the board meeting is a gigantic exercise in passivity and that board members are only expected to listen to long, detailed accounts of things that have already happened. Is it any wonder then that it is hard to recruit good board members?

Another thing that makes boards of directors so hard to manage is that their structure for getting things done is often frozen in time like an insect in amber. There's the executive committee, and the finance committee, and the nominating committee, and guess what happens in each one of these committees? Right—more reports!

So, let's begin with the assumption that the Willows' End board of directors and staff worked hard developing their desired strategic position and that they believe in it. Let's further assume that they are willing to organize themselves so as to provide the best chance of implementing it successfully. Let's also acknowledge that groups do not really accomplish much unless they hold themselves accountable. The logical outgrowth of these assumptions is that the board's sub-committee structure should match the components of the desired strategic position.

This means that the board will form three new subcommittees: the flagship committee, the local caregiver employer of choice subcom-mittee, and the revenue subcommittee (covering both types of rev-enue, fee-for-service and targeted philanthropy). What about the existing subcommittees? Get rid of them. Chances are, at least some were drawn directly from the original bylaws, which in turn came from legal boilerplate as opposed to careful thought about what the orga-nization will need. Keep the finance committee and perhaps the exec-utive committee, but this is a good time to make sure the organization has the committees it needs, not the ones set up with-out much regard for strategy implementation.

Any standing committees the board decides to keep should be redirected toward the three components of the strategic position that require intensive implementation. So, the finance committee should be responsible for figuring out the financial implications of being a flagship organization (constant theme: How can we afford to become a flagship within the constraints of our resources?). They will target any fundraising energies toward local homeowners and targeted phil-anthropic opportunities, and so on. Finance committees can fall into a comfortable rut just dealing with routine events such as the annual audit or overseeing any endowment managers, so these routine mat-ters should always be considered in the context of what they mean for the three major components.

For example, implicit in the flagship-as-community-crossroads strategy is that the WEAL building itself must remain attractive and well maintained. In turn, that means that the finance committee must stay on top of investments in the building such as major repairs and upgrades, not to mention ordinary maintenance. Financial matters are the easiest to benchmark, so part of the committee's job is to fig-ure out how to keep track of its progress. More on that later when we talk about staff-level responsibilities.

Creating the Strategic Agenda

With a fully defined strategic position and the outline of an imple-mentation plan, the board of directors can create meaningful agendas and specific, concrete ways for individual members and subcommit-tees to contribute. We call this the strategic agenda.

If the strategic position for the organization really means some-thing, it should recur over and over again on many different levels of the organization. In effect, the strategic position should become the shape of each board meeting's agenda. This is how Willows' End can avoid the common mistake of seeing the board's oversight of its strategy as simply a list of reports. Still, it is hard for a board to shift from a passive and reactive approach to one that is truly affirmative and future-oriented. Let's look at ways the Willows' End board might do that.

Fitting Agenda Items to the Strategic Agenda

The board must begin to see its deliberations and decisions through the framework of its strategic position. To do this, it will use the strategic position as an overlay and sorting mechanism for its actions. In order to illustrate how this would work, we will create a mythical series of items that the board must take up during its next meeting.

- The finance committee is considering two major capital invest-ments, creating an additional 10 parking spots in the back of the building and purchasing the empty half-acre adjacent to the

facility's current plot of land. Both would require the organization to borrow money, and it has the capacity to do one of them.

- A board member has resigned due to an out-of-state job transfer.
- A professor from the local college has requested that Willows'
  End serve as a research site for a national program she is
  designing that would examine the relationship between the
  onset of Alzheimer's disease and the presence of Down syndrome in patients' immediate family.
- The board needs to authorize the submission of a $250,000
  grant proposal to a major national foundation for the creation
  of a pilot program to create oral histories of World War II veteran residents' experiences in aging.

Virtually every board meeting agenda should be constructed
around the following items:

- Welcome
- Approval of consent agenda
- Flagship through crossroads of learning objective
- Caregiver of choice
- Targeted revenue strategy

These are not necessarily in priority order, since for any given
meeting there may be other items of a lower priority that must take
a higher position, and in some meetings there may be no items at all
for a particular category. Each of these components of the desired

THE CONSENT AGENDA

Clear out some of the procedural underbrush by using a
consent agenda. The principle behind a consent agenda is
to routinize approvals that might otherwise take up valuable board time. In advance of the meeting, bundle up all
of the reports and motions that are expected to require little or no discussion in a single package. Make sure that all
board members have copies of each item on the consent
agenda well in advance. Then, at the beginning of the
board meeting, move for adoption of the consent agenda
with the proviso that any single board member can remove
any item they desire from the agenda for specific attention
and discussion. Members vote on the remaining consent
agenda in a single up-or-down vote.

strategic position can also have more than one action item assigned to it. There are two reasons for this aspect of the strategic agenda. First, the components themselves provide a ready guide for planning the sequence and priority of discussion items; and second, the constant repetition of the components of the strategic position serves to reinforce their legitimacy and power.

Examining the action items, the meeting planners decide to fit them into the framework as follows:

1. Welcome
2. Approval of consent agenda
3. Flagship through crossroads of learning objective
   a. Professor's request to serve as research site
   b. Board member replacement
4. Caregiver of choice
   c. Finance committee recommendation on parking lot expansion
   d. Finance committee recommendation on purchase of adjacent lot
5. Targeted revenue strategy
   e. National grant application approval

Their reasoning for this design goes like this. The professor's request for Willows' End to serve as a research site obviously fits under the flagship component because it is the kind of initiative that can place the organization in a leadership role in the care of the elderly. The board member resignation and the search for a replacement could arguably fit anywhere, so planners put it under the first category with the rationale that any such free-floating action item should be automatically tied to the top priority, if possible. Placing the two capital items under the caregiver of choice component may seem odd until one considers why the parking lot expansion is being considered. Finance committee members point out that an increasing number of employees are driving to work, and during certain peak times there are not enough parking spaces for them. Since the capital investment has to be for one item or the other, and since the purchase of the adjacent lot was offered to WEAL and is being considered primarily to protect property interests rather than for any special purpose, both items go under the caregiver category. Finally, the national grant application approval is clearly a revenue matter.

How They Might Decide
With the strategic agenda drawn directly from the strategic position, the board can now carry out its leadership responsibilities within

cleanly drawn lines. The professor's request is likely to be enthusiastically approved. With appropriate provisions that would allow residents and their families to choose whether to participate, and with
safeguards for the privacy of the data, it is hard to see much of a
downside to the proposal. As an additional benefit, the project might
help one or more staff members gain experience in systematic
research on a national stage, and linking the facility's name to the
findings would be a positive.

The empty board seat would be given to the nominating committee to fill. The real role of the board here would be to have a
discussion about the kind of person they are looking for. Many nonprofit boards tend to fill board seats on an implied quota basis—one
lawyer, one banker, a religious leader, choices for ethnic diversity, and
so on. Willows' End can turn this rather sterile and impersonal
approach upside down and look for a person who fits certain characteristics that would help it achieve the flagship strategy.

The parking lot expansion/adjacent lot purchase is destined to be
a trickier discussion because it is an either/or proposition. Some will
undoubtedly argue that expanding the parking lot is a necessary part
of remaining (or becoming) the caregiver employer of choice; 10 parking spaces for staff is a major statement of support for the staff.
Others may question putting funds into a parking lot when a half-acre
abutting lot might be purchased by someone interested in using the
space for purposes detrimental to WEAL. A counter-argument could
be that the extra parking spaces during off-peak hours might be useful in relieving the strain on the parking spaces available to community and elder service leaders when attending a flagship-supporting
meeting at Willows' End. In all likelihood, the question will slant in
favor of the parking lot expansion due to its lower cost and the lack
of any other use for the half-acre lot that would support some aspect
of the desired strategic position.

If the board is committed to its strategic position and pays attention to its nuances, it will reject the national application as unsup-
portive of its strategy. First of all, this is a national foundation, and
groups like Willows' End rarely have an unaccompanied chance to
succeed at getting national monies on this scale. More important, the
strategy of elephantine national grants for purposes only incidentally
connected to the organization is the opposite of the tightly targeted
philanthropic strategy that it has decided to pursue.

In this case, the board members would have to fully explain the decision to whatever staff person was involved with the proposal. The board may even want to apologize that the process got this far before being turned down, pointing out that this is the first board meeting since the new strategic position was crafted and showing how future grant applications could be designed to be more consistent with the new grant revenue strategy.

These actions and decisions are worth examining for several reasons. In every instance, the board used standing committees such as finance and nominating to help achieve the strategic position, not as generators of reports about what has already happened. In fact, the nominating committee probably would appreciate the board's approach in providing concrete guidance about the type of candidate they sought, while leaving the process of seeking individuals up to the committee itself.

Second, the process was mutually educational both for the way it connected to the strategy and in the details of how different courses of action were evaluated against their ability to help achieve the strategy. There was an underlying message of mutual accountability as well. Finally, the clarity of the strategy and the board's previously stated commitment to it should have been enough to cushion the rejection of the national foundation proposal and to have showed that it was not afraid to take potentially unpopular decisions in support of the larger strategic position.

It is also helpful to note that the strategic agenda does not preclude the board from doing routine organizational maintenance chores such as accepting the yearly audit or approving the yearly budget. What it does do is supply a framework within which these things fit, rather than taking them up as separate, apparently unconnected events. For example, the yearly budget would be approved according to how well it supports the desired strategic position, and the yearly audit could be discussed for what it says about Willows' End's ability to achieve its strategy, not as a document that simply needs to be processed. Equally important, the strategic agenda will help board members think in a more integrated fashion. It is conceivable, for instance, that it might occur to a board member interested in targeted grant seeking that the rejected lot purchase might be converted into a targeted revenue opportunity, either by trying to convince the owners to donate it and take a tax deduction, or by searching out a way to get a donation specifically to purchase the land for self-protection purposes.

(Re)Organize the Staff

Now that the board of directors is suitably organized, staff may need to be as well. The implementation task is far more complicated, and there are far more variables for the staff than for the board, so it is not as easy to speak about staff reorganization plans that will be applicable across all organizations. What is applicable, however, are a few fundamental principles of how a nonprofit's staff should organize itself to implement a desired strategic position.

Assign Responsibility

The primary organizational step for a staff trying to implement a strategic position is to assign responsibility for each component of the strategy. Responsibility in most nonprofit organizations is a complex idea. Assigning responsibility is necessary to keep processes running smoothly, but the assignment itself may or may not say anything about who will do the majority of the work, and it says nothing at all about how the work should get done. One of the subtle benefits of an organization trying to achieve a strategic position as opposed to a list of big goals is that it can help establish a team focus. Willows' End staff will assign each of the three components requiring substantial implementation activity to a specific individual, but as was already suggested in the parking lot discussion above, many different individuals and types of skill will be needed to do justice to most decisions.

The other reason for clearly assigning responsibility in a nonprofit is to minimize ego battles. In the for-profit world, money makes a lot of things clear. An executive may not get credit publicly for success in his or her area, but the oversized bonus check at the end of the year says that someone knows the true story. What's at stake in most nonprofits is largely bragging rights. Ego battles are the most bruising and most unfair kind of internal struggles, corroding morale and team spirit because there is no easy way of resolving them. "Tinkers to Evers to Chance" was the most famous double-play combination in baseball, a clockwork-like chain of events that resulted in almost certain outs for the opposition and led to a World Series championship for the Chicago Cubs in the early twentieth century. Less well known is that Tinkers and Evers hated each other off the field, in spite of their success on it. Disputes in nonprofits are not as easily mediated by baseball-style measurable outcomes. If Tinkers, Evers, and Chance had existed in most nonprofit environments they'd probably just be three more staff members who never talked to each other.

Willows' End should assign responsibility for the three components to three different staff members, if possible. Since the flagship/community crossroads component is so close to the overall strategic position, the executive director would in all likelihood assume responsibility for it. The caregiver employer of choice is an obvious assignment for the human resource person, at least at first glance: as an employer, Willows' End is large enough to warrant a full-time human resource professional.

The problem that Willows' End will face in this assignment is that, candidly, the type of person the organization is likely to have attracted to be the human resource officer is probably not the kind of person needed to lead an initiative of such broad scope and complexity. If this is the case, the organization may need to give the responsibility to an assistant director or someone of similar stature.

The revenue strategy assignment also will pivot not on technical skill but on strategic and people skill. The chief financial officer may seem to be a natural for it, but, as with the caregiver employer of choice assignment, this is less a technical initiative than a visionary, creative one. The development person might be a good alternative, although once again the type of development personnel that a Willows' End would have attracted would not necessarily be a good fit for the kind of consumer-oriented marketing that half of the task would require. In the end, the executive director or some other senior executive may have to take this on as an assignment.

The quiet corollary to responsibility is authority. The two should be given out in matched pairs, with responsibility never exceeding authority. This is another reason why responsibility may flow up the organizational chart, since many middle-level managers can never have the authority necessary to carry out key pieces of the strategic position.

Devise Measures of Success

The difficulty of measuring the success of the assisted living model is undeniable, but that does not mean that measures cannot be devised for success in achieving the components. It may take some creativity to come up with measures that can easily be tracked, but it can usually be done.

Set Up Feedback Mechanisms

Metrics mean nothing without a system for tracking and reporting them. We call these systems feedback loops, as explained earlier. Again, they should not be highly complicated. Be ready to sacrifice elegance and precision for practicality.

Creating Management's Work Plan—Devising Ways of Achieving the Desired Strategic Position

We move now to what management will do to implement the desired strategic position. For each component, there are many things management could accomplish to make that part of the desired strategic position a reality. We call these management goals, for the unabashed reason that executives prefer to motivate managers by setting goals. To show how reasonable goals can be formulated, we will suggest several possible management goals for the first component, picking one of them to document in the form found in Appendix E. We will do the same for the second component, the caregiver employer of choice piece.

A complete work plan would be composed of several management goals for each of the three components. For each component, there could be the usual 3–7 goals, meaning that the three components in total should represent no more than about 21 goals, preferably closer to the 10–15 range. As with components of the strategic position, only a handful of these goals are likely to get strong organizational attention. But there is the added benefit that even though the organization may not be able to work on more than a small number of objectives at one time, assigning each goal to a manager increases the chances that a motivated individual can accomplish something toward the goals even if they do not have a lot of institutional support.

As with the process of setting the desired strategic position, there are an unlimited number of ways one might attempt to achieve each element. Common to all of the good ones is a thoughtful, reality-based attempt to get at the things that will really make a difference in positioning the organization. Planning fatigue at this point can make organizations want to get it over with quickly by just getting something down on paper. Another temptation is to use prefabricated

THE SEVEN VARIABLE RULE AGAIN

As discussed earlier, individuals have a limited tolerance for variables. So do organizations. Try to keep the total number of individual activities for each component in the 3–7 range. Any more than that, and managers will push back. As well they should.

expressions such as those from a workbook on strategic planning. If it helps, remember that these are the things that management will be spending its time on for the next several months or even years, so it is worth taking the time to carefully craft the planned activities.

Good methods start with the desired result and work backwards. A way to think about methods for achieving elements of the strategic position is to ask what the hallmarks of success would be and then reason backward to come up with ways that the entity might be able to achieve that success. This is largely a process of asking "if . . . then" about each of the hallmarks. "If this hallmark of success is true, then what had to have been in place to accomplish it?"

Flagship/Community Crossroads Component—Management Goal #1
This ambitious flagship strategy will have a chance of succeeding only if Willows' End is not only widely seen as providing high-quality service but does in fact provide it. High-quality service, which for others is merely an aspiration, for Willows' End has to be a threshold that it routinely achieves. Only then can the flagship strategy work. This is not easy in an industry where there is no JD Powers to issue a seal of approval, or even a widely accepted metric of success (this is true of much of the nonprofit world, incidentally—for that matter, it is true of some of the for-profit world, too). Without these advantages, any assertion of quality has to be regarded skeptically until it is proven.

The catalyst in achieving flagship status is communication. Most highly respected organizations do not get that way as the result of an explicit plan to be the best. Usually what gets expressed is a vague commitment to the goal that is boosted by one or more gifted managers somewhere in the organization plus a lot of hard work on a lot of people's part. The purpose of a communication plan is to draw attention to positive things that otherwise might go unnoticed. Here are some of the activities that Willows' End management might undertake to accomplish its goal of winning over opinion leaders (WEAL splits opinion leaders into generic community opinion leaders and opinion leaders who operate solely in the elder care realm). Each of these activities is a candidate to appear either explicitly or implicitly in the bullets that are expected to accomplish the goal. It will be the responsible person's job to decide exactly what activities to employ to accomplish the desired status in the desired time frame.

Get the Pols and the Vols on Your Side In any community there are a relatively small number of community-wide opinion leaders that can shape public perceptions of a place like Willows' End. These are the pols and the vols, the people who spend whole careers and/or much free time in elected office or volunteer roles planning, deliberating, and taking actions that they believe will help the community. They are the political figures and good-deed-doers who seem to populate just about every neighborhood and small town in this country. The Willows' End staff's task is to identify those leaders and get to them with proof of their quality and with constant reminders of what it can mean for the community they have in common.

WEAL's staff members' first task is to decide who those opinion leaders are. Undoubtedly, Willows' End already knows and has relationships with some of them if only because it is hard to start and operate a program of this size without coming into contact with at least a few. Nevertheless, if they truly want to achieve their desired position they now have to become much more strategic and methodical about this goal.

This means that they will have to do several things. We will track them one by one to suggest ways an organization can go about creating a work plan that will help achieve this one specific aspect of their strategic position.

Change the WEAL Mindset The most powerful thing that WEAL staff can do is cheap yet difficult: change its mindset. Most organizations in their position have a haphazard approach to influencing opinion leaders, including not feeling it necessary to do so at all. Willows' End will need to go after these leaders rather than waiting for them to call on WEAL. That spells a fairly aggressive mindset that has to extend through at least the first level of middle managers, so that everyone understands how important it is to support the courting of local opinion leaders. This can be accomplished through constant explanations of the desired end position, and repeated demonstrations of the positive attention that opinion leaders can bring. Clinical people are well known for sensibly resisting blatant or manipulative management programs, however, so it is all the more important that management be clear that it is simply trying to communicate the good work already being done rather than fooling people into thinking something is true that really is not.

Identify the Local Elder Care Opinion Leaders At first it makes sense to cast a wide net in search of opinion leaders to target. You simply never know who might build your reputation. But the core targets of your community opinion leader strategy will be mostly those who have credibility in caring for seniors. They will be specialists, consumers, other providers, and opinion-shapers such as advocates. They are the ones who should be on all the mailing lists, all the special-invitations lists, and whose names are top-of-mind for anyone connected with the organization.

Next, Willows' End managers need to narrow the list of local opinion leaders. At this point, the list needs to be electronic, and it needs to capture information about each leader ranging from basic contact information to professional interests to the nature of their influence. Unlike personal contact information, this data needs to be widely known among key staff and board members, and it should be part of each manager's responsibility to study it.

Incidentally, do not miss the subtlety in this search for leaders. The word "leaders" is not a synonym for donors. We are dealing with power and influence here, and while it is true that these two commodities are often bunkmates with money, carrying out a flagship strategic position turns more on power and influence than on a big check during the annual appeal. It is also likely to be more difficult. Getting leaders to use their power on your behalf requires that they feel invested in your organization's success, and that they understand how they can help achieve it.

Touch each opinion leader regularly Just as repetition is the essence of advertising (say it three times), regular contacts facilitate a favorable perception. Willows' End needs to find ways to constantly "touch" local opinion leaders. Newsletters are a good, albeit uninspired, example of how to touch people. The advent of email has made it easier and much cheaper to touch a constituency regularly. Advisory committees are another way. Periodic phone calls—as long as they serve some mutually constructive purpose—are yet another. In truth, the vehicle itself does not matter as much as does the contact itself. People who are regularly and skillfully sought out by an organization, including commercial interests such as banks and real estate firms and supermarkets, will tend to have at least slightly positive associations with the organization.

Get Leaders on Site Regularly Even in a bits-and-bytes world, it is hard to become a community crossroads without getting people physically on site regularly. But first, note that there is a double-entendre quality to this component. At its highest and best interpretation, being a community crossroads means that elder care leadership decisions of many different kinds often would include Willows' End.

HOW MANY OPINION LEADERS?

Pretend you are a Willows' End planner staring at a blank piece of paper after being asked to identify the opinion leaders in your region. How many names should be on the paper when you are done? There is no easy answer to this question, but here is a way to go about answering it.

In most populations, there are relatively few true opinion leaders as we have defined them here (leave aside those who are momentarily moved to express a strong opinion based on either a positive or negative experience). As a starting point, take 1 percent of the community's population. This represents most of the pols and vols, as well as other shapers such as major employers, media types, and so on. In most communities, there simply is not room for many more local opinion leaders. Remember, the global CEO or nationally renowned professor is not an opinion leader for WEAL's purposes—they may not even know where the facility is located.

Next, discard about 70–80 percent of the 1 percent as being uninterested in matters of health, elder service, or community affairs. Then start naming names. Build the list from the ground up. Seek names everywhere, but make sure to stick close to potential referral sources. Chances are, the total of the names you identify will fit within the number you originally calculated (another way of approaching this is to shoot for approximately three tenths of 1 percent of your community's population as the opinion leaders in matters of health care and elder services).

At a more immediate, concrete level, it literally means that people often use the facility for functions related to elder care but not necessarily directly related to Willows' End.

Proximity breeds familiarity. With outside elder care leaders accustomed to routing elder-care matters unofficially through the demonstrable leaders on the staff of Willows' End, it will begin to feel natural for the organization to take initiatives, represent the voice of at least a part of the community, and stake out leadership positions.

THE POWER OF BRIDGE

One assisted living facility used games of bridge to bring large numbers of seniors to their building. The local senior center management objected to the bridge games, feeling that they had grown way beyond the physical capacity of the center's building, were crowding out other activities, and—most irksome for the town-funded center—were attracting mostly players from out of town. The homeless bridge game turned to the assisted living program for assistance, and suddenly dozens of bridge-playing seniors, future potential residents all, were showing up at the facility several hours a day—kind of a mass test drive before buying.

With standing elder-related committee meetings, recurring events, and special gatherings using Willows' End's facilities at cost or for free, the physical location will begin to feel like the center of important activities.

Arrange for a Well Known Pol or Vol to Become a Resident What better testimony can Willows' End receive than to be chosen by a retired community opinion leader? There is no way to be sure that such a leader would even be interested in Willows' End, of course, but there is a fair chance that it would happen, especially if the organization makes a point of becoming visible to this market.

A tactical note. Some might think that it would be better to serve an opinion leader's family member than the leader him or herself— the leader's parent, spouse, sibling, and so on. While this could be helpful, it is not as desirable as serving the leader. Why? Program staff at places like Willows' End know that dissatisfied residents will tell program staff only positive things, while aiming their complaints at a family ear. If the opinion leader's family takes these complaints too seriously or is unaware of this dynamic, the opinion leader will create a powerful source of negative reviews that will have the reverse of the intended effect.

A Sample of One Fully Articulated Management Goal to Help Achieve the Flagship Strategic Position (Identify Local Elder Care Opinion Leaders) A possible work plan for the management goal of identifying local elder care opinion leaders is laid out below. The point of the format is to get planners to think about several things. For one, they should assess where they are—the status quo. For another, they need to think about where they want to be within a certain period of time (note the parallel to the larger future scan/internal scan/strategic positioning steps). They need to devise logical, objective ways of measuring their own progress. They need to be clear about who "owns" the goal, in order to hold themselves accountable. And they need to do it all in a succinct, practical fashion.

With that in mind, carefully examine the wording of the goal and consider what it means in practical terms. All management is doing in this goal is identifying the local elder care opinion leaders. And their target is a mere 30 leaders. Any three senior managers at Willows' End who have been in the field for more than a few years can probably name 15 leaders without thinking hard. What's more, this goal calls simply for a bit of research and documentation. Chances are they could do this in a half-hour of brainstorming. And putting the names into a computer database could mean anything from a sophisticated contact management system available throughout the organization to a few columns on a spreadsheet.

All of which is not to downplay the importance of this goal. Chronologically it has to be one of the first, and future goals should build on it (touching opinion leaders regularly might be a standalone

Work plan for component of strategic position: Become the flagship provider/ community crossroads			
Management Goal #1: Identify the local elder care opinion leaders			
Status Quo	Desired Situation in Three Months	Objective Measure	Person Responsible
Many informal relationships No systematic way of using them No systematic way of developing more such relationships No systematic way of tracking efforts	Identify ~30 local opinion leaders Collect information about them in a centralized, accessible fashion Familiarize key managers and managers and any appropriate staff with these opinion leaders	Create and maintain electronic database of local elder care opinion leaders Populate database with 30 local names and associated information	XXXXX XXXXX

goal. Getting them on-site a certain number of times per year might be another). It may help that this is an early goal precisely because it is so doable. In all honesty, it ought to be accomplished well within the three month time frame, if only because so much else is contingent on other work with the identified opinion leaders.

Caregiver Employer of Choice Component—Management Goal #1
When in planning mode and feeling creative and energized, many boards of directors happily sign on to a proposal to be a world-class employer. Later, when the momentary intoxication has passed, they wisely pretend to be busy doing something else whenever anyone asks what happened to the idea. Anyone who has ever tried to become an employer of choice (whatever that means) knows that it is expensive, time consuming, maddeningly imprecise, and the entire designation turns out to be a moving target anyway. Exactly what is it that employees want today that they did not want yesterday?

Yet the sentiment is laudable, and it is an effort worth making. For a variety of reasons, nonprofit organizations over the years have often extracted the steepest price from their own employees in the form of low salaries, poor benefits, and substandard working conditions. A board's stated intention to reverse that tendency is a great starting point. It can also be smart business. Satisfied employees turn into mini-goodwill-pumpers, and their good feelings create enormous social capital for the company. Willows' End has started down this classic roadway paved with good intentions. It is now the staff's responsibility to see that they get where they want to be with a minimum of detours and dead ends.

Willows' End will never be included on any national publication's list of 100 best places to work, and it will never be featured in a human resource officers' journal for its innovations in employee relations. But that is not the right aspiration for this organization anyway. The key modifier in this component of their desired strategic position is the word "local." Just as the numeric majority of its residents come from within a few miles of the facility, so do the majority of their staff. Willows' End's task is to appeal to staff and potential staff within a simple commute from the building. The idea of becoming the local caregiver employer of choice also goes far beyond the capabilities of any single individual, so although the human resource person may or may not be equipped to take overall responsibility for this component, the entire management staff will have to be involved in achieving the desired position.

Willows' End management and board members must accept that this part of the strategic position puts them in head-to-head competition with other organizations, including nonprofits with whom they might be collaborating on other matters. The potential caregiver labor pool is limited, and they have chosen to attempt to win a decisive percentage of it. This is simply another way in which nonprofits are learning to be competitive.

We will assume that Willows' End has the basic human resource systems in place such as recruiting, screening, hiring, supervising, and terminating employees. Otherwise, instituting those systems would need to be part of the implementation plan. We will concentrate instead on describing those things that, if properly done, would help move them beyond being simply a reasonably well-managed place to work to the kind of prized employer to which they aspire. As with the illustration above, we will select one of the goals for more detailed planning in the goal management sheet.

Understand Fully Other Caregiver Employers' Salary and Benefits Offerings Willows' End needs to know what other caregiver employers offer. They may not be able to match it dollar for dollar—hospitals, for instance, often can pay higher average wages than assisted living facilities—but at least they will know what they are competing against. Current or new staff coming to Willows' End from another caregiver employer can be a good source of this information on an anecdotal basis. A time-tested way of getting reliable statistical information is through targeted surveys administered by a third party. Such surveys are available for purchase from various sources and are often specific to a state or even a large region. It is also conceivable that Willows' End could collaborate with the other caregiver employers in the region to commission a study unique to their shared labor market. The results would have to be available to every participant, but then they would all know where they stand. Besides, there is a gap between their labor pool competitors knowing the market and actually doing something about it.

Create a Culture of Recognition Recognition is the strongest and least expensive way to retain employees, and we are not just talking about a special parking space for the employee of the month. The best recognition does not even happen through a formal program, which is what makes it so powerful. Senior executives at WEAL would have to agree to deliberately create a culture of recognition by acknowledging in small, highly individualized ways the little things that good employees do every day. This is a delicate undertaking, and the culture it creates is perishable without constant maintenance, but it can be a powerful motivator.

Create a Culture of Affiliation Similarly, service-providing organizations like WEAL tend to attract employees with high affiliation needs. For them, the pleasure of their coworkers and the sense of being part of a caring team is an important part of job satisfaction. This is harder to do with credentialed professionals (ever had a new dentist comment on the excellent work your previous dentist did?), but there are not many of these in an assisted living organization. Willows' End managers will need to determine the desired profile of direct service employees, then try to hire personalities who complement it. There are essentially two different styles of managing employees—managing through positions and managing through relationships. Organizations that manage through positions tend to have clearly defined job categories and a reward system based on them (this is how most publicly held companies operate). By contrast, managing through relationships tends to occur in smaller work settings with deliberate shaded lines of definition. These organizations are frequently misunderstood by outsiders as cults, cliques, clubs, and the like. Willows' End staff will want to be on the side of relationships, so management should oblige them.

After Money, Give Time A high affiliation workforce, once compensation levels are satisfactory, will prize time over money. While Willows' End cannot afford to even imply that adhering to scheduled work hours is optional, it can find ways to offer flexible schedules, offer job sharing, and so on. Earned time, in which vacation days, holidays, and sick days are combined to offer an individualized time bank from which employees cover time off, is practically mandatory. So are flexible spending accounts for child care and health care. Caregiver employees are often caregivers in their private lives too, so Willows' End will earn maximum credit by making reasonable adaptations to individuals' personal needs. The organization is not large enough to be able to offer on-site day care or similar benefits to employees, but it may be able to find small ways to support employees' dependent care needs.

Fix Their Transportation Problems Caregiver employees, like most lower-paid staff members, will almost always have transportation problems that are proportionately larger for them than for those who have deeper financial resources with which to solve them. Doing something creative here will earn Willows' End good will. A regular employee shuttle to a public transportation hub might work. Maybe Sam the maintenance guy could double as an emergency chauffeur (limit of five rides per year). Or the facility might negotiate discounted rates with a local cab company. Advocating with the regional transit authority for more frequent bus service on their route could produce results and in any event would be symbolically important.

Ask Finally, Willows' End should do something straightforward: ask their employees what kind of benefit structure and personnel policies they would value. They could do this with a survey, but smaller, more individualized dialogs would produce more qualitative information. A cautionary note: caregiver employees will not be able to answer this question in human resource speak, so managers should take care to ask specific, concrete, focused questions about possible benefits and practices.

Work plan for component of strategic position: be the local caregiver employer of choice			
Management Goal #1: Understand fully other caregiver employers' salary and benefits offerings			
Status Quo	Desired Situation in One Year	Objective Measure	Person Responsible
Compensation and benefits were historically set, have never been revisited Three years of raises below consumer price index Turnover rate of 45% in direct service jobs Anecdotal evidence of staff migration to higher-paying caregiver jobs	Turnover rate at or below 35% Thorough knowledge of competitor employer compensation and benefits levels Budgeted raises of 3–5%, depending on results of above	Documentation of most caregiver employer compensation and benefits levels Turnover rate	YYYY YYYYYY

A further problem for Willows' End planners is that, if services are truly already of a high quality, they will have to work very hard to produce even small gains. Plus, there is no readily-agreed upon way to achieve those gains anyway. Discussion around this goal could split the staff and must be handled very carefully. Here are some activities that might raise the level of care even further, assuming that Willows' End does not already do them.

Conduct a Client and Family Satisfaction Survey Of course, the baseline task for any organization wishing to operate a flagship is the same two-headed master: mission and margin. Any organization must excel in providing its mission services, and it also has to make sure its financials are in order. Only after those things are accomplished can the entity think about truly becoming a flagship.

Some groups, like Willows' End, may understandably regard maintaining a high quality of service to be the first and most important goal in achieving their desired strategic position. This is a laudable objective, of course, but here's the paradox: high quality is an operations goal, not a strategic one. There is not much strategic in the basics of managing an operation at a high level, because most of it is tactical. It may sound daunting, but good service is a starting point, not an end in itself. The basics of hiring, supervising, scheduling, training, maintaining the building, and all the other components of quality need to be tended to, but they are on a separate plane. Strategic positioning in this sense reaches beyond simple operations. It is, frankly, an additional layer of work. That's what makes achieving it so hard.

Creating a Strategic Financial Plan

Strategic positions do not implement themselves, and implementation plans do not work without some thought being given to their financial underpinnings. We call this final phase of strategic positioning the strategic financial plan. One of the recurring failures of traditional strategic planning is that both the people who think grand thoughts and the people who think implementation details often do not communicate with the people who manage the money. If they did, the grand thinkers might find a way to make their strategic position more achievable, and the people who think about the implementation details might find that they achieve their goals more efficiently.

A strategic financial plan need not be grand. It also need not be highly detailed, with cross-references and footnotes stretching endlessly. It just has to be realistic. A strategic position with a well-thought-out financial plan has a very good chance of working. A strategic position without a well-thought-out financial plan will fail, and few will understand why.

The Three Areas to Cover
A strategic financial plan will cover three areas of financial activity: cash flow, capital structure, and profitability. Depending on the organization and its strategic position, two of these areas are likely to be most important. The key is recognizing which are the two areas, and what to do in each. First, some background. Much of what follows in the next few sections is covered in greater depth in *Streetsmart Financial Basics for Nonprofit Managers*, so we will touch on each briefly.

Liquidity   Liquidity refers to the ability of an organization to meet its liabilities in the ordinary course of its business. Conventionally, short-term assets are defined as cash and any other type of asset that could potentially be converted directly to cash within that business cycle. Short-term liabilities are those obligations to pay a future party money that will come due during the same business cycle.

For nonprofit organizations, cash is king. With cash, a nonprofit can take advantage of unexpected opportunities or cope with unexpected problems. Without cash, an organization struggles and can even go out of business entirely.

Capital Structure   Think of capital as sticky money. Capital is given to an organization by an outside source, and it stays in the organization (contrast this with flowing funds below). The identifying characteristic of capital is that it is often connected directly to an outside party that, under certain circumstances, could pull that capital back for itself. Nonprofits have three meaningful sources of long-term capital—profit, loans, and capital donations (for-profits also have three, with stock sales replacing capital donations).

Many nonprofits are undercapitalized and do not realize it. They see the symptoms of poor cash flow and low profit margins or high expenses and do not appreciate that these are often rooted in inadequate sticky money. Some think that the "bottom line" means profit or that it is somehow related to operations. The real bottom line, in the sense of a point beyond which no nonprofit can go, is the inability to bring capital into the organization.

Profitability   Everyone recognizes what profit is, and by now most in the nonprofit sector accept that it is necessary for a nonprofit to

PROFIT BY SERENDIPITY

Unhappily, most nonprofit organizations, including their boards and funders, have not yet reached the stage where they can have an honest dialog resulting in a budgeted level of profit. So they have to conduct a bit of a sham exercise each year in which management presents a budget studded with profitability possibilities (such as not filling authorized positions), hoping that one or two of them can actually produce a profit. This is profit by serendipity, a bit of collusion that does not fool anyone and saves face all around. But in an industry where something like 60 to 80 percent of most spending is on personnel, it is not hard to see what has to flex in order to produce that profit. Would it not be better to start out with an explicit, shared plan in the beginning?

make a profit if it wants to be around for a while. Profit is not the sole reason for a nonprofit's existence, but it is a requisite. No margin, no mission.

How They Relate
A strategic financial plan recognizes how the three areas interact with each other. Consistent profitability brings in capital—sticky money—more easily and with less direct cost than either borrowing or getting capital donations. Capital facilitates things like investment in buildings and equipment, and liquidity allows operations to continue uninterrupted.

Different strategic positions will put differing pressures on these three areas. Rapid growth always strains liquidity unless there is a reliable source of expansion capital or high profits, both of which are unlikely in a nonprofit setting. Institutions that rely on a heavy investment in capital assets, such as universities and hospitals, will be limited in the amount of money they can invest in their campuses and equipment if profitability is low and they cannot borrow additional funds.

The Implications for Strategy Strategy leaders must recognize these interactions and then find ways to work with them. While all strategies are based in a unique time and set of circumstances, it is possible to illustrate how common strategies can be supported by emphasizing one or two of the three basic areas. The following chart shows common organizational strategies on the left, with some appropriate financial strategies on the right. Other strategies beyond those listed might also work. So much of the choice has to depend on the characteristics of the organization. For instance, nonprofits that do not require major capital assets will handle growth very differently than those that do.

The Strategy Options chart shows how it is often possible to hold steady in one of the three areas, while emphasizing one or both of the remaining two. For instance, rapid growth demands high liquidity to cover all the short-term costs associated with growth (such as taking on new staff and paying expenses that will only be recovered later on). It also practically demands high profitability—which is probably one of the signs that high growth is necessary and possible. But even nonprofits that use a large amount of capital assets such as vehicles or land and buildings can coast a bit here if they wish, investing only in additional assets proportionate to the percentage of growth expected. Nonprofits that must shrink in size will want to get rid of excess assets, which benefits liquidity without much effort, but they need to be very disciplined about reducing expenses in parallel with their reduced revenue.

STRATEGY OPTIONS

Strategy	Liquidity	Capital	Profitability
Rapid growth	Rapid growth needs high liquidity	Borrow only within range supported by profit	Must maintain high profitability
New programming	Increase proportionate to amount of new programming	Invest in additional capital only from profit	Enough profit to cover risk of failures and new capital
Recovery	Keep at least even, hopefully increase	Hold off investing, possibly sell	Must break even, prefer at least some profit
Shrink in size	Should improve if budget balanced	Sell off assets to reduce debt	Reduce expenses to create profit
Merge	Keep temporarily high	Consolidate assets if possible	Expect diminished profit near term, higher in long term

Willows' End's Strategic Financial Plan

A strategic financial plan for Willows' End would be relatively simple because the financial ramifications of their desired strategic position are for more of the same rather than any abrupt or massively expensive shift in focus. Implications of the strategy, by major component, would look like this:

Flagship Provider/Crossroads of Learning This part of the strategic position requires constant investment in facility upkeep. Willows' End already has a relatively newly renovated building with adequate space and an attractive future for a steady flow of outsider visitors, which is one of the reasons for their confidence that they can implement this component. In the future, their strategy of making the program an easy meeting place both literally and symbolically will demand that they keep it that way.

But there is another dimension to this requirement that is equally important: ongoing profitability. Many organizations cope with declining revenues or profitability by the time-tested strategy of putting off repairs and maintenance. The leak in the corner of the meeting room

BENCHMARK YOUR CAPITAL ASSETS

Nonprofits needing major investments in buildings and equipment to provide services can easily see whether they are keeping pace. The measurement is called the accounting age of plant and equipment. To calculate it, go to your IRS Form 990 and find line 57b, the accumulated depreciation of your tangible assets. Divide it by line 42A, the total depreciation charged for that year. The result is a ratio that gives you insight into whether you are staying current with your investment level. Lower is better because it indicates your assets are "younger." But the real power of the ratio comes over time, as you see from year to year what the number is doing. If it is trending higher, you are not staying on top of the investment needed for your assets. If it is steady or even declining, it means that you are keeping up with the investment in tangible assets. Hospitals find this number very helpful, since they have to have up-to-date buildings and equipment.

gets fixed, but the ceiling does not because there is no provision for cosmetic repairs. The elevator really needs to be completely over-hauled after the shaft flooded but there is only enough money in the operating budget to keep applying band-aids and the insurance pol-icy does not cover the damage because someone selected a high deductible to save money.

With their strategy, Willows' End will not have that luxury. Deferred maintenance starts biting back surprisingly quickly. The organization has no choice but to fund its maintenance and upkeep needs fully, or else watch the physical plant begin to slide out of the flagship zone. Managers need to be certain to create enough margin both for scheduled upkeep and unexpected repairs. Major, periodic renova-tions will also be needed.

Caregiver of Choice Much of the caregiver employer of choice com-ponent of their strategy will rely on behavioral changes and only mar-ginally on economic ones unless their research suggests that their compensation and benefit levels are not competitive. In that case, the economic impact would be substantial. In any event, the pressure point will be operations in general and profitability in particular.

Suppose that Willows' End decides it needs to increase salaries for all staff. Like most nonprofits with a heavy labor need, Willows' End spends about 70 percent of its total expenses on compensation and benefits. That means that if the organization generates an additional 1 percent profit it can offer all of its staff an average raise of about 1.4 percent. If it can raise prices at an overall level higher than the impact of inflation on wages, it will have some of the difference to spend on raising salaries.

The trade-off for pleasing the labor force with good compensation and benefits is that Willows' End must be absolutely relentless about cost control. Willows' End has to assume that eventually the growing popularity of assisted living will make it a commodity business in which providers will differentiate themselves mainly on the basis of price. When that occurs, for Willows' End to continue as a flagship provider and a crossroads of community learning, it will need to find a way either to provide services at a lower cost than their peers or to supplement their revenue through non-marketplace means. If they already have a strong cost control culture, it will be easier to simply sustain it. The promise of the crossroads part of the strategy is that by the time the industry is turned into a commodity Willows' End's reputation will give it the option of making additional revenue through activities like consulting with other providers, licensing parts of their service technology, or simply creaming the local market.

Targeted Revenue Strategy Willows' End's revenue strategy is to maintain a balance between fee-for-service and targeted philanthropy. There are no government entitlement programs for assisted living, and in fact the only government assistance WEAL administrators will see comes directly to individuals from low-income and military-pension-related sources. As a consequence, the organization has the advantage of not having to operate in a highly regulated marketplace, and the disadvantage of being almost totally dependent on private individuals and select donors.

Some would feel that WEAL has an advantage in its freedom from government funding, but paradoxically this could be a source of difficulty. The very intricate, cost-conscious nature of most government funding forces nonprofits to be cost-conscious themselves: the temptation at Willows' End will be to act as if cost control is not important because no external party demands it. Executives have to ensure that this does not happen, especially if the above analysis of the need for cost controls in a commodity-like market is correct.

Because Willows' End charges private clients a month in advance, cash flow should not be a major issue. However, capital financing could be a problem in the sense that profitability could always be threatened, and it would take considerable future success in the community crossroads strategy to build enough community support to sustain a successful capital campaign. Banks are likely to be their major source of funds for capital investment for the near term.

Introduction to Appendices

For those who want them, there are recipe cards in this book. At the end of the main sections, in segments appropriately titled Recipe Cards, we include some practical, step-by-step directions on how to implement the grand ideas presented earlier in those sections. We do not spend much time on this part, admittedly, but that's because we feel that every intelligent reader is capable of using his or her own tools to put these ideas into action. In some cases, the Recipe Cards are further amplified by items in the appendix. Other times, we leave the elaboration to the reader. In any case, Recipe Cards are only meant to be adapted to each situation.

Quick Start

Here's a Quick Start version. The basics of strategic positioning are included right here: everything else is just details and thinking.

Strategic positioning is made up of two kinds of work: planning strategy and planning work. Planning strategy is done by leaders, mostly board members, senior executives, and (hopefully) some level of participation by lower level managers and staff. Planning work is done exclusively by management.

In strategic positioning the organization answers two fundamental questions: Where do you want to be in 5–10 years, and what will you have to do to get there? To answer these two questions, an organization will go through a total of six distinct steps. The first question should be answered by some combination of the board of directors and senior management, while the second is purely the responsibility of management, with board approval.

WHERE DO YOU WANT TO BE?

A strategic position aims at some point in the future to place the organization into predefined relationships with a handful of key elements in its future. In short, it answers the question "where do you want to be in 5–10 years?" in several different ways. There are four distinct steps in deciding "where you want to be."

1. **Create or reaffirm your mission.** This step is close to self-explanatory. For existing organizations, double-check that your mission is still viable, relevant, and desirable. Modify it if necessary. For

new organizations, articulate the mission as succinctly and compellingly as possible.

2. **Scan Your Future.** Stand at the front door of your organization and look outside. Imagine what you will be seeing there in 5–10 years. This is a monstrously ambiguous topic, but here's some help. Break your future into seven distinct elements, and examine the trends in each one:

   a. The NEED or demand for the type of service you offer—what is the nature of the need for your services? Most nonprofits are formed in response to things like illness, lack of education, the inaccessibility of cultural experiences, and so on. Research the pure need for your service extensively.

   b. The population—USERS—you choose to serve—basic demographic trends. What does this population look like now? What will it look like in a few years?

   c. Your chosen GEOGRAPHY—does this organization focus on a specific neighborhood, a region, a multiple-state area, or the entire country?

   d. Your COMPETITORS—if you are squeamish you can call them alternatives to your services. These are the things that can take your revenue away Be sure to cover both direct competitors and indirect competitors. Slide rule companies went out of business not because they lost to direct competitors but because electronics were miniaturized. Paradox: usually, only your competitors will be interested in being your collaborators.

   e. Your FUNDERS—who provides the funds to pay for the service? Government? Foundations? Individual donors? Fee for service?

   f. Your LABOR force—someone has to do the mission-related work. What does this labor force look like now, and how will it change in the next 5–10 years?

   g. The role of special ASSETS in providing your services (technology, buildings, intellectual capital, etc.).

3. Scan your internal strengths. Now do another scan, this time focusing internally instead of externally. Pattern your internal scan along exactly the same lines as your future scan, except for one catch—the only thing that should show up is strengths. Why? You are building

a foundation for the future. Would you rather build it on strengths or weaknesses? We thought so.

Examine the services you offer. What's your service model? Under what circumstances does it work best? Research the users of your service. Revisit your assumptions about geography. Research your funders and what they like about you. Why do you fit with their motivations, capacities, and so forth? Study your labor force with a clear eye. What special assets do you already have that are helpful in the delivery of your services?

4. Decide where you want to be in 5–10 years. Compare your future trends with your strengths and decide where you want to be with respect to each of your future trends in 5–10 years. This is the essence of your strategic position. To get it, line up every one of your future trends and match it with your internal strengths, if any. Go down the list one by one, literally putting a trend and your strength(s) in that area side by side. Examine the lists very closely. Think through the implications of the match-up (or lack of it) between a future trend and your internal strength. If you do not have a strength to match a trend, do not worry about it right now— that will be management's job later on. Right now, strive for a conceptual conversation.

Leaders—stop right here. Turn this over to the managers to plan the implementation.

WHAT DO YOU HAVE TO DO TO GET WHERE YOU WANT TO BE?

The leadership of the organization has decided where it wants to be in 5–10 years; now it is management's job to figure out what to do to get there. This is work planning. Management should now go away for a few weeks and do two things:

5. Craft a succinct statement of the desired strategic position, and . . . put into as few words as possible a description of where the organization's leadership wants to be five years from now with respect to each of those seven elements. This is not just playing with words. A simple one- or two-sentence description of the desired strategic

position should play a primary role in educating, guiding, and motivating everyone in the organization for the next several years.

6. Devise a work plan for getting there. This is where you figure out how to bridge the gaps between current strengths and the desired position. It is management's job to figure out ways to capitalize on strengths, build or acquire new strengths, and minimize or mitigate weaknesses.

Once the work plan is complete, it needs buy-in from leadership. With that in hand, the focus becomes one of implementation. Again, that's management's job, but now they will have a clear statement of the desired strategic position to guide them.

Strategic positions should ordinarily endure for years, whereas work plans change, sometimes frequently. Two questions, six steps, and you have a two-part, long-lived product.

National Research with Personal Perspectives

 oing national research is like going on a fishing trip in a proven rich fishing ground. The question is not whether you will catch something, the question is what you will catch? Here are some groups to help make it more likely that you can use what you catch. To add richness to your research, try getting insiders' perspectives.

ASSOCIATIONS

Associations are some of the best ways to research national trends and patterns. Try to pick trade associations as opposed to advocacy groups. You will need to critically examine the results of conversations with either type of group, but advocacy organizations tend to push specific points of view, while trade groups will push a point of view but often back it up with original research.

The first associations to start with are the ones you in which your organization holds a membership. The reasons for this are obvious (you pay their salary), but there are some less overt advantages too. Foremost among them is that your good questions help them mark a member organization that is above average in its energy level and sophistication.

Associations are usually quite manageable for the stranger. Hitting an association's website is always a good starting point, but personal conversations with association staff can be very productive. The average staff size of most associations according to the American Society of Association

Executives is 28, but half have fewer than 13 staff members. That means you cannot go too far wrong if you call without an introduction.

In a very large association, go for people with titles like "policy analyst" or "research director" or "issues coordinator." Even if you can reach the CEO you might not want to: they may be tempted to spin not only the issue but the association's role in it. Professional association executives often use the initials "CAE" after their name to indicate that they are certified association executives. This involves a lengthy and fairly involved course of study and suggests a professional executive who may very well be managing a different type of association next year. But since this designation does not necessarily relate to a particular association's industry, these people may be more expert in process than in content.

Other association employees sometimes resemble university faculty or foundation staff members in their mindsets, and can be surprisingly willing to challenge their own association's orthodoxy to give what they see as the straight story. Most can be a fountain of knowledge if approached on a subject in their comfort zone.

FOUNDATIONS

Major foundations, the ones with large research efforts that release an important paper more frequently than many of us balance our checkbooks, are a trove of information. Much of it is now available online, but as with all other national sources it is most helpful to be able to talk directly with knowledgeable staff.

Unlike associations, in which the unspoken culture is to be part of the member services team, foundation cultures tend to breed individuals pleased to be out front on their individual issues. Direct approaches are always the best unless your favorite college professor's wife is the foundation's specialist in your area.

Be aware that foundation staffs often are not experts in any particular kind of content so much as they are facilitators and conveners. They may very well be knowledgeable in a subject, but not deeply. Often their role has been to identify and support an outsider with the skills and position to develop deep knowledge about your desired target area. You may find that the real experts are simply on the receiving end of the foundation's largesse, spending most of their time in academia.

ACADEMICS

Outside of future Nobel laureates and recent presidential appointees, most academic researchers will be happy to share their expertise with you. The sweet spot for academic informants about national trends is academics in their early thirties. These are the people who are just one side or the other of tenure decisions, with still-fresh ideas and enough energy and passion to pursue them. They and their cause are rising, and they should see you as an opportunity to educate and perhaps proselytize a bit.

Do not forget the specialized societies of academics. Name a corner of our economy that is large enough to attract and hold the attention of academics numbering in the three figures, and you will probably find a society dedicated to it. These can also be great sources of information, papers, and even leads on topic areas.

GOVERNMENTS

National and big state governments are great sources of strategic trend information—if you can find the right person. There is an invisible (to the outsider) line in most governments between the appointed government executive and the lifer. Technically, it is probably described as those positions requiring appointment and those subject to civil service or some equivalent regulations, such as collective bargaining provisions.

For seasoned big-picture perspectives, try to stay just beneath the appointed positions. This is not easy to do, since officials do not display special codes, but if you can find those people they can be a great source of information. So can the appointed official, for that matter, but he or she is more likely to have just started, to have no particularly deep knowledge of the field, or to have a deep personal agenda that does not include educating you. The risk in the civil service type positions is that you will get a determined little-picture person, but that can still be somewhat helpful, especially if you have already gotten big-picture stuff elsewhere.

Brainstorming/ Clustering Technique

Here is a good way to start with just the energy of a small group and end up with a handful of clusters or themes. This technique can be used with virtually any type of process, including strategic positioning and work planning.

BRAINSTORMING

Ask the group to brainstorm ideas—expressed as a word, phrase, or short sentence. Write the ideas exactly as expressed on a flip chart. At the same time, have someone copy entries to large yellow sticky notes, one per sticky.

CLUSTERING

Put the stickies on a wall in random order. Ask the group to stand in front of the wall and sort the stickies into groups *that make sense to them* using the following ground rules:

1. This is intended to be a thinking exercise, not a competition. Let the clusters shape and reshape your thinking as they emerge. The objective is to arrive at a set of clusters (i.e., themes) that may not be perfect from each individual's perspective but that are workable.
2. Take as much time as you need.
3. When you are satisfied with the clusters that have emerged, stay with the group. If you grow unsatisfied, reenter the clustering process.

4. Stickies need only be in a recognizable cluster—they do not need to be grouped horizontally or vertically as long as they can be seen as a cluster or theme.

5. During the entire process, group members may not talk with each other.

The facilitator may want to apologize for the hokeyness of the exercise; on the other hand it works, so no apologies are necessary in the end.

This exercise works best with groups of 5–10 people. If necessary, a larger group can be split into smaller groups. In this case, build in a second step to integrate the results of the subgroups (this could be a final sticky exercise).

Groups will almost always settle on about 3–7 categories (it is so spookily predictable that it must be a law of nature). Often, when there are six or more categories, it is because at least one or two are one-word "categories" or are items that really are not on the same level as the other entries.

To prioritize the results, see the Appendix D.

D

Weighted Voting Technique

To set priorities or to settle disputes, consider weighted voting. There are many ways to arrange a weighted voting exercise, but here is our favorite.

1. Start with a list of items to be voted upon that is listed on a flip chart. The list can be any length, but the process will be most effective if there are 5–12 items. Make sure that participants know exactly what each item means. Also, be sure that there is a logical reason for each item being separate. If there is not enough clarity between all the items, consider doing a clustering exercise.

2. Purchase a package of brightly colored dots at a stationery store. Each dot is a "vote." The kind of package with columns of seven dots works best because seven votes is a large enough number to produce clear variances without being so small that a single voter can unduly sway a vote.

3. Give each "voter" a set of seven dots.

4. Tell them to place their dots on the flip chart on (or near) the items being voted upon.* If they wish to spend all their dots on one item, that's fine. If they wish to split their seven votes among two or more items, that's fine too. Emphasize that putting multiple dots on a single item means you feel strongly about that item being given a high priority.

*It helps to reproduce the items being voted on in a horizontal grid fashion, with plenty of white space after or below each item to accommodate the dots.

5. Turn the flip chart around and ask participants to line up to go "behind the chart" to place their dots in private.*

6. Ask participants to vote all at the same time. Encourage those who hang back to vote at the same time as their peers.

7. The winning items are the ones which receive the largest number of dots.

*This style of voting is only necessary if the group is an internal one. Every group of human beings is prone to exaggerate strengths or to downplay internal rivals' strengths. To counteract this natural tendency, have participants vote in private. Only the second person in line will know with complete assurance what any other person's "vote" was, and since they are so early in the voting process there is little they can do to exploit that knowledge. Privacy in voting cuts down on the intimidation and manipulation factor.

Media Markets

Rank	Designated Market Area (DMA)	TV Households	% of US
1	New York, NY	7,375,530	6.692
2	Los Angeles, CA	5,536,430	5.023
3	Chicago, IL	3,430,790	3.113
4	Philadelphia, PA	2,925,560	2.654
	Boston (Manchester, NH)	2,375,310	2.155
6	San Francisco-Oakland-San Jose, CA	2,355,740	2.137
7	Dallas-Ft. Worth, TX	2,336,140	2.120
8	Washington, DC (Hagerstown, MD)	2,252,550	2.044
9	Atlanta, GA	2,097,220	1.903
10	Houston, TX	1,938,670	1.759
11	Detroit, MI	1,936,350	1.757
12	Tampa-St. Petersburg (Sarasota), FL	1,710,400	1.552
13	Seattle-Tacoma, WA	1,701,950	1.544
14	Phoenix (Prescott), AZ	1,660,430	1.507
15	Minneapolis-St. Paul, MN	1,652,940	1.500
16	Cleveland-Akron (Canton), OH	1,541,780	1.399
17	Miami-Ft. Lauderdale, FL	1,522,960	1.382
18	Denver, CO	1,415,180	1.284
19	Sacramento-Stockton-Modesto, CA	1,345,820	1.221
20	Orlando-Daytona Beach-Melbourne, FL	1,345,700	1.221
21	St. Louis, MO	1,222,380	1.109
22	Pittsburgh, PA	1,169,800	1.061
23	Portland, OR	1,099,890	0.998
24	Baltimore, MD	1,089,220	0.988
25	Indianapolis, IN	1,053,750	0.956

*Estimates as of September 2005. Copyright Nielsen Media research

Rank	Designated Market Area (DMA)	TV Households	% of US
26	San Diego, CA	1,026,160	0.931
27	Charlotte, NC	1,020,130	0.926
28	Hartford & New Haven, CT	1,013,350	0.919
29	Raleigh-Durham (Fayettville), NC	985,200	0.894
30	Nashville, TN	927,500	0.842
31	Kansas City, MO	903,540	0.820
32	Columbus, OH	890,770	0.808
33	Milwaukee, WI	880,390	0.799
34	Cincinnati, OH	880,190	0.799
35	Greenvllle-Spartanburg, SC-Asheville, NC-Anderson, SC	815,460	0.740
36	Salt Lake City, UT	810,830	0.736
37	San Antonio, TX	760,410	0.690
38	West Palm Beach-Ft. Pierce, FL	751,930	0.682
39	Grand Rapids-Kalamazoo-Battle.Creek, MI	731,630	0.664
40	Birmingham (Anniston and Tuscaloosa), AL	716,520	0.650
41	Harrisburg-Lancaster-Lebanon-York, PA	707,010	0.641
42	Norfolk-Portsmouth-Newport News, VA	704,810	0.640
43	New Orleans, LA	672,150	0.610
44	Memphis, TN	657,670	0.597
45	Oklahoma City, OK	655,400	0.595
46	Albuquerque-Santa Fe, NM	653,680	0.593
47	Greensboro-High Point-Winston.Salem, NC	652,020	0.592
48	Las Vegas, NV	651,110	0.591
49	Buffalo, NY	644,430	0.585
50	Louisville, KY	643,290	0.584
51	Providence, RI-New Bedford, MA	639,590	0.580
52	Jacksonville, FL	624,220	0.566
53	Austin, TX	589,360	0.535
54	Wilkes Barre-Scranton, PA	588,540	0.534
55	Albany-Schenectady-Troy, NY	552,250	0.501
56	Fresno-Visalia, CA	546,210	0.496
57	Little Rock-Pine Bluff, AR	531,470	0.482
58	Knoxville, TN	516,180	0.468
59	Dayton, OH	513,610	0.466
60	Richmond-Petersburg, VA	510,770	0.463
61	Tulsa, OK	510,480	0.463
62	Mobile, AL-Pensacola (Ft. Walton Beach), FL	501,130	0.455
63	Lexington, KY	478,560	0.434
64	Charleston-Huntington, WV	477,890	0.434
65	Flint-Saginaw-Bay City, MI	475,500	0.431
66	Ft. Myers-Naples, FL	461,920	0.419
67	Wichita-Hutchinson, KS Plus	446,820	0.405
68	Roanoke-Lynchburg, VA	440,390	0.400
69	Green Bay-Appleton, WI	432,810	0.393
70	Toledo, OH	426,520	0.387
71	Tucson (Sierra Vista), AZ	422,480	0.383

Rank	Designated Market Area (DMA)	TV Households	% of US
72	Honolulu, HI	414,960	0.377
73	Des Moines-Ames, IA	413,590	0.375
74	Portland-Auburn, ME	407,050	0.369
75	Omaha, NE	399,830	0.363
76	Syracuse, NY	398,240	0.361
77	Springfield, MO	395,820	0.359
78	Spokane, WA	389,630	0.354
79	Rochester, NY	385,460	0.350
80	Paducah, KY-Cape Girardeau, MO-Harrisburg-Mt. Vernon, IL	383,330	0.348
81	Shreveport, LA	382,080	0.347
82	Champaign & Springfield-Decatur, IL	378,100	0.343
83	Columbia, SC	373,260	0.339
84	Huntsville-Decatur (Florence), AL	370,820	0.336
85	Madison, WI	365,550	0.332
86	Chattanooga, TN	354,230	0.321
87	South Bend-Elkhart, IN	333,190	0.302
88	Cedar Rapids-Waterloo-Iowa City & Dubuque, IA	331,480	0.301
89	Jackson, MS	328,350	0.298
90	Burlington, VT-Plattsburgh, NY	325,720	0.296
91	Tri-Cities, TN-VA	323,690	0.294
92	Harlingen-Wesalco-Brownsville-McAllen, TX	318,800	0.289
93	Colorado Springs-Pueblo, CO	315,010	0.286
94	Waco-Temple-Bryan, TX	310,960	0.282
95	Davenport, IA-Rock Island-Moline, IL	308,380	0.280
96	Baton Rouge, LA	305,810	0.277
97	Savannah, GA	296,100	0.269
98	Johnstown-Altoona, PA	294,810	0.267
99	El Paso (Las Cruces), TX	290,540	0.264
100	Evansville, IN	288,800	0.262
101	Charleston, SC	283,730	0.257
102	Youngstown, OH	276,720	0.251
103	Lincoln & Hastings-Kearny, NE	274,150	0.249
104	Ft. Smith-Fayetteville-Springdale-Rogers, AR	273,000	0.248
105	Greenville-New Bern-Washington, NC	271,130	0.246
106	Ft. Wayne, IN	270,500	0.245
107	Myrtle Beach-Florence, SC	265,770	0.241
108	Springfield-Holyoke, MA	264,840	0.240
109	Tallahassee, FL-Thomasville, GA	261,250	0.237
110	Lansing, MI	256,790	0.233
111	Tyler-Longview (Lufkin & Nacogdoches), TX	255,770	0.232
112	Reno, NV	255,090	0.231
113	Traverse City-Cadillac, MI	247,600	0.225
114	Sioux Falls (Mitchell), SD	246,020	0.223
115	Augusta, GA	245,590	0.223
116	Montgomery-Selma, AL	245,090	0.222
117	Peoria-Bloomington, IL	241,800	0.219

Rank	Designated Market Area (DMA)	TV Households	% of US
118	Fargo-Valley City, ND	234,190	0.212
119	Boise, ID	230,100	0.209
120	Macon, GA	229,870	0.209
121	Eugene, OR	229,280	0.208
122	Santa Barbara-Santa Maria-San Louis Obispo, CA	224,290	0.204
123	La Crosse-Eau Claire, WI	224,090	0.203
124	Lafayette, LA	220,030	0.200
125	Monterey-Salinas, CA	218,080	0.198
126	Yakima-Pasco-Richland-Kennewick, WA	211,610	0.192
127	Columbus, GA	205,300	0.186
128	Bakersfield, CA	201,850	0.183
129	Corpus Christi, TX	192,380	0.175
130	Chico-Redding, CA	191,190	0.173
131	Amarillo, TX	190,250	0.173
132	Columbus-Tupelo-West Point, MS	186,510	0.169
133	Rockford, IL	183,090	0.166
134	Wausau-Rhinelander, WI	182,620	0.166
135	Monroe, LA-El Dorado, AR	174,370	0.158
136	Topeka, KS	170,650	0.155
137	Duluth, MN-Superior, WI	168,650	0.153
138	Columbia-Jefferson City, MO	167,860	0.152
139	Wilmington, NC	167,810	0.152
140	Beaumont-Port Arthur, TX	167,430	0.152
141	Medford-Klamath Falls, OR	163,090	0.148
142	Erie, PA	158,660	0.144
143	Sioux City, IA	156,950	0.142
144	Wichita Falls, TX & Lawton, OK	154,960	0.141
145	Joplin, MO-Pittsburg, KS	153,720	0.139
146	Lubbock, TX	152,150	0.138
147	Albany, GA	152,140	0.138
148	Salisbury, MD	147,890	0.134
149	Bluefield-Beckley-Oak Hill, WV	145,850	0.132
150	Terre Haute, IN	145,630	0.132
151	Bangor, ME	142,790	0.130
152	Rochester, MN-Mason City, IA-Austin, MN	142,770	0.130
153	Palm Springs, CA	142,730	0.130
154	Wheeling, WV-Steubenville, OH	142,020	0.129
155	Anchorage, AK	141,290	0.128
156	Binghamton, NY	138,560	0.126
157	Panama City, FL	136,450	0.124
158	Biloxi-Gulfport, MS	135,540	0.123
159	Odessa-Midland, TX	135,100	0.123
160	Minot-Bismarck-Dickinson (Williston), ND	133,910	0.122
161	Sherman, TX-Ada, OK	124,060	0.113
162	Gainesville, FL	117,190	0.106
163	Idaho Falls-Pocatello, ID	114,560	0.104
164	Abilene-Sweetwater, TX	112,510	0.102

Rank	Designated Market Area (DMA)	TV Households	% of US
165	Clarksburg-Weston, WV	108,730	0.099
166	Utica, NY	106,130	0.096
167	Hattiesburg-Laurel, MS	105,000	0.095
168	Missoula, MT	104,700	0.095
169	Quincy, IL-Hannibal, MO-Keokuk, IA	103,890	0.094
170	Yuma, AZ-El Centro, CA	103,170	0.094
171	Billings, MT	102,620	0.093
172	Dothan, AL	98,370	0.089
173	Elmira (Corning), NY	97,210	0.088
174	Jackson, TN	95,010	0.086
175	Lake Charles, LA	94,090	0.085
176	Alexandria, LA	93,120	0.085
177	Rapid City, SD	91,070	0.083
178	Watertown, NY	90,930	0.083
179	Jonesboro, AR	89,530	0.081
180	Marquette, MI	89,160	0.081
181	Harrisonburg, VA	85,870	0.078
182	Greenwood-Greenville, MS	76,800	0.070
183	Bowling Green, KY	75,420	0.068
184	Meridian, MS	71,210	0.065
185	Lima, OH	70,940	0.064
186	Charlottesville, VA	69,750	0.063
187	Grand Junction-Montrose, CO	65,190	0.059
188	Laredo, TX	64,410	0.058
189	Great Falls, MT	64,130	0.058
190	Parkersburg, WV	63,990	0.058
191	Lafayette, IN	63,330	0.057
192	Twin Falls, ID	60,400	0.055
193	Butte-Bozeman, MT	59,300	0.054
194	Eureka, CA	58,340	0.053
195	Cheyenne, WY-Scottsbluff, NE	54,320	0.049
196	Bend, OR	54,250	0.049
197	San Angelo, TX	53,330	0.048
198	Casper-Riverton, WY	52,070	0.047
199	Ottumwa, IA-Kirksville, MO	51,290	0.047
200	Mankato, MN	50,930	0.046
201	St. Joseph, MO	45,840	0.042
202	Zanesville, OH	33,080	0.030
203	Fairbanks, AK	32,310	0.029
204	Presque Isle, ME	31,140	0.028
205	Victoria, TX	30,250	0.027
206	Helena, MT	25,810	0.023
207	Juneau, AK	24,130	0.022
208	Alpena, MI	17,790	0.016
209	North Platte, NE	15,320	0.014
210	Glendive, MT	5,020	0.005
Total		**110,213,910**	**100.000**

Future Scan Form

Theme:

Key Fact-Based Trends:

Implications:

Work Plan for Element of Strategic Position #1:			
Management Goal #1:			
Status Quo	Desired Situation–1 year	Objective Measure	Person Responsible
			XXXXXX YYYYYY

Data Sources for
Competitor Research

There is a fairly rich array of sources for competitor research. Since research like this is a hit-or-miss proposition and any one source might produce only a scrap of information (if that), it helps to try more than one source. It may also help to know which ones are free and which ones are not.

FREE

Guidestar.org The mother lode of nonprofit information sources for nonprofit public charities. Lots of financial information, but also juicy tidbits like programs and services, executive salaries and (often) board of directors info plus whatever else the reporting nonprofit decided to include.

Other websites Too numerous to mention. Use your favorite search engine.

State and local paper records Often overlooked, the state capital and local cities and towns often have useful info on local competitors that has not found its way online yet. State records are good for corporate information (usually filed with the secretary of state or equivalent), while local municipalities may have information on property held and local activities. Of course, it helps to be located physically near the office where the information is kept, or else it could turn into a long and fruitless trip.

NOT FREE

(Hint: many of these services are subscription-based. To get access to them, consider asking your auditing firm or attorney if they would be willing to do the research and get reimbursed for the direct costs, which are usually minimal. With luck, they will do the research and not ask for the reimbursement).

> **Dun & Bradstreet reports** Financial information, as well as corporate information and some evaluative comments.
>
> **Lexis Nexis** Legal records (Lexis) and general information (Nexis). Can be quite revealing in some situations.

PRESENTATION OF THE DATA

Presenting the data is just as important as the data itself. Depending on how ambitious the group is, the presentation can range from simple lists of competitors and key characteristics (revenue, numbers of programs, funding sources, profitability, etc.) to more nuanced displays.

Attention Board Members and Staff: Develop Your Own Personal Strategic Position

$\mathbb{N}$ ow that that marathon Saturday strategic-positioning session is over, it is time for you to develop your own parallel personal strategic position. One of the least appreciated aspects of strategy development is that individuals, including board members, managers, and executives, need to be aligned to the strategy just as much as the structure and other major processes of their organization do. A little proactive thinking on everyone's part about how they can fit into the new strategy will help both parties.

If you want to get an idea of where an organization is headed, watch where its best people go. When a part of the organization is growing or innovating, those on the inside know it and it is usually in everyone's interests for them to make a shift. The resources and management attention directed to that part tend to act like a magnet for talent. Similarly, when a nonprofit is drifting or downright failing it is an open secret, and the best people start moving out of the organization.

How can you best position yourself to take advantage of the opportunities created by the new strategy? The answer is to follow the personal equivalent of strategic positioning: examine your future environment (in this case, the organization), take an inventory of your personal strengths, decide where you want to be relative to the organization over the next several years, then create a personal development plan that will get you there. We will describe each of these steps in order.

SCAN YOUR ENVIRONMENT

As an insider, your personal environment is the organization. What the organization will look like in 5–10 years, what it will emphasize and what it is trying to become will have a lot to say about your professional development. There are a handful of variables that will largely determine your happiness and success as a professional. Examine them closely.

Demand for Services

What general market or markets for its services does your organization want to be in? How do those markets differ from where the organization is now? What are the demographics and related trends in those markets? Is the demand growing, contracting, or staying the same?

Users of the Services

Within those markets, who are the projected users of the services, and how are they the same or different from the ones currently being served? If your theater plans to supplement its symphony series with country and western acts, the future overall portrait of attendees will look very different from the way it looks now, which could have implications for you.

Geography

All nonprofits are geographically oriented. Will your organization's geographic range be changing? Will sites be added or subtracted, or will they remain unchanged? Within that geography, what are the expected trends? New geographic areas bring new opportunities.

Coworkers

Coworkers and other board members often make a pivotal difference in a nonprofit role. How will they change? Will there be additional numbers of employees, more turnover, less turnover? Might there be a contraction of the workforce? Will the skill level and socioeconomics of your future coworkers change appreciably? Where will the new people be coming from? Will they create a more competitive environment, or simply add to an existing base? Coworkers are enormously powerful in changing an organization's culture, which is a big factor in most people's comfort level. Can you intuit where tomorrow's workers will come from and what cultural values they will bring?

Personal Assets

What type of personal assets—education, skills, and knowledge—will your organization need to rely on in its board and staff members to carry out the strategy? How will this differ, if at all, from what it currently needs? Pay particular attention to the future skills that the strategy will require. Technical skills often go in and out of demand, whereas generic abilities like people skills or communication skills tend to be steadily in demand.

INVENTORY YOUR PERSONAL STRENGTHS

Next, critically examine your existing strengths against the same categories listed above. Look honestly for your strengths, because that's what you will build your personal strategic position on.

For market-related questions, consider the implications for you of any new markets. Ask yourself whether you will be comfortable serving a new market, or giving up an old one if that's the case. Do the same for future users of the services. You may not like country and western music, but do you like its fans?

Geography may be out of your control, but at least understand what it means for you personally. Typically, people in higher paid and/or professional positions tend to have a broader range of acceptable geography, whereas other positions tend to be filled by people from a narrower geographic range. Is the future geography going with you, against you, or staying unchanged?

As with users of your organization's services, future coworkers are not a controllable variable. Assessing where your coworkers and board members are currently strong will help you better understand what the organization is going to require in the future to build on those strengths.

Finally, everyone in an organization is expected to make a deposit in the knowledge and skill bank. What is the nature of your current contribution?

What things are you good at? What contributions of yours do others seem to value most? The most critical and manageable part of adapting to your organization's future strategic position is your unique stock of professional assets. These are your strengths, and it is what you will build on for much of your future personal strategy.

WHERE DO YOU WANT TO BE IN FIVE YEARS?

Considering all of the above, decide where you want to be in five years (or less, for board members with term limits). This is essentially a process of recognizing and deciding to accept the implicit incentives laid out in the strategy. If the changes you project in your environment come true, do you expect to stay put? If so, it is time to decide what your personal strategic position in the organization will look like. One by one, decide where you want to be with respect to each of the first four variables—the projected demand for the organization's services, the expected users, the desired geography, and your anticipated coworkers. These are all factors that will facilitate your future happiness and success.

YOUR PERSONAL DEVELOPMENT PLAN

The above factors are also the least controllable, from an individual's perspective. What is quite controllable is the store of personal assets you bring. The benefit to you of a well-crafted organization strategy is that the handwriting is already on the wall, so you know what to plan for, and you have some time.

This is also a good time to launch your personal development plan by adding some skills that will grow more valuable as the larger strategic position is implemented. Depending on your role, these skills could be cultivated in areas like new groups of users or changing program models for the new demand for services. Happily, in five years you will also be more experienced and more knowledgeable. So, if nothing else make sure that the experience comes in the direction toward which your organization is moving. Education is the obvious way of achieving this, whether it is formal or informal, on site or online.

On the other hand, if you do not like where you see the organization being in five years, then you have already made the preliminary decision to leave. That's okay for now. You still have plenty of time, and things can always change. If not, at least you have established where you want to be and it will be easier to recognize an organization that will help you achieve that.

Organizations have strategic positions, and so should their people. Peer into the future, assess your strengths, decide where you want to be, then launch your personal development plan. And you will not have to spend a whole Saturday doing it.

Index

LaVergne, TN USA
09 September 2010
196379LV00002B/67/A